Webometric Studies And Libraries

WEBOMETRIC STUDIES AND LIBRARIES

Akhandanand Shukla
Assistant Professor
Department of Library & Information Science
Mizoram University, Aizawl – 796 004
&
Aditya Tripathi
Assistant Professor
Department of Library & Information Science
Banaras Hindu University, Varanasi – 221 005

Ess Ess Publications
New Delhi

Webometric Studies and Libraries

ISBN: 978-81-7000-746-3

First Published 2015

Published by:
Ess Ess Publications
4831/24, Ansari Road,
Darya Ganj,
New Delhi-110 002.
INDIA
Phones: 23260807, 41563444
Fax: 41563334
E-mail: info@essessreference.com
www.essessreference.com

Cover Design by *Patch Creative Unit*

Printed and bound in India at Salasar Imaging Systems.

CONTENTS

Preface

The World Wide Web (WWW or Web) is a system of inter-connected web pages available over the Internet, started in 1989 by Tim Berners-Lee and Robert Cailliau at European Organization for Nuclear Research (CERN) in Geneva, Switzerland. Web is increasing day by day in terms of webpages, URLs, search engines, domains/sub-domains, website traffic, web usage, online tools, social networking etc. Web is measured to check the effectiveness of various services provided over it. Some popular types of measurement of Web are search engine performance, recall and precision, query analysis, indexing of databases, and behaviour. Web can be also measured with website usage analysis, content analysis, and URL analysis. An interesting measure of Web can be established through measuring depth of the Web and qualitative analysis of Web documents. All these can be categorized into four major groups,

- Link analysis (including web impact factor analysis)
- URL analysis
- Web citation analysis and
- Web content analysis.

Webometrics (metrics of the Web) analyses hyperlinks, hyperlink types, hyperlink structure, and usage of the Web. In the area of Webometrics, Web Impact Factor is an important parameter to measure the popularity of a website. Webometrics studies the quantitative growth of Web that is measured through application of statistical methods and principles of bibliometrics, scientometrics and informetrics studies. The concept of Webometrics was conceived in 1997 and still offers a good scope for study. Search engines are widely adopted tools for Webometric research. These are particularly useful for counting of pages over large area of the Web. Besides search engines, there are number of online tools and software programs available to conduct Webometric researches.

Libraries are information resource centres which perform preservation, processing, and dissemination of knowledge through Information Communication Technology (ICT) to serve user needs in a better way. Websites for libraries are a good medium through which knowledge can be disseminated to every nook and corner of the world. The content of Library websites depend on the library collection, services, facilities etc. Content awareness of these library websites indicate qualitative and quantitative aspects of information provided by the libraries to their users and it can be a method for measuring usefulness of library websites. Further, Web Impact Factor is one aspect of evaluating the library websites through backlinks or web citations. In the book examples of Webometric studies have been given for the Universities and Institutes of India using four popular search engines.

The book is presented in five chapters. First chapter introduces the web, webometrics and web impact factor. Second chapter deals with conceptual approach to the webometrics and its related disciplines. Third chapter presents content awareness evaluation criteria for library websites and evaluative status of their content awareness. Fourth chapter presents measured web impact factor data and analysis of the Central Universities and Institutes of National Importance library websites with solutions for increasing the web impact factor of library websites. Fifth and last chapter presents implications of webometrics in library and information science and its future in the field for further studies.

This book is useful for the students, teachers and researchers of Library Science and Computer Science. Librarians may find this book helpful in conducting Webometric studies related to library website usage.

- *Authors*

1

WEB, WEBOMETRICS, AND WEB IMPACT FACTOR

1.1 INTRODUCTION

Since the mid-1990s, increasing efforts have been made to investigate the nature and properties of the World Wide Web (WWW), by applying modern informetrics methodologies to its contents, link structures and search engines (Björneborn & Ingwersen, 2001). Library and information science (LIS) is concerned with how different information resources and information structures (inter-relations of information resources) are generated, organized, distributed and utilized by different users in different contexts (Björneborn, 2004). Library and information centres are the appropriate medium to disseminate variety of information resources through services locally as well as globally. For measuring the effectiveness of library and information center's services, various researches have been conducted. The libraries have adopted vide application of advanced technologies, mainly computer and information and communication technology (ICT). The World Wide Web has become the main component of ICT. By the application of ICT, services become faster and easy accessible. The application of WWW has emerged as a new research area in library and information science because the WWW has now become one of the main sources of information for academic and research community. Therefore, it provides an excellent platform to test new methods of evaluating webometric activities.

Webometrics (also known as "cybermetrics") is the study of web through which we analyze the number of hyperlinks, types of hyperlinks, structure of the hyperlinks and usage of the web. Webometrics is evolved from bibliometrics and covers the concepts of scientometrics and informetrics. Link structure analysis, web page content analysis, web usage analysis and web technology analysis are the core areas of webometrics (Björneborn, 2004).

Since the evolution of World Wide Web, academic and research institutes have web spaces to disseminate knowledge and information globally. Academic and research institutes, at world level, share knowledge and recognize contributions of each other. This type of attachment (linking) of one organisation to other organisation creates a mesh of inter-relationship between organisations at world level. Webometrics studies the creation, development, destruction, usage and behaviour of this mesh.

Web Impact Factor (WIF) is an important parameter to measure the popularity of a website. A popular website is a website which is viewed and used by many. Hence, it can be concluded that a good website must be useful for users in terms of services and rendered information over web. For instance, a good library with good services definitely would render information about library services as well as would render library services online. The present approach of libraries is to ensure library services through online access. In that case library website is going to be a key measure for measuring quality of library. Hence, Web Impact Factor automatically becomes important indicator towards measuring of quality of library. Case studies of Central University (CU) libraries and Institute of National Importance (INI) libraries are illustrated in succeeding chapters.

1.2 THE WEB

The World Wide Web is commonly known to public as Web. It is a system of interconnected hypertext documents available over the Internet. Hypertext documents are known as web pages contain text, images, audios, videos and other multimedia items interconnected with hyperlinks and can be seen on web browsers over Internet. The World Wide Web was started in 1989 by Tim Berners-Lee and Robert Cailliau at European Organization for Nuclear Research (CERN) in Geneva, Switzerland. In 1990, Tim Berners-Lee and Robert Cailliau built a "Hypertext project" called World Wide Web to store data that would be viewed in hypertext pages.

In 1993, CERN announced that the World Wide Web would be free to anyone, with no fees. The terms Internet and World Wide Web are interchangeably used by the public which has much distinction. Internet is a global data communications system which requires hardware and software infrastructure for inter-connectivity between computers whereas World Wide Web is one of the services communicated over the Internet by inter-connected hypertext documents and other resources. Briefly we can understand it as the web (Wikipedia).

1.2.1. Growth of The Web

Tim Berners-Lee, in 1990, developed the "hyper text transfer protocol" (HTTP), the "hyper text markup language" (HTML), the first web browser, the first HTTP Server and the first web page. On August 1991, the web was made open for public.

> *"The World Wide Web (WWW) project aims to allow all links to be made to any information anywhere. [...] The WWW project was started to allow high energy physicists to share data, news, and documentation. We are very interested in spreading the web to other areas, and having gateway servers for other data. Collaborators welcome!"*
>
> *—from Tim Berners-Lee's first message (History of the World Wide Web).*

The growth of web is increasing day by day in all the dimensions; we can assume these as services of the web, techniques of the web and so like. Popular growing dimensions of the web are: number of hypertexts, number of URLs, number of search engines, number of websites / domains, number of sub-domains, number of Top Level Domains (TLDs), number of country code TLDs (ccTLDs), website traffic, web usage, online tools, software(s), online research, social networking, file sharing, online applications, web programming languages, search engine optimization (SEO), information retrieval techniques etc.

According to Internet Usage Statistics, the Internet users globally increased up to more than 8 times till June 30, 2014 (3,035,749,340) in comparison to December, 2000 (360,985,492) and global penetration of web usage reached up to 42 percent among world population. In India, there are about 243,000,000 Internet users (till 30 June, 2014) having penetration rate of 19.7 percent of total population of India.

Fig. 1.1, 1.2 and 1.3 illustrate that there are about 1386.2 million Internet users in Asia region which have quite large data than rest of the world but low Internet penetration rates (34.7%) than any others. North America has highest Internet penetration rate (87.7%) than any of the continent while world's average of Internet penetration ratio is 42.3 percent.

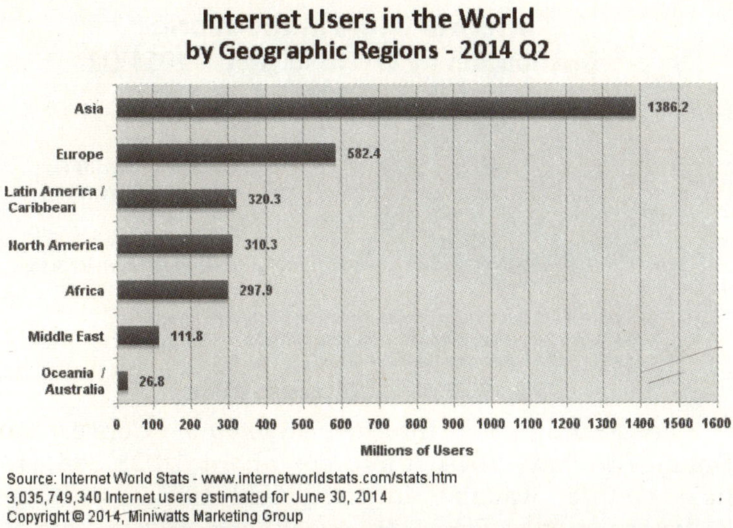

Fig. 1.1: Internet Users in the World by Geographic Regions

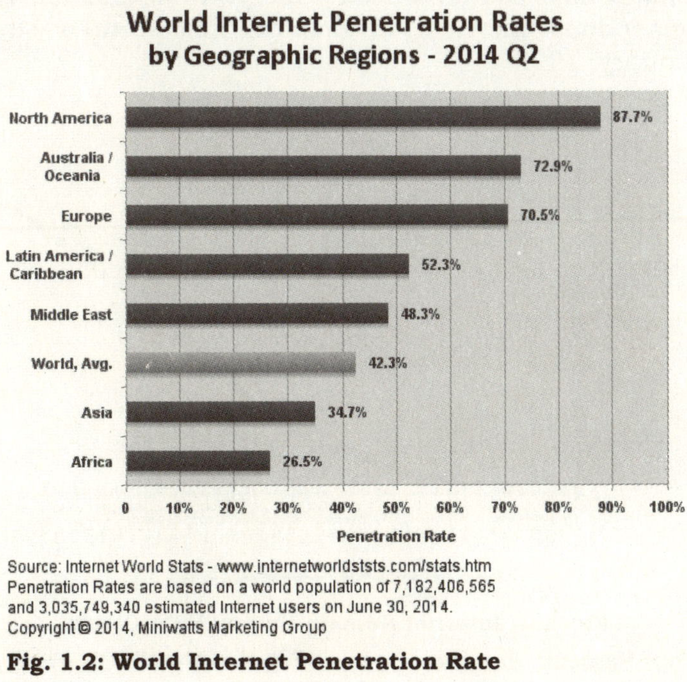

Fig. 1.2: World Internet Penetration Rate

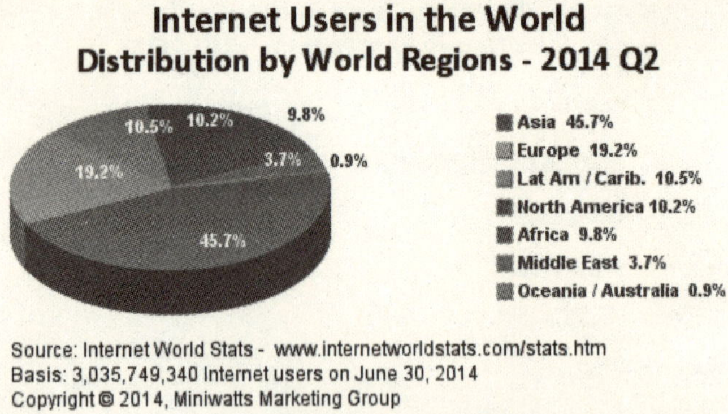

Fig. 1.3: World Internet Users

According to Internet Systems Consortium Domain Survey, 2014, there are about 1,028,544,414 host counts available in the world till July, 2014. Following graph (Fig. 1.4) reveals the growth rate of domain host counts since January, 1994 and there is tremendous increase in domain host counts since January, 1999.

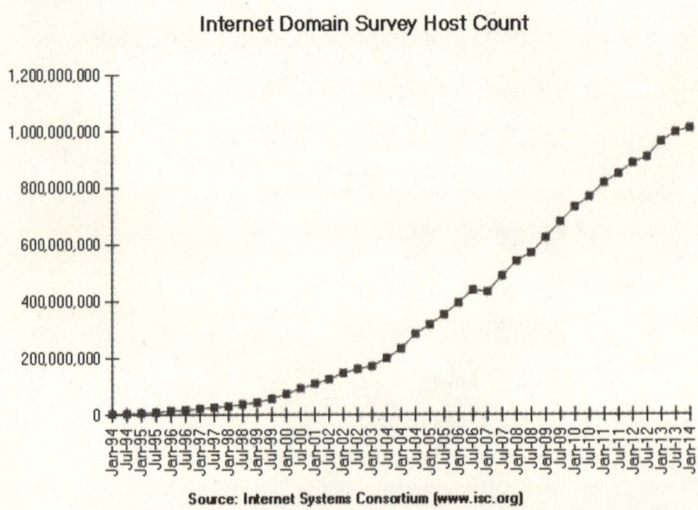

Fig. 1.4: Internet Domain Survey Host Count

Search Engine Land (February 2013) records Google leads in number of searches and popularity in the web search done worldwide. Google search is still the number 1 search service when ranked by total searches done till December, 2012, with 114.734 billion total searches representing 65.2 percent of all search queries conducted during the month.

1.2.2. Measurement of the Web

The web is measured to check the effectiveness of various services provided over it. There have been many researches conducted to measure the web in various dimensions. Several researchers (Rodríguez i Gairín, 1997; Ingwersen, 1998; Smith, 1999; Snyder & Rosenbaum, 1999; Bar-Ilan, 2000; Thelwall, 2000; Thelwall, 2001; Smith & Thelwall, 2002; Thelwall, 2002; Kousha & Horri, 2004; Noruzi, 2005; Shukla, 2009a; Shukla, 2009b; Shukla & Tripathi, 2009; Easley & Kleinberg, 2010; Frías, 2010; Shukla & Vanlalfeli, 2014; Shukla & Tripathi, 2014) have studied the web and results obtained by them are one aspect of measurement of web. The most popular types of measurement of web is search engine performance, recall and precision of search engines, search engine query analysis, indexing of search engine databases, behaviour of search engines, website usage analysis, website content analysis, URL analysis, depth of the web, qualitative analysis of web documents and so like.

1.2.2.1. Link Analysis

As earlier alluded (cf. Section 1.2) that, the web is consisted of inter-connected hypertext documents with hyperlinks. The hyperlinks are mostly made for navigational purposes of the web which direct to relatively similar content. The hyperlinks are usually known as "*outlink*" of the hypertext document. The total number of hypertext documents in any website / domain can be measured by inbuilt text command (site: website address) in search engines. There are various inbuilt text commands available by which one can measure the total number web pages, *self-links*, *outline*[1], *inlinks*[2] etc. There have been much studies conducted to analyse links and web pages with commercial search engines (Rodríguez i Gairín, 1997; Ingwersen, 1998; Smith, 1999; Snyder & Rosenbaum, 1999; Henzinger, 2000; Thelwall, 2000; Thelwall, 2001; Smith & Thelwall, 2002; Thelwall, 2002; Kousha & Horri, 2004; Noruzi, 2005; Shukla, 2009a; Shukla, 2009b; Shukla & Tripathi, 2009; Easley & Kleinberg, 2010; Jalal et al., 2010; Jeyshankar, 2011; Thelwall, 2011; Maharana et al., 2012; Shukla & Vanlalfeli, 2014; Shukla & Tripathi, 2014).

1.2.2.1.1 Web Impact Factor (WIF)

In the decade of 1990's, there have been efforts made to search the significance of the web for scientific communication, by using bibliometric techniques (Larson, 1996; Turnbull, 1996). These bibliometric techniques also known as webometrics (Almind & Ingwersen, 1997) can be defined as the "*study of quantitative aspects of the construction and use of information resources, structures and technologies on the web, drawing on bibliometric and informetric approaches*" (Björneborn, 2004). Web impact factor (WIF) is the quantitative indicator for calculating webometric activities. Ingwersen (1998) developed the idea of web impact factor (WIF) based on journal impact factor (JIF). Web impact factor is nothing but measuring average link frequencies and is based on hyperlinks and their citations. In more concrete words,

> "*Web impact factor (WIF) is the number of outside web pages linking to a website which is divided by the number of web pages in that very website at a time*".

---

1 Links going from the site to other website. Also known as "outgoing links".

2 Links coming to website from outside the website.

That means, the numerator is the number of link pages made to a website and the denominator is a measure of the size of that very website.

This very idea was adopted from the Journal Impact Factor (JIF), originally proposed by Eugene Garfield in 1972. The WIF is extemporaneous result of search engines' database at a specific time. It provides quantitative tools for ranking, evaluating, categorizing, and comparing websites, top-level domains and sub-domains.

There are three kinds of Web Impact Factors (WIF) based on three types of links found i.e. *inlinks*, *outlinks*, and *self-links*. Links coming into a site from another site is *inlinks* (also known as *backlinks*), links outgoing from a site to another site is *outlinks*, and links coming from the same site is *self-links*. The *self-links* are made for navigational purposes only. The Web Impact Factor (WIF) based on links properties are:

(a) Overall WIF: It is calculated by the total number of combining *inlinks* pages and *self-links* pages;

(b) Inlink (Revised) WIF: It is calculated by the total number of *inlinks* pages coming from outside; and

(c) Self-link WIF: It is calculated by the total number of *self-link* pages of the website.

Calculation of Web Impact Factor (WIF) : The web impact factor (WIF) can be calculated by using the following formula where:

A = total links to a website (all *inlinks* and *self-links* pages)

B = *inlinks* to the website (subset of A)

C = *self-links* within the same website

D = total number of web pages present in the website at a time.

A. Calculation for Overall WIF

$$\frac{A = \text{total links to a website (all } \textit{inlinks} \text{ and } \textit{self-links} \text{ pages)}}{D = \text{total number of web pages present in the website at a time}}$$

Overall WIF= A/D

B. Calculation for Inlink (Revised) WIF:

$$\frac{B = \textit{inlinks} \text{ to the website}}{D = \text{total number of web pages present in the website at a time}}$$

Revised WIF=B/D

C. Calculation for Self-link WIF:

$$\frac{C = \textit{self-links} \text{ within the same website}}{D = \text{total number of web pages present in the website at a time}}$$

Self-link WIF= C/D

Limitations of WIF : The Web Impact Factor (WIF) can be influenced by many of the factors. Noruzi (2006) has identified the following reasons, which can affect Web Impact Factor (WIF):

The Web Impact Factor (WIF) depends on search engines' web coverage. The search engines' web coverage varies between countries. Search engines' database coverage is not constant (Ingwersen, 1998; Lawrence & Giles, 1998; Shukla, 2009a; Shukla, 2009b; Shukla & Vanlalfeli, 2014; Shukla & Tripathi, 2014).

The web impact factor (WIF) may vary by English and non-English language websites. Japanese websites have very low Web Impact Factor (WIF) than any other country (Ingwersen, 1998). Websites in English language web pages have higher web impact factor (WIF).

The coverage of subject strongly determines Web Impact Factor (WIF). Interdisciplinary websites attract more *backlinks* and thus have higher Web Impact Factor (WIF). Different disciplines exhibits different Web Impact Factor (WIF). So, websites may be analysed in context of their specific field.

1.2.2.2. URL Analysis

The URL analysis has connotation with link analysis. There is very minute demarcation line between link analysis and URL analysis. Link analysis is the study of mathematical calculation of incoming links and outgoing links to any particular website / domain whereas URL analysis is the study of analyzing the structure and properties of URLs embedded in interlinks web pages (i.e. incoming links or outgoing links), between one website / domain to another website / domain or in any single website. Thus we can understand URL analysis is the study of characteristics and behaviour of web pages address of websites. The URL analysis includes study of top level domains (TLD[3]), country code TLDs (ccTLD[4]), generic TLDs (gTLD[5]), sites / domains, sub-sites / sub-domains, file types of web pages, structure of URLs etc. (Shukla & Vanlalfeli, 2014).

1.2.2.3. Web Citation Analysis

Earlier, web links were treated as citation. Later on it was observed that web links are *backlinks* from one website to another website. These *backlinks* may come from journal articles, conference papers, research reports, personal home pages, web curriculum vitae[6] and simple web pages etc. The citation analysis is the measurement of scholarly communication of documents and web citation analysis is the measurement of scholarly communication of documents on the web parlance. The term web citation

---

3 Top-level domain is the last part of the domain name. e.g. http://www.google.com, .com is TLD.

4 Country code top-level domain is the last part of the domain name reserved for a country. For e.g. http://www.bhu.ac.in, .in is ccTLD.

5 Generic top-level domains are the category of TLDs. The core gTLDs are .com, .info, .net and .org.

6 Personal resume available on the World Wide Web.

describes the number of web links that any online article or online journal has received during a given time. Search engines Google, Yahoo!, AltaVista, AlltheWeb etc. are used in the web link analysis. However, Google Scholar (Mukherjee, 2007) is used in extraction of web citation from scholarly resources. As mentioned in Google Scholar's Support for Scholarly Publishers website "Google and Google Scholar have boosted the worldwide visibility and accessibility of [the] content. [They] work with publishers of scholarly information to index peer-reviewed papers, theses, preprints, abstracts, and technical reports from all disciplines of research and make them searchable on Google and Google Scholar".

1.2.2.4. Web Content Analysis

Neuendorf (2002) defined content analysis as *"content analysis is an in depth analysis using quantitative or qualitative techniques of messages using a scientific method (including attention to objectivity, inter subjectivity, a priori design, reliability, validity, generalizability, replicability and hypothesis testing) and is not limited as to the types of variables that may be measured or the context in which the messages are created or presented"*. Content analysis is also considered a scholarly methodology in the humanities by which texts are studied as to authorship, authenticity, and their meaning. Lasswell (1948) formulated the core questions of content analysis "Who says what, to whom, why, to what extent and with what effect?" Thus content analysis of web documents is known as web content analysis which is now prevalent in the area of web to check the authenticity and quality of information available over the Internet. Recall and precision efficiency of search engines is also one aspect of web content analysis.

1.2.3. Search Engine as a Tool for Measurement

The "web search engine" is a tool designed to search information on the World Wide Web (Wikipedia). The search results are usually presented in a list and are commonly called hits. The information may consist of web pages, images, information and other types of files. Search engines retrieve data from open directories, databases, web directories, digital repositories etc._WordNet Search - 3.0 defines search engines as "*a computer program that retrieves documents or files or data from a database or from a computer network (especially from the Internet)*".

Search engines are suites of computer programs that automatically find and download web pages, then store them in a database. Search engine include programs that link the database to a user interface, normally in the form of a web page, so that it can be interrogated through the Internet, often by a keyword search (Thelwall, 2001).

A crawler based search engine is made of three major parts: the crawler, the indexer and the query engine (Brin & Page, 1998). Web crawler[7] collects data by visiting URLs of the web. Indexer analyses the contents (words, headings and Meta tags) of each web pages to determine how it should be indexed. Analyzed data of web pages are stored in an index database. The query engine examines the index database and returns a listing of best matching web pages to the users who made the query. Most of the search engines support Boolean operators AND, OR and NOT to specify the search query. Few of the search engines provide advanced search feature called proximity search through which one can search the distance between keywords.

---

7 An automated web browser that follows every link it sees is also known as spider.

Search engines are divided into four categories: robots (programs that reside on a host computer and retrieve information from sites on the web using standard protocols, e.g. AltaVista, Excite, Lycos), directories (rely mainly on people to identify and group resources, e.g. Yahoo!, SOCIG), meta-search engines (which utilize databases of other search engines, e.g. Metacrawler, Dogpile) and software tools (software programs for searching the web that is installed on user's workstation, e.g. Copernic 98, Websleuth) (Oppenheim et al., 2000). There are many such studies conducted in the field of webometrics based on various search engines (Rodríguez i Gairín, 1997; Ingwersen, 1998; Smith, 1999; Snyder & Rosenbaum, 1999; Thelwall, 2000; Thelwall, 2001; Smith & Thelwall, 2002; Thelwall, 2002; Kousha & Horri, 2004; Noruzi, 2005; Mukherjee, 2007; Shukla, 2009a; Shukla, 2009b; Shukla & Tripathi, 2009, Shukla & Vanlalfeli, 2014; Shukla & Tripathi, 2014).

As earlier alluded (cf. Sections 1.2.2, 1.2.2.1 – 4) that search engines can be used as an important tool for measuring the web in the field of webometrics. Besides this, search engines are normally used as information retrieval tool for variety of purposes.

1.3. LIBRARY WEBSITES OF INDIAN ACADEMIC AND RESEARCH INSTITUTES

A website is an important medium to convey the aim / purpose / mission, educational courses run, scholarships, infrastructure, facilities and many more information to the potential students, general public, faculty, professionals, organizations etc. Libraries of universities and institutes play a vital role in the development of students and teachers in their study, teaching and research. Library websites disseminate knowledge and information among users and attract potential users by showing richness of collection / resources, variety of services, number of facilities etc. A survey suggests (Shukla, 2009b) that about 42 percent universities and institutes have no separate library website (domain) / sub-site (sub-domain) or any single web page for library. This population also covers universities and institutes, who have library websites but are not working due to certain reasons. The same study also reported that there is lack of separate library websites in India in general. Library websites of Indian universities and institutes are mostly available in web pages rather than websites. Website is collection of hypertext documents (web pages) with a home page. A home page is the first page of the website also known as index page and is a single hypertext document.

1.4. WEB IMPACT FACTOR AS QUALITY MEASUREMENT INDICATOR

There is enormous growth in academic and research institutes in the last 50 years around the world. These academic and research institutes conducts various academic (study and teaching) programs, research projects (directly or through scholarship) and training programs (professional and vocational courses). These academic and research institutes provide better infrastructure, environment and facilities to students for conducting their study, teaching, research and training. There are various governmental and non-governmental organizations which have been setup to examine and analyze the annual performance of these academic and research institutes. These governmental and non-governmental organizations (examining and analyzing) conduct surveys and publish their reports year-by-year, in which they provide ranking to such academic and research institutes with other statistical data. The ranking of academic and research institutes may help one to select his best choice for study, teaching, research and training. When we talk about infrastructure, facilities and environment of any academic and research institute: library, sports complex, hostels, cafeteria / canteen, computer centre, bank, electric supply, water supply, air cooled buildings, classrooms, scholarships, research laboratories, transport etc. are included in the survey ranking in which each of the item plays a role to make the ranking high. Library is the most important among all of them because; richness of the library attracts more students. Times Higher Education Supplement (THES) conducts similar type of survey for world's educational and research institutes since 2004 and provides ranking to the educational and research institutes in various categories like life sciences and biomedicine, engineering and IT, natural sciences, social sciences, arts and humanities etc.

WIF is a very popular concept in UK especially in library parlance however in India it is still in its infancy and lot more applications to be developed by libraries. In future this indicator can become a marketing tool to attract users and popularize library services and the host institution. It can become a comparative tool for students, faculties, institutions, the government and the public in general. In libraries one of the usage criteria could be the richness of library and its usability. Libraries play a vital role in dissemination of knowledge and information among users. So, rankings of them will actually reflect the status and standing of such organisation. Now almost all the academic and research institutes have their websites for self and for libraries. An investigation about how the websites of these institutional libraries are being used in order to disseminate information to their users can bring out many interesting results.

In this context, studies like evaluation of library websites in the light of their content through WIF would provide an excellent ranking mechanism for measuring quality of library.

1.5. SIGNIFICANCE OF WEBOMETRIC RESEARCH

There has been a continuous growth in the web and webometric techniques used to study the growth of web. Webometrics based researches are prevalent in European countries (mainly UK). In India, few researches have been undertaken in the area of webometrics and there is lack of such researches in library and information science perspective and libraries are still far from this. By analyzing link counts, URL counts and calculating web impact factor (WIF), websites and their hosts can be very well evaluated; and the findings based on quantitative and qualitative analysis may help users, librarians, faculties, professionals and general public to understand the strength and weaknesses of institute (host institute where the library website is hosted). Such studies will also reveal the content awareness of libraries for their websites and help to adopt best practices to increase the web impact of library websites. The comparative ranking may help users and librarians to understand the current position of their library among others in the same group. This will also help the librarians and webmasters of libraries to improve upon web interface of their library. In India, we still lack such kind of evaluative studies.

REFERENCES

Almind, T. C. & Ingwersen, P. (1997). Informetric analyses on the World Wide Web: methodological approaches to webometrics. *Journal of Documentation, 53*(4), 404-426.

Backlink Analyzer. (n.d.). [computer software]. Retrieved June 17, 2009, from eKstreme.com. Available at http://ekstreme.com/backlink-analyzer

Backlink Analyzer. (n.d.). [computer software]. Retrieved June 17, 2009, from SEOTOOLS. Available at http://tools.seobook.com/backlink-analyzer/

Backlink Watch!. (n.d.). [online software tool]. Retrieved June 17, 2009, from BACKLINK WATCH!. Available at http://www.backlinkwatch.com/index.php

Bar-Ilan, J. (2000). Evaluating the stability of the search tools HotBot and Snap: a case study. *Online Information Review, 24*(6), 439-449.

Björneborn, L. (2004). *Small-world link structures across an academic web space: a library and information science approach (Doctoral Dissertation).* Copenhagen, Denmark: Royal School of Library & Information Science.

Björneborn, L. & Ingwersen, P. (2001). Perspectives of webometrics. *Scientometrics, 50*(1), 65-82.

Brin, S. & Page, L. (1998). The anatomy of a large-scale hypertextual web search engine. *Computer Networks and ISDN Systems, 30,* 107-117.

Easley, D. & Kleinberg, J. (2010). Link Analysis and Web Search. In *Networks, Crowds, and Markets: Reasoning about a Highly Connected World.* Chapter 14. Cambridge University Press.

Frías, E. R. (2010). *Application of webometric techniques to the study of accounting and financial variables (Doctoral Dissertation).* University of Granada.

Garfield, E. (1972). Citation analysis as a tool in journal evaluation. *Science, 178*(4060), 471-479.

Google Scholar's Support for Scholarly Publishers. (n.d.). Retrieved June 8, 2009, from Google Scholar: http://scholar.google.co.in/intl/en/scholar/publishers.html

Henzinger, M. (2000). Link analysis in web information Retrieval. *Bulletin of the IEEE Computer Society Technical Committee on Data Engineering, 23*(3), 1-7.

History of the World Wide Web. (n.d.). Retrieved from Wikipedia: http://en.wikipedia.org/wiki/History_of_the_World_Wide_Web

Ingwersen, P. (1998). The calculation of web impact factors. *Journal of Documentation, 54*(2), 236-243.

Internet Systems Consortium Domain Survey. (2014, July). Retrieved January 21, 2015, from Internet Systems Consortium:http://ftp.isc.org/www/survey/reports/current/

Internet Usage Statistics. (n.d.). Retrieved Janaury 21, 2015, from Internet World Stats: http://www.internetworldstats.com/stats.htm

Jalal, S. K., Biswas, S. C., & Mukhopadhyay, P. (2010). Web impact factor and link analysis of selected Indian

Universities. *Annals of Library and Information Studies, 57*(1), 109-121.

Jeyshankar, R. (2011). Link analysis and Web Impact Factor of Indian nationalised banks. *International Journal of Information Dissemination and Technology, 1*(3), 171-179.

Kousha, K. & Horri, A. (2004). The relationship between scholarly publishing and the counts of academic inlinks to Iranian university websites: exploring academic link creation motivations. *Journal of Information Management and Scientometrics, 1*(2), 13-22.

Larson, R. R. (1996). Bibliometrics of the World Wide Web: an exploratory analysis of the intellectual structure of cyberspace. *In* S. Hardin (Ed.), *Proceedings of the 59th Annual Meeting, ASIS 96, Baltimore, Maryland* (pp. 71-79). Medford, NJ: Learned Information.

Lasswell, H. (1948). The structure and function of communication in society. *In* L. Bryson (Ed.), *The communication of ideas* (pp. 37-51). New York: Harper & Brothers.

Lawrence, S. & Giles, C. L. (1998). Searching the World Wide Web. *Science, 280,* 98-100.

Link Checker Pro. (n.d.). [computer software]. Retrieved June 17, 2009, from Link Checker Pro. Available at http://www.link-checker-pro.com/

Maharana, R. K., Panda, K. C., & Sahoo, J. (2012). Web impact factor (WIF) and link analysis of Indian Institute of Technologies (IITs): A webometric study. *Library Philosophy and Practice (e-journal). 789,* 1-11.

Mukherjee, B. (2007). *Scholarly communication on the web: an investigation of open access electronic journals in library and information science (Doctoral Dissertation).* Varanasi, India: Department of Library & Information Science, Banaras Hindu University.

Neuendorf, K. A. (2002). *The content analysis guidebook..* Thousand Oaks, CA: SAGE.

Noruzi, A. (2005). Web impact factors for Iranian universities. *Webology, 2*(1), Article 11. Retrieved from http://www.webology.ir/2005/v2n1/a11.html

Noruzi, A. (2006). The web impact factors: a critical review. *The Electronic Library, 24*(4), 490-500.

Oppenheim, C., Morris, A., McKnight, C. & Lowley, S. (2000). The evaluation of WWW search engines. *Journal of Documentation, 56*(2), 190-211.

Rodríguez i Gairín, J. M. (1997). Impact assessment of information on the Internet: AltaVista, the citation index of the web. *Revista Española De Documentación Científica, 20*(2), 175-181.

Search Engine Land. (2013, February). Retrieved August 12, 2014, from Search Engine Land: http://searchengineland.com/google-worlds-most-popular-search-engine-148089

SearchEngineWatch.com. (n.d.). Retrieved June 6, 2006, from Search Engine Watch: http://searchenginewatch.com/ (currently page not exists)

Search Commands. (n.d.). Retrieved June 5, 2006, from Search Commands: http://www.searchcommands.com/ (Last accessed on 24.06.09)

Search Thingy Top Ten Search Engines. (n.d.). Retrieved June 5, 2006, from Search Thingy: http://www.searchthingy.com/search.asp

Shukla, A. (2009a). Measuring effectiveness of institutional websites: a case study of central universities of India. *Research Digest, 4*(3).

Shukla, A. (2009b). *Evaluating Indian academic and research library websites based on web impact factor analysis (Doctoral Dissertation).* Varanasi, India: Department of Library & Information Science, Banaras Hindu University.

Shukla, A. & Tripathi, A. (2009). Webometric analysis of institutes of national importance in India. *IASLIC Bulletin, 54*(3), 165-180.

Shukla, A. & Tripathi, A. (2014). *Backlinks* analyses of institutes of national importance and premier management institutions library websites. *Journal of International Academic Research for Multidisciplinary (JIARM), 2*(7), 560-575.

Shukla, A. & Vanlalfeli. (2014). Webometric analyses of library websites of Indian Institutes of Technology. *Journal of Advancements in Library Sciences, 1*(2), 34-48.

Smith, A. G. (1999). A tale of two web spaces: comparing sites using web impact factors. *Journal of Documentation, 55*(5), 577-592.

Smith, A. G. & Thelwall, M. (2002). Web impact factors for Australasian universities. *Scientometrics, 54*(3), 363-380.

Snyder, H. & Rosenbaum, H. (1999). Can search engines be used for web-link analysis? A critical review. *Journal of Documentation, 55*(4), 375-384.

Thelwall, M. (2000). Web impact factors and search engine coverage. *Journal of Documentation, 56*(2), 185-189.

Thelwall, M. (2001). The responsiveness of search engine indexes [Electronic version]. *Cybermetrics, 5*(1), Paper 1. Available at http://www.cindoc.csic.es/cybermetrics/articles/v5i1p1.html

Thelwall, M. (2002). Evidence for the existence of geographic trends in university website interlinking. *Journal of Documentation, 58*(5), 563-574.

Thelwall, M. (2011). A comparison of link and URL citation counting. *Aslib Proceedings, 63*(4), 419 - 425.

Thomas, O. & Willet, P. (2000). Webometric analysis of departments of librarianship and information science. *Journal of Information Science, 26*(6), 421-428. doi: 10.1177/016555150002600605

Times Higher Education Supplement. (n.d.). Retrieved June 2, 2009, from Times Higher Education: http://www.timeshigher education.co.uk/

Top Ten Search Engines. (n.d.). Retrieved June 4, 2006, from seoconsultants.com: http://www.seoconsultants.com/search-engines/

Turnbull, D. (1996). Bibliometrics and the World Wide Web (Technical Report FIS-12-19-1996-1). Faculty of Information Studies, University of Toronto. *University Grants Commission.* (n.d.). Retrieved April 27, 2006, from University Grants Commission (UGC): http://www.ugc.ac.in/

Walia, P. K. & Kaur, P. (2008). Webometric analysis of library associations' websites of India. *IASLIC Bulletin, 53*(3), 131-143.

Web search engine. (n.d.). Retrieved June 9, 2009, from Wikipedia: http://en.wikipedia.org/wiki/Search_engines

Wordnet search - 3.0. (n.d.). Retrieved June 9, 2009, from WordNet: http://wordnetweb.princeton.edu/perl/webwn

World Wide Web. (n.d.). Retrieved June 8, 2009, from Wikipedia: http://en.wikipedia.org/wiki/World_Wide_Web

2
WEBOMETRICS

2.1. INTRODUCTION

The chapter deals with the origin of webometrics from bibliometrics, scientometrics, and informetrics; and relation with them. The relation amongst bibliometrics, scientometrics, informetrics, cybermetrics, and webometrics has been discussed here. Webometrics concepts including its origin, development, tools & techniques, growth in academic arena, web impact factor and its related tools & techniques have been elaborated in the chapter.

2.2. BIBLIOMETRICS

Bibliometrics is the method which deals with study of published literature. Cole and Eale's (1917) study on "The history of comparative anatomy. Part I: a statistical analysis" is considered to be the first bibliometric study. The expression "statistical bibliography" was first time used by Hulme (1923) in his literature and later it was used by many others. Ranganathan in 1948 at the Aslib Conference in Leamington Spa, suggested that it is necessary for librarians to develop "librametry" on the lines of biometry, econometry and psychometry, since "*many of the matters connected with library work and services involve large numbers*" (Aslib 1949). An information scientist, Paul Otlet (1934) had earlier used the term "bibliometrie". Pritchard (1969) outlined bibliometrics widely, to be *"the application of mathematical and statistical methods to books and other media of communication"*. He advocated the term "bibliometrics" in preference to "statistical bibliography". In a study, Wittig (1978) observed the historical development of the term "statistical bibliography" and indicated that "The root of the term 'statistical bibliography' can be traced to its first use by Hulme in 1923".

The above discussion of librametry and bibliometrics show that librametry primarily aims at the quantitative analysis of the management of libraries and bibliometrics is limited to recorded knowledge. The literature concerning both fields suggests that in librametry and bibliometrics, one examines the statistical distributions of the processes relating to the utilization of documents, library staff, and library users to establish a theory for the structural aspects of library (Ravichandra Rao, 1983). He further stated that bibliometrics and librametry are commonly defined areas in which one studies: *"Information processes and information handling in libraries and information centres by quantitatively analyzing the characteristics and behaviour of documents, library staff, and library users"*.

Many attempts have been made to define the term "bibliometrics" and "statistical bibliography". An earlier approach made by Pritchard to elaborate the statistical bibliography as *"to shed light on the processes of written communication and of the nature and course of development of a discipline (in so far as this is displayed through written communication), by means of counting and analysing the various facets of written communication ... the application of mathematics and statistical methods to books and other media of communication ..."*. In the same year, Fairthorne (1969) defined bibliometrics as *"the quantitative treatment of the properties of recorded discourse and behaviour appertaining to it"*. The Glossary of Documentation of Terms (BS 5408:1976) explained bibliometrics as the study of *"the use of documents and patterns of publication in which mathematical and statistical methods have been applied"*. Hawkins (1977) has interpreted bibliometrics as *"the quantitative analysis of the bibliographic features of a body of literature"*. Similarly Potter (1981) has defined bibliometrics as *"the study and measurement of the publication patterns of all forms of written communication and their authorship"*. White and McCain (1989) have defined it as *"bibliometrics is the quantitative study of literature as they are reflected in bibliographies. Its task, immodestly enough, is to provide evolutionary models of science, technology, and scholarship"*.

Bibliometric Distribution and Measurements

Bibliometric distributions are used to study: frequency of occurrence of words in a text (Zipf's law), productivity of authors in terms of scientific papers (Lotka's law), and scattering of articles over different journals (Bradford's law). These distributions are characterized as positively skewed, long-tailed and reverse-J shaped respectively. A similar characteristic is also observed in distributions relating to library size, citation of papers, book usage, and obsolescence of literature. Citation counting, bibliographic coupling and co-citation studies are prevalent measurement techniques in bibliometrics. Citation counting is a technique that determines how many citations a given document, author, journal etc. has received over a period of time. Citation analysis was first time used by Gross and Gross (1927). Impact Factor, developed by Garfield (1972), is another modified measure of bibliometric approaches. He defined the term "Impact Factor" as *"the ratio of the number of times a journal is cited in a given time period to the total number of source items published in the journal, during specified period of time"*. In 1956, the concept of bibliographic coupling was first time identified by Fano and later on Kessler (1983) elaborated, tested and coined the term "bibliographic coupling". Bibliographic coupling is the number of common references cited in two documents that indicates the degree of similarity of contents of the citing papers. In an independent study, first time Small (1973) and Marshakova (1973) suggested the concept of co-citation. The concept of co-citation has emerged from the citation analysis. In this, two documents are cited together in subsequent literature and frequency of their co-citation represents the strength of the two cited documents.

2.3. SCIENTOMETRICS

Scientometrics is nothing but the study of quantitative aspects of science. Wikipedia defines *"Scientometrics is the science of measuring and analysing science"*. Practically, scientometrics is the study of scientific literature by applying bibliometric and statistical techniques. According to Nalimov and Mulchenko (1969), scientometrics is *"the application of those quantitative methods which are dealing with the analysis of science viewed as an information process"*. In another definition by Tague-Sutcliffe (1992), scientometrics is *"the study of the quantitative aspects of science as a discipline or economic activity"*. Thus, scientometrics is concerned with the quantitative features and characteristics of science. Modern scientometrics is mostly based on the work of Derek J. de Solla Price and Eugene Garfield. The former one is known as "father of scientometrics". He formulated his theory on the exponential growth of science in 1963 whereas Garfield founded the Institute for Scientific Information (ISI) which provides the data and tool for scientometric analysis.

2.4. INFORMETRICS

Informetrics is nothing but the study of quantitative aspects of information. The term was originally coined in German "informetrie" by Nacke in 1979. In the following year, Nacke et al. (1980) declared scientometrics as a sister field of informetrics within information science. At the first international conference on "Bibliometrics and Theoretical Aspects of Information Retrieval" in 1988, Brookes stated that *"this new term is being used to cover both sciento- and biblio- metrics impartially. It has produced no distinctively new ideas of its own but as it implicitly covers both documentary and electronic forms of communication, it may have a future"*. As a general field of study, it includes the earlier fields bibliometrics and scientometrics. During the second conference, Brookes (1990) approved "informetrics" as a general term for scientometrics and bibliometrics. After two years later, Tague-Sutcliffe (1992) has defined informetrics as *"the study of the quantitative aspects of information in any form, not just records or bibliographies, and in any social group, not just scientists"*. Thus it covers the quantitative aspects of formal, informal communication and recorded information of any social community with intellectual community. According to Ingwersen and Christensen (1997), informetrics *"designates a recent extension of the traditional bibliometric analyses also to cover non-scholarly communities in which information is produced, communicated, and used"*. In 1999, Wilson has outlined the field of informetrics which includes citation analysis, obsolescence studies, word-related analyses, author studies, growth studies of the informetrics laws (Lotka, Zipf, and Bradford) and webometrics.

2.5. WEBOMETRICS

The science of study of web was named as "webometrics" by Almind and Ingwersen (1997) however the term "cybermetrics" is used for the same by Journal of Cybermetrics. Webometrics is the combination of theories of informetrics, scientometrics and application of bibliometrics. For example, counting and analysis of outgoing links from the website, known as *outlinks*, and of links pointing to the website, called *inlinks*, can be seen similar to citation analysis (Björneborn & Ingwersen, 2001). Later, Björneborn (2004) elaborated webometrics as *"the study of the quantitative aspects of the construction and use of information resources, structures and technologies on the web, drawing on bibliometric and informetric approaches"*. He further stated that there are four areas of webometric research: web page content analysis; web link structure analysis; web usage analysis; and web technology analysis. Webometric researches mainly cover search engines' coverage and quality analysis, web page property analysis and web impact factor (WIF) analysis, domain and sub-domain analysis, and TLDs analysis.

2.5.1. Beginning of Webometrics

Webometrics is nothing but the quantitative study of web based phenomena, has analogy with bibliometrics. It was originally formulated by the application of citation analysis methods of Institute for Scientific Information (ISI) citation databases. First time Almind and Ingwersen (1997) coined the term "webometrics" whereas first time basic idea of webometrics has been identified by Rodríguez i Gairín (1997) and further pursued by Aguillo (1998). Larson (1996) was the first researcher who extensively explored link structure analysis. First time Rousseau (1997) studied the informetric analysis of the web.

2.5.2. Relation with Bibliometrics, Scientometrics and Informetrics

The primary aim of development of web was sharing of global document network for scholarly use (Berners Lee & Cailliau, 1990) and now inhabited by a diversity of users, the web constitutes an obvious research area for information scientists, statisticians and mathematicians. There are many more new terms which emerged since the mid-1990s, for example, *netometrics* (Bossy, 1995); *internetometrics* (Almind & Ingwersen, 1996); *webometrics* (Almind & Ingwersen,

1997); *cybermetrics* (Isidro Aguillo, 1997) etc. Webometrics and cybermetrics are currently the two most widely accepted synonymous terms in information science.

Björneborn and Ingwersen (2004) have proposed a different terminology to distinguish between studies of web and Internet applications. Björneborn (2004) defined webometrics as *"the study of the quantitative aspects of the construction and use of information resources, structures and technologies on the WWW, drawing on bibliometric and informetric approaches"*. The definition covers quantitative aspects of both, the construction side and the usage side of web, embracing the four main areas of present webometric research: web page content analysis; web link structure analysis; web usage analysis (exploiting log files for users' searching and browsing behaviour); and web technology analysis (including search engine performance). All four main research areas include long term studies of changes on the dynamic web, for example, of page contents, link structures and usage patterns. Further, Björneborn and Ingwersen (2004) have proposed "cybermetrics" as a generic term for *"the study of the quantitative aspects of the construction and use of information resources, structures and technologies on the whole Internet, drawing on bibliometric and informetric approaches"*. Both the definitions are same however the former (webometrics) is restricted to WWW whereas later (cybermetrics) is study of Internet. Thus, cybermetrics includes statistical studies of discussion groups, mailing lists, and other computer mediated communication on the Internet (Bar-Ilan, 1997; Herring, 2002) including the web, quantitative measures of the Internet backbone technology, topology and traffic (Molyneux & Williams, 1999). This makes large overlaps in the coverage of cybermetrics and webometrics during the analyses of web contents, link structures, web usage and web technologies. Likewise webometrics, there are also number of such new terms which have emerged since the mid-1990s, for example, *cyber geography / cyber cartography* (Girardin, 1996; Dodge, 1999), *web mining* (Etzioni, 1996; Kosala & Blockeel, 2000), *web graph analysis* (Chakrabarti et al., 1999; Broder et al., 2000) etc.

There is significant difference among concepts of informetrics, bibliometrics and scientometrics as defined by Björneborn and Ingwersen (2004). The diagram in Fig. 2.1 (Björneborn & Ingwersen, 2004) shows the field of *informetrics* embracing the overlapping fields of *bibliometrics* and *scientometrics* following widely adopted definitions by Brookes (1990), Egghe and Rousseau (1990) and Tague-Sutcliffe (1992).

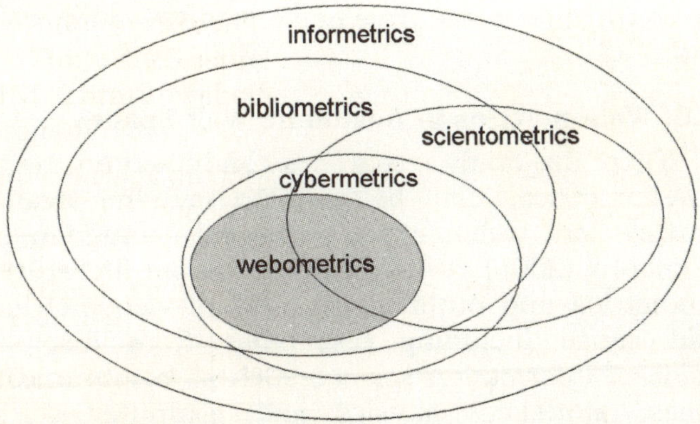

Fig. 2.1: Infor-, Biblio-, Sciento-, Cyber-, and Webo-metrics (*Source*: Björneborn & Ingwersen, 2004)

In this context, the field of webometrics may be seen as entirely encompassed by bibliometrics, because web documents, whether text or multimedia, are recorded information stored on web servers. This recording may be temporary, just as not all paper documents are properly archived. In the diagram, webometrics is partially covered by scientometrics, as many scholarly activities today are web based. Furthermore, webometrics is totally included within the field of cybermetrics as defined above.

In the fig. 2.1, the field of cybermetrics exceeds the boundaries of bibliometrics, because some activities in cyberspace normally are not recorded, but communicated synchronously as in chat rooms. Cybermetric studies of such activities still fit in the generic field of informetrics as the study of the quantitative aspects of information "*in any form*" and "*in any social group*" as stated by Tague-Sutcliffe (cf. Section 2.4).

The inclusion of webometrics expands the field of bibliometrics. As ideas rooted in bibliometrics, scientometrics and informetrics have contributed to the emergence of webometrics, ideas in webometrics might now contribute to the development of these embracing fields.

2.5.3. Webometrics in Academic Web Spaces

There are many researches conducted on the area of webometrics, can be counted by the available literature on webometrics. Thelwall, Vaughan and Björneborn (2005) reviewed the available literature on webometrics and outlined the field of webometrics in broad sense including researches from disciplines outside of information science such as communication studies, statistical physics and computer science. Further, they elaborated types of link analysis and areas beyond webometrics, including web log file analysis. They realized, the quantitative methods that originally designed for bibliometric analysis of citation patterns of scientific journal articles, could be applied to web by using commercial search engines, AltaVista, Yahoo!, AlltheWeb, MSN, HotBot, and Google, to provide the raw data. In another study by Noruzi (2006), he reviewed the literature on webometrics to know developmental history of web impact factor (WIF) and applied the webometric methodology in case of University of Tehran by using search engine Yahoo! Before this, Bossy (1995) suggested how "*netometrics*" could supplement bibliometrics and scientometrics in observing *"science in action"* on the Internet, enabling *"new ways of measuring the impact of scientific contribution that take into account the cooperative aspect of science"*.

The pioneer approach for webometrics was made by Larson (1996), in his paper *"Bibliometrics of the World Wide Web: an exploratory analysis of the intellectual structure of Cyberspace"*, investigated link structures in academic web spaces for the first time. He used search engine AltaVista in a co-citation analysis for a set of earth science related websites and could produce clusterings of websites that had topical similarities. After that, two scholars Almind and Ingwersen (1997), in their study, introduced the term *"webometrics"* and observed the webometric methodology in Nordic portion of the web.

Before the evolution of webometrics, McKiernan (1996) for "*backlinks,*" coined the term "*sitation*" to make it different from the term "*citation*" because *backlinks* are originated from the web. Further Rousseau (1997) analyzed the patterns of distribution of websites, site *backlinks* and site *self-links*. The search string *informetrics OR bibliometrics OR scientometrics* were retrieved by AltaVista and findings showed that the distribution of TLDs (top level domains, such as .edu, .uk, .dk) for the investigated sites followed the ubiquitous (often encountered) power-law-like Lotka distribution. He also used the term *"sitation"* in his study.

The concept of "web impact factor" (WIF) was first introduced by Ingwersen (1998), also demonstrated this by a study of seven small and medium scale national domains and four large web domains as well as six institutional websites of Nordic origin. He conceptualized the web impact factor (WIF) from ISI's "journal impact factor" (JIF) which has close analogy with citation analysis. Prior to Ingwersen, Rodriguez i Gairin (1997) had introduced the concept of "*information impact*" on web in a Spanish documentation journal but this article was not as influential as Ingwersen's. Furthermore, Ingwersen defined the concept of *"external Web Impact Factor"* (known as r*evised WIF*) for a given website (or TLD) as the number of external pages (pages in other sites or TLDs) with links to the given site (or TLD) divided by the number of indexed pages (in search engine's databases) available at the site (or TLD). He used search engine AltaVista for calculating the web impact factor. However, the fluctuations in results of search engine created problems which lead to variations in the calculation of web impact factor. On the basis of his study, he confidently stated that national, sector and larger web segments' web impact factor are more reliable as compared to small institutional web segments. As a consequence, Thelwall measured and developed the WIF as evident from his several papers (Thelwall, 2000; 2001b; 2001c; 2001d; 2002a; 2002d; 2003a; 2003b; Smith & Thelwall, 2002; Thelwall & Tang, 2003). Further, Thelwall (2001c; 2001d) introduced an important methodological improvement for webometric investigations of academic web spaces by deploying specially designed personal web crawlers.

In academic web spaces, interlinking studies are carried out to study the correlation of *backlinks* count and ranking of departments within a scientific domain. Thomas and Willett (2000) first time studied UK based library and information science (LIS) departments and found no significant correlation between *backlinks* counts and research ratings. Significant differences between *backlinks* counts and US newspaper rankings were found later for US library and information science (LIS) schools (Chu et al., 2002). Since then, in a number of different studies, significant research and *backlink* count correlations have been found for UK computer science departments (Li et al., 2003), US psychology and US chemistry departments (Tang & Thelwall, 2003).

The international linking patterns between universities are focused in few studies too. Smith and Thelwall (2002) compared linking among UK, Australian and New Zealand universities, and found that New Zealand was relatively isolated on the web. In another subsequent study on journals by Glänzel (2001), he found that international *backlinks* were very less as compared to national *backlinks*. In a significant study, where AltaVista was used to map the interlinking among universities in Asia-Pacific region (Thelwall & Smith, 2002), four types of diagrams: raw link counts; links divided by target system size (total number of web pages in all universities in the target country); links divided by source system size; and links divided by source and target system size were analysed and found that all four diagrams were very different, but it showed that Australia and Japan were at the heart of the web in the region, with Australia being a common target of links and Japan having a more balanced *incoming* and *outgoing links*.

Countrywide universities' network has been the focus for *backlink* analysis to analyze the interlinking pattern among all of the universities and institutes of a single country domain. The first attempt in this direction was made by Ingwersen (1998) who analyzed the online impact of six (6) university websites. In another study, Noruzi (2005) calculated the WIF for Iranian universities by using AltaVista. He found that Iranian universities have low *inlink WIFs*. His study demonstrated significant correlation between English language pages and *backlinks* counts. Further he concluded that due to linguistic reasons Iranian university websites are not attracting the attention over web. Smith and Thelwall (2002), in a study, calculated WIF for Australasian universities. They used specially designed web crawler and compared results with AltaVista and AlltheWeb, and found roughly proportional results for only Australia. In another study, Thelwall (2002e) explored inter relationship between UK university websites by link analysis and found that there are no techniques available to extract all the links. He used multivariate statistical analysis to count links in sets of 96 UK university websites. For studying structure of web links of university websites, in a study, Thelwall (2002f) analyzed the *backlink* structure of the top 100 linked-to pages on UK university websites, and characterized the page types of these 100 pages. In a similar kind of study of Israeli universities, Bar-Ilan (2004), explored the nature of links of academic institutes to characterize the links and the source and the target pages. His findings showed that the average source page and link are created by a person from mathematics, computer science, engineering or statistics for professional purposes.

Further investigations have given more insight into to the understanding of the phenomenon of academic website interlinking. Study conducted by Thelwall (2002a) investigated the alternative sources of links classified by top-level domains and found that links to UK universities from .edu sources produced results very similar to .ac.uk sources and suggested that academic link attractiveness is a phenomenon that is numerically similar on an international scale within a single country. In another study, hyperlink patterns of Canadian university websites were analyzed by a mathematical modeling approach which shows that faculty quality and the language of the university are important predictors for links to a university website. Higher the faculty quality means more number of links. It has been found that French language universities attracted significantly fewer links than English language universities (Vaughan & Thelwall, 2005).

The majority of studies in academic web spaces have analyzed inter-university links as outlined above, either within a discipline, within a national university system, or in international university comparisons.

However, some studies have focused instead on links between universities and other sectors of society, such as commerce, industry and government, for example, a study by Chen et al. (1998) and Leydesdorff and Curran, (2000).

Academic institutes and universities are centre for education and research. The scholarly productivity of universities is centered with its research activities and this has much influence on the web. Thelwall (2001a) made an attempt to assess the correlation between research productivity of 25 UK universities and link counts, and found significant correlation. This study had given the first concrete evidence of a real association between research and links. He used AltaVista and an information science web crawler for this study, both had given similar results. Another similar relationship was later found for Australia (Smith & Thelwall, 2002) and Taiwan (Thelwall & Tang, 2003). In this context, the most significant quantitative result of all was that the quantity of research produced by academics was the main reason for attracting links. Researchers of universities have attracted more links because they produced more qualitative web content (Thelwall & Harries, 2004).

In another study, geographic factors for interlinking of academic web spaces have also been investigated. Thelwall (2002c) developed a methodology to analyze the patterns of interlinking among university websites and used it to indicate that the degree of interlinking decreases with distance in UK. This gives an insight that as distance increases hyperlinking patterns of websites decreases.

Many webometric studies of academic web spaces have chosen scholars as the basic unit of analysis, for example, collecting data of invocations: the mentioning of a scholar's name in any context in a web page. Cronin et al. (1998) found academics to be invoked on the web in a wide variety of contexts, including informal documents such as conference information pages and course reading lists. In another study conducted by Thelwall et al. (2003) identified the academic subjects that have most impact on the web for Taiwan and Australia. The basis for the characterization was domains not web pages. For knowing the factors which affect web impact of scientist's personal homepages, Barjak et al. (2007) conducted a study and found that scientists' personal and institutional characteristics are the significant reasons for higher impact. Further they suggested that for increasing online visibility, one should include full text journal articles, discussion papers, draft manuscripts, conference presentations etc. in their personal homepages. In another study on Nobel laureates' homepages, Nelson (2005) showed that the pages of prize winners in chemistry received significantly fewer links than the pages of economics. Previous researches at other levels (Tang & Thelwall, 2003, 2004; Thelwall, Harries & Wilkinson, 2003) have shown that web linking is discipline dependant.

Problems persist while counting of web pages in a site using search engine or doing it manually. For this, Thelwall and Harries (2003) investigated the connection of web links to research based web pages of UK universities and classified the pages into four categories and an advanced web document model is described. Before this, Thelwall (2002b) introduced the *Alternative Document Models* (ADMs), particularly applied in academic web spaces as aggregated units of analysis. He used the terminology for four main ADMs which are in use: the *page, directory, domain* and *site* ADM. The *page* ADM was the default unit consisting of individual files on a web server. In the *directory* ADM, all pages in the same web server directory identified through the URL file name path, are counted as one unit – as an aggregated "macro document". The *domain* ADM aggregates all pages with the same (subsite) domain name in its URL into a common unit of analysis. The *site* ADM (originally called the *university* ADM) aggregates all derivative domain names into a single unit of analysis by specifying the domain name ending. The ADM models have been useful for avoiding irregularities in link data and conceptual problems with counting pages. Thelwall (2002b) applied the ADM models to the UK academic web spaces with a data set of 108 universities. In particular, the aggregated directory and domain (subsite) ADMs produced more significant results that correlated better with the aforementioned Research Assessment Exercise[1] (RAE) governmental research productivity measures.

There have been few noteworthy efforts made by researchers to reveal the motive of linking of websites. The first exhaustive approach made by Kim (2000), conducted a survey, by using HotBot, for finding the motive of hyperlinking pattern in scholarly electronic articles. Nineteen (19) hyperlinking motives have been identified and categorized into three classes: scholarly, social, and technological. The study found that in scholarly electronic environment scholars use hyperlinks for a variety of scholarly and non-scholarly purposes and these hyperlinks usually offers only a partial reflection of the scholarly impact or influence of the hyperlinked source. In another study, Wilkinson et al. (2003) investigated the motivation for academic website interlinking and found that scholarly activities conducted by academic institutions has significant reason for interlinking.

2.5.4. Tools for Webometric Studies

Search engines are widely adopted tools for webometric research. These are particularly useful for counting of pages over large areas of the web. AltaVista

---

1 Research Assessment Exercise is an exercise of the UK higher education funding councils HEFCE, SFC, HEFCW, and DEL to evaluate the quality of research undertaken by UK higher education institutions.

allows advanced Boolean queries to combine information requests about pages, links and domains (Almind & Ingwersen, 1997). It can be used to return counts of pages or link pages that satisfy given criteria. However, commercial search engines have a number of drawbacks. They never return complete results and cover only 16 percent of the whole web (Lawrence & Giles, 1999). The results returned by them are also unreliable and fluctuate (Ingwersen, 1998; Rousseau, 1999; Snyder & Rosenbaum, 1999; Bar-Ilan, 1999; Mettrop & Nieuwenhuysen, 2001, Shukla & Vanlalfeli, 2014; Shukla & Tripathi, 2014). In another study, it has been found that the results returned by search engines are problematic because their coverage is variable and they provide different results over a short period of time (Thelwall, 2001d). He further conducted study on personally designed web crawler which has returned significant and reliable result. Nevertheless, AltaVista has been found to be more reliable than any other (Thelwall, 2001e; Vaughan & Thelwall, 2003) and have good coverage of academic websites (Thelwall, 2001c). Researchers should always take steps to assess the accuracy and coverage of results because the algorithms are subject to change without notice, and the effect of the advanced commands are not always fully documented (Thelwall, Vaughan & Björneborn, 2005). Accuracy of search engines' can be checked by testing a sample of the pages returned by AltaVista to ensure that they do contain the features specified in the query. However, coverage is more difficult to check, but for any given study it may be possible to use AltaVista's *host:* command to check the number of pages indexed by AltaVista (Thelwall, Vaughan & Björneborn, 2005). Björneborn and Ingwersen (2001) recommend the use of sampling and filtering to clean up data from search engines, though it is difficult to perform. An alternative strategy is to employ multiple search engines, and average the results. Li et al. (2003) used AltaVista for data collection and confirmed that to calculate the WIF the size of site which is denominator in formula is not reliable. Noruzi (2005) has done a time series WIF for the University of Tehran in order to monitor performance of AltaVista and shows that there large fluctuation in WIF during the time.

It is found that commercial search engines display national biases in site coverage. In a study conducted for four countries showed that US sites were much better covered by three major search engines than China, Taiwan and Singapore. Though, website language did not cause any difficulty in coverage (Vaughan & Thelwall, 2004). Time series data can be obtained from some search engines and also the Internet archive. For example, AltaVista allows searches of pages by their last modified (or creation) date (Leydesdorff & Curran, 2000). The Internet Archive Wayback Machine gives genuine time series data because it records all the dates on which a page was found (Thelwall & Vaughan, 2004). Bar-Ilan (1999) examined the performance of search engines over time and found search engines loose the information content and relevant URLs. In another study by Snyder and Rosenbaum (1999) investigated the performance and problems of search engines, HotBot and AltaVista. They further suggested that commercial search engines have limited scope for the webometric research. Further, Thelwall (2000) conducted a study to check the WIF reliability based on AltaVista results. Further he tested the coverage of search engines and suggested that search engine should be used for web based researches as they have high coverage of the actual pages in website. Again Bar-Ilan (2000), in a study, examined search performance of two search engines "HotBot" and "Snap" over a period of ten days and found Snap's results were rather stable than "HotBot". In another study, Thelwall (2001e) investigated the responsiveness of search engines AltaVista, HotBot, and Yahoo! over a period of seven months and found evidence that only Google is able to respond quickly to changes and capable of finding new websites (as per results seen after the integration of Yahoo! with Google in June, 2000) whereas AltaVista's results were very stable over time. Bar-Ilan (2002) also evaluated performances of search engines over time by using a set of measures. The measures introduced were: technical relevance; technical precision; relative coverage; new and totally new URLs; forgotten, recovered and lost URLs; well-handled and mishandled URLs; self-overlap; number of rounds in which the URL is retrieved; and persistent URLs. These measures are illustrated through specific examples. In a very recent study, Thelwall (2008) carried a research to extract accurate and complete results from search engine Windows Live. He introduced two new methods (automated query splitting and automated domain & TLD searching) to extract extra URLs from search engines. He found both the methods were successfully identifying additional URLs. He further confirmed that there is no way to get complete list of URLs or accurate hit counts from Windows Live also.

2.6. CONCEPTUAL FRAMEWORK OF WEB IMPACT FACTOR (WIF)

Björneborn (2004) in his doctoral dissertation made an attempt to build a basic consistent conceptual framework for webometric link structure analysis. The conceptual framework used in the present web impact factor (WIF) analysis is as follows:

2.6.1. Basic Link Terminology

Since the emergence of webometric research, there has been lack of appropriate terminology and concepts. First time Björneborn (2004) conceptualized various terms in the field of webometrics. Earlier Ingwersen (1998) has also used the terms related to web impact factor (WIF) analysis. However, following are the link terminologies which provide more insight to the present WIF analysis:

Web node: It denotes a unit of analysis like a web page, directory or website but could also be an entire top level domain of a country.

Incoming link: Also referred as *inlink*, *backlink*, *inbound link*, *inward link* and *citation*. The link coming to a website from another website is known as *incoming link*. McKiernan (1996) and Rousseau (1997) used *"sitation"* for *incoming links* with clear connotations to bibliometric citation analysis. This is to be noted that Rousseau used *"sitation"* for web based citation.

External link: An external link referred as a link pointing out from a website. Often referred as synonymous to *outlink*.

Outlink: Also referred as *outbound link*, *outward link* and *outgoing link*. The link outgoing from a website to another website is known as *outlink*.

Self-link: Also referred as *internal link*, *navigational link* or *inside link*. The link coming from different web pages of a website to any web page of that very website is known as *self-link*. *Self-links* are only made for navigational purposes.

Reciprocal link: The links which are mutually incoming and outgoing between two websites are known as *reciprocal link*.

Transversal link: A link that is directly linked to dissimilar nodes across directed link path. These links function as shortcut between two web nodes.

Fig. 2.2 below illustrates the terminology used to describe different link topologies, i.e. different degrees of cohesiveness and connectedness of link structures on the web.

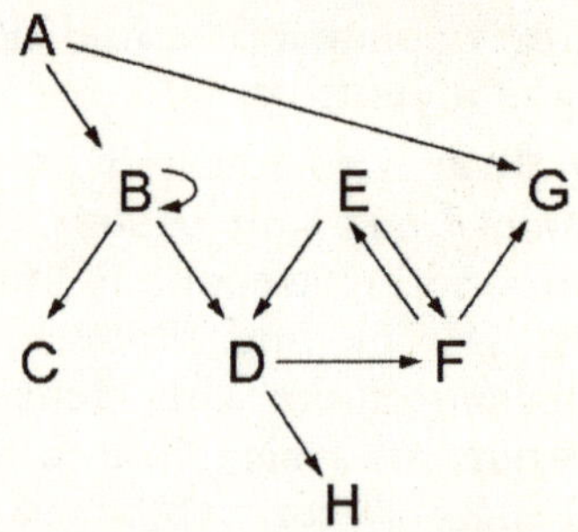

- B has an *inlink* from A; B is *inlinked*; A is *inlinking*
- B has an *outlink* to C; B is *outlinking*; C is *outlinked*
- B has a *self-link*; B is *self-linking*
- E and F have *reciprocal links*; E and F are *reciprocally* linked
- A has a *transversal* outlink to G: functioning as a shortcut

Fig. 2.2: Basic Webometric Link Terminology (Björneborn, 2004)

Letters A-H represents different web node levels such as web pages, web directories, websites, or top level domains of countries or generic sectors.

The terms *inlink* and *outlink* were used in computer science based web studies by Broder et al. (2000), Chen et al. (1998), and Pirolli et al. (1996). The terms *outlink* and *inlink* have analogous characteristics with the terms *reference* and *citation* in bibliometrics, respectively. Price (1970) has elaborated the conceptual difference between the terms *reference* and *citation* and matched the difference between *outlink* and *inlink*.

On the web, *self-links* are used for a variety of purposes. This reflects a special case of the general difference between *outlinks* / *inlinks* and *references* / *citations* (Björneborn, 2004). *Self-links* are of two types: *page self-links* and *site self-links*. The *page self-links* point from one section to another within the same page while *site self-links* are basically navigational pointers from one page to another within the same website. *Reciprocal links* are mutual *inlinks* and *outlinks* between two web nodes. *Transversal links* (Björneborn,

2001; 2004; Björneborn & Ingwersen, 2001) span across dissimilar topical domains on the web.

2.6.2. Web Impact Factor Data Retrieval Tools and Techniques

There are number of tools available for measuring web impact factor. There are following types of tools available for webometric studies:

2.6.2.1. Online Tools

The WIF data can be collected using available online tools. There is diverse variety of online tools. These online tools are freely available. A few significant of them are:

Domain Inbound Links Checker : This is a free online computer program which analyzes up to 1000 *backlinks* of arbitrary page (or website) and shows domains of *backlinks*. It also shows separately different classes of URLs like .edu, .mil, .com, .net, .gov and other. It collects all the *backlink* web pages from the same website at a place by which one can count the number of *backlinks* from a website.

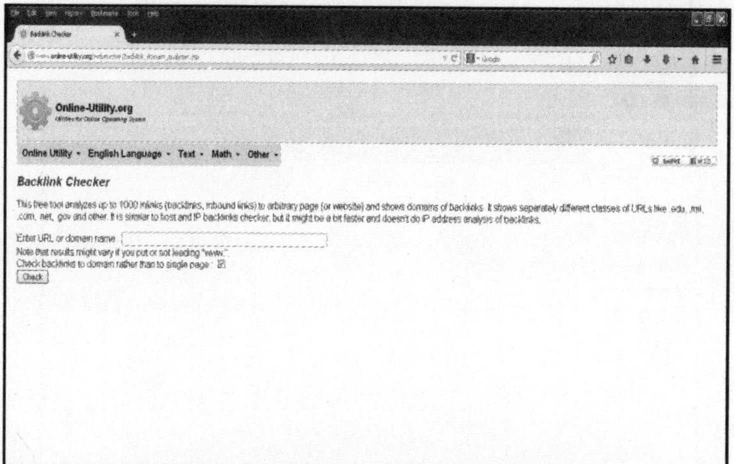

Fig. 2.3: Domain Inbound Links Checker

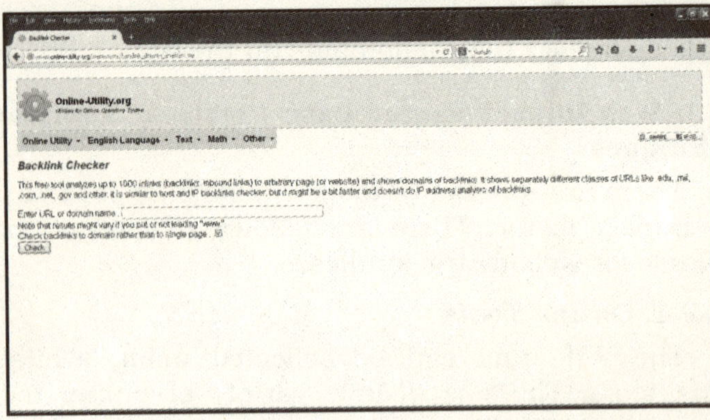
Online-Utility.org
Online Utility · English Language · Text · Math · Other
Backlink Checker
This free tool analyzes up to 1000 inlinks (backlinks, inbound links) to arbitrary page (or website) and shows domains of backlinks. It shows separately different classes of URLs like .edu, .mil, .com, .net, .gov and other. It is similar to host and IP backlinks checker, but it might be a bit faster and doesn't do IP address analysis of backlinks.
Enter URL or domain name :
Note that results might vary if you put or not leading "www"
Check backlinks to domain rather than to single page :
Check

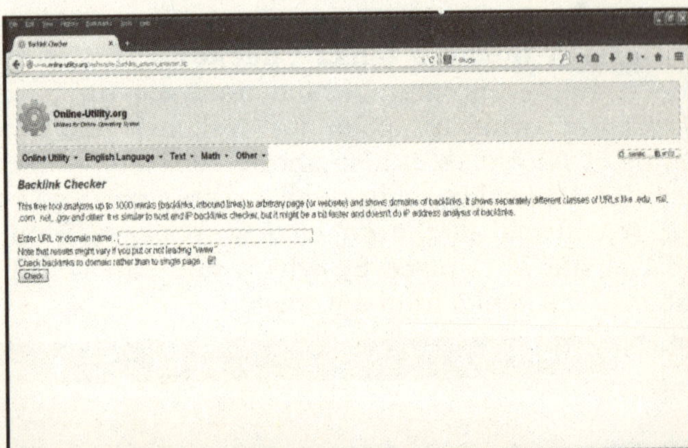
Online-Utility.org
Online Utility · English Language · Text · Math · Other
Backlink Checker
This free tool analyzes up to 1000 inlinks (backlinks, inbound links) to arbitrary page (or website) and shows domains of backlinks. It shows separately different classes of URLs like .edu, .mil, .com, .net, .gov and other. It is similar to host and IP backlinks checker, but it might be a bit faster and doesn't do IP address analysis of backlinks.
Enter URL or domain name :
Note that results might vary if you put or not leading "www"
Check backlinks to domain rather than to single page :
Check

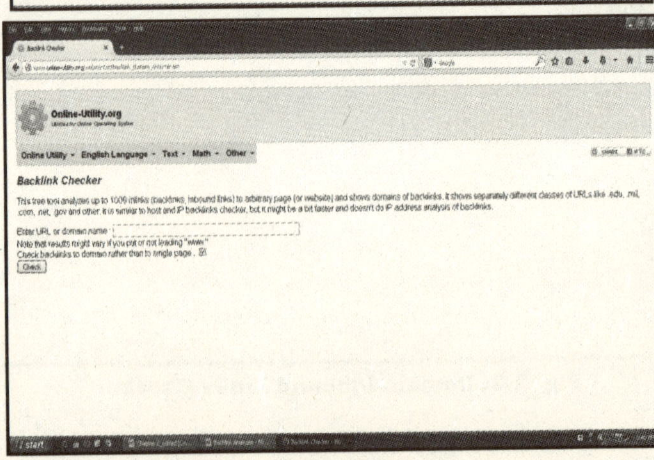
Online-Utility.org
Online Utility · English Language · Text · Math · Other
Backlink Checker
This free tool analyzes up to 1000 inlinks (backlinks, inbound links) to arbitrary page (or website) and shows domains of backlinks. It shows separately different classes of URLs like .edu, .mil, .com, .net, .gov and other. It is similar to host and IP backlinks checker, but it might be a bit faster and doesn't do IP address analysis of backlinks.
Enter URL or domain name :
Note that results might vary if you put or not leading "www"
Check backlinks to domain rather than to single page :
Check

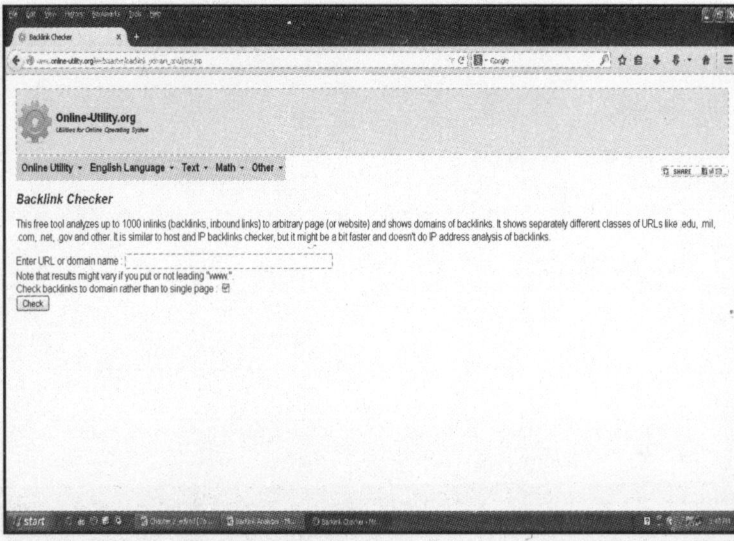
Backlink Checker
Online-Utility.org
Online Utility
English Language
Text
Math
Other
Backlink Checker
This free tool analyzes up to 1000 inlinks (backlinks, inbound links) to arbitrary page (or website) and shows domains of backlinks. It shows separately different classes of URLs like .edu, .mil, .com, .net, .gov and other. It is similar to host and IP backlinks checker, but it might be a bit faster and doesn't do IP address analysis of backlinks.
Enter URL or domain name :
Note that results might vary if you put or not leading "www.".
Check backlinks to domain rather than to single page :
Check
start

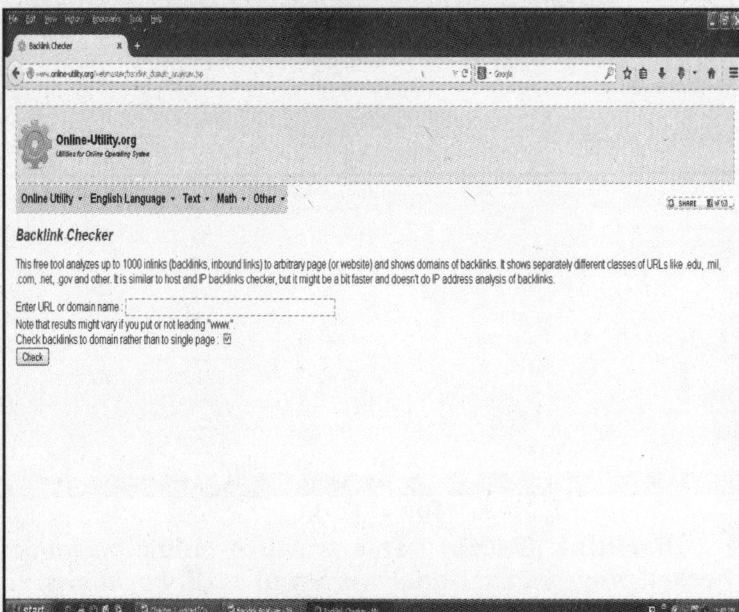
Backlink Checker
Online-Utility.org
Online Utility
English Language
Text
Math
Other
Backlink Checker
This free tool analyzes up to 1000 inlinks (backlinks, inbound links) to arbitrary page (or website) and shows domains of backlinks. It shows separately different classes of URLs like .edu, .mil, .com, .net, .gov and other. It is similar to host and IP backlinks checker, but it might be a bit faster and doesn't do IP address analysis of backlinks.
Enter URL or domain name :
Note that results might vary if you put or not leading "www.".
Check backlinks to domain rather than to single page :
Check
start

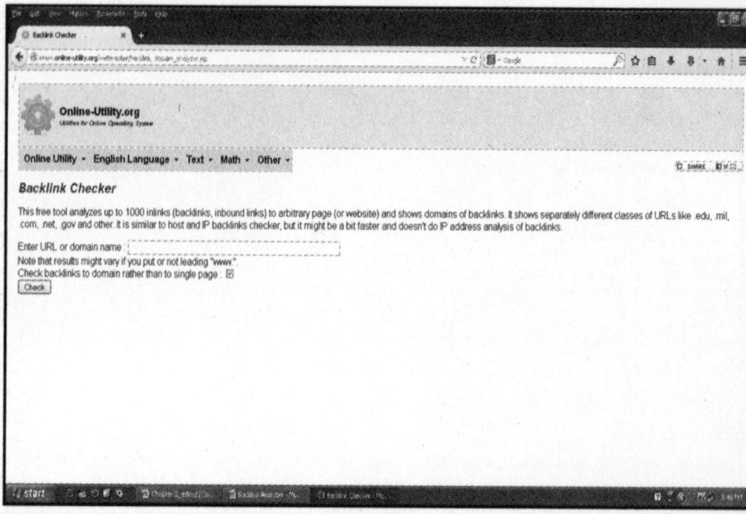

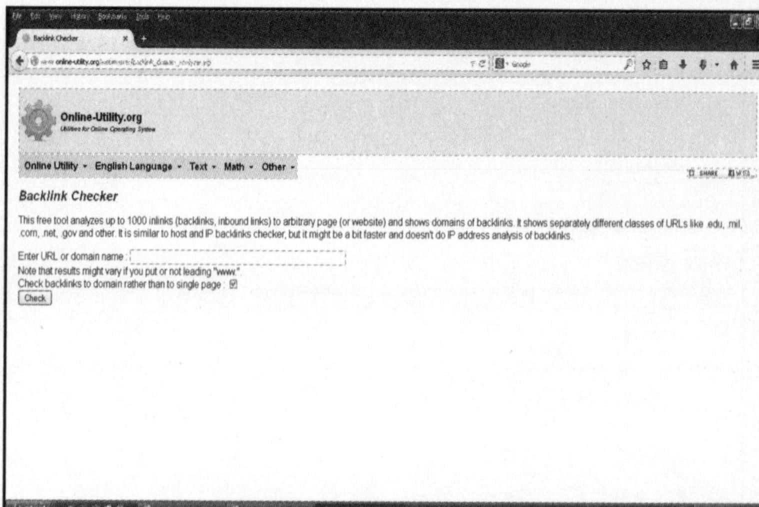

Top of Form

Backlink Watch! : This is a free online *backlink* checker program that analyzes up to 1000 *backlinks* to any web page as well as domain of any website. It shows URLs of *backlinks* with anchor text, page rank, *outbound link* of a *backlink* giving page and so on.

Though, it analyses up to 1000 *backlinks* but also shows the number of all *backlinks* for given URL or domain. It also returns all the *backlinks* from the same source but doesn't organize them.

Fig. 2.4: Backlink Watch!

Link Popularity : This is another free online *backlink* checker program. It analyzes unlimited *backlinks* to any web pages as well as domain of any website. The results returned by this are based on commercial search engines Ask.com, Yahoo Site Explorer, Google, AlltheWeb and AltaVista. It functions as meta-crawler.

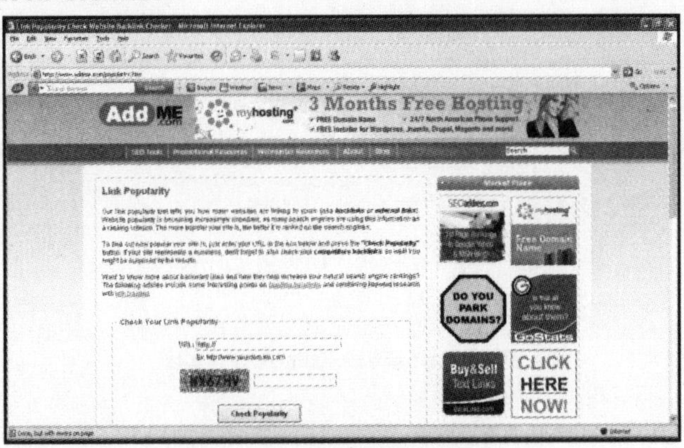

Fig. 2.5: Link Popularity

2.6.2.2. Software Tools

There are number of search engine optimization (SEO) firms, providing the free software tools to measure the web impact factor calculation. Following are significant ones:

Backlink Analyzer : It is a free link analysis tool which can be downloaded from http://tools.seobook.com/backlink-analyzer/. It offers number of *backlinks*, detailed list of top level domains, pointing pages, link type relationship, deep link ratio, anchor text, IP addresses of *backlink* giving URLs, Alexa data[2], page title, number of links on a page and number of *outbound links* on a page etc. The software program takes a minimum of 5 minutes to maximum 5 hours for an institution depending on the structure and size of the website. It collects data from Google, Yahoo!, MSN and AlltheWeb at a time, if selected. The crawled data returned by it can be save in excel / spreadsheet.

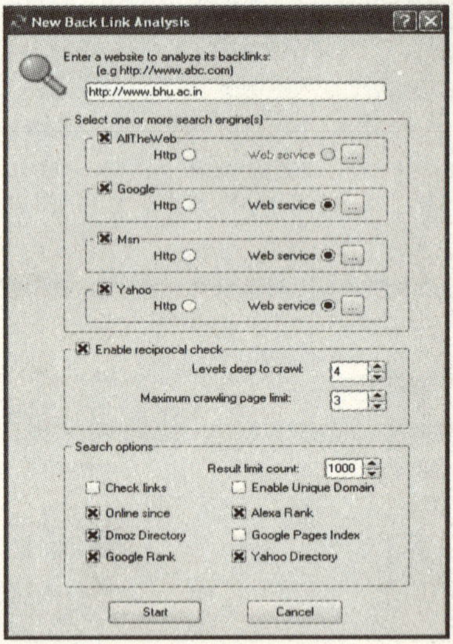

Fig. 2.6: Backlink Analyzer

---

2 Alexa data includes website's traffic rank, related links, links pointing in, contact information etc.

PR Weaver : PR Weaver is browser based software which displays Google search results with PageRank. It is designed for search engine optimization (SEO) experts. The results returned by it can be saved as a hypertext markup languagae (HTML) sheet or in a comma separated value (CSV) list. PR Weaver retrieves the text of *backlinks* and returns analysed link text (anchor text) and alt text (Alt Img text). It filters *self-links* and *backlinks*. It also displays results according to language and country.

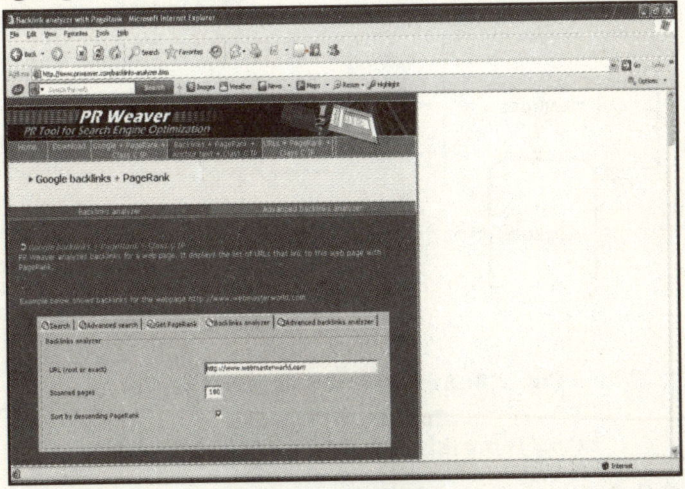

Fig. 2.7: PR Weaver

The other software tools available for *backlinks* retrieval from the web are Data Doctor Backlink Checker (version 2.0.1.5) and Link Popularity Check 3.0.3 etc.

2.6.2.3. Personal Web Crawlers

Personal web crawlers come into the category of search engines. A crawler (also known a spider, robot) is a piece of software that can automatically and iteratively download pages, and extract as well as download their links (Heydon & Najork, 1999; Thelwall, 2001f). Web crawlers search new pages by following links. They also miss isolated pages, links to pages which crawler cannot understand, for instance JavaScript pages, password-protected pages, pages with robots exclusion protocol and temporarily down condition of server. This shows crawlers also don't cover 100 percent of the websites.

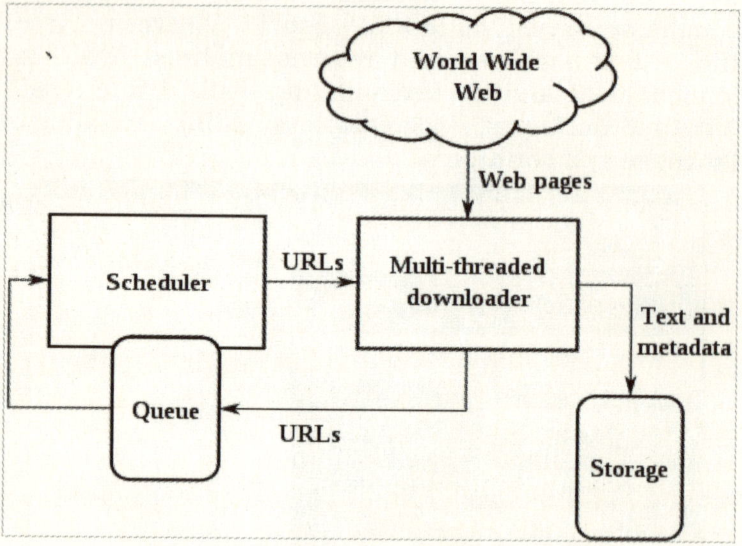

Fig. 2.8: Architecture of Web Crawler

(*Source*: Wikipedia: http://en.wikipedia.org/wiki/Web_crawler)

2.6.2.4. Search Engines

Search engines are widely used as information retrieval tools. These are extensively used in the webometric research for retrieving data from the web. There are number of search engines available with distinct features. The most widely used search engines are AltaVista, Yahoo!, Google, AlltheWeb, Lycos, MSN, Excite and Metacrawlers HotBot, Dogpile etc. Search engine AltaVista (Rodríguez i Gairín, 1997; Almind & Ingwersen, 1997; Ingwersen, 1998; Smith, 1999; Snyder & Rosenbaum, 1999; Thelwall, 2000; Thelwall, 2001c; Smith & Thelwall, 2002; Thelwall, 2002c; Kousha & Horri, 2004; Noruzi, 2005; Shukla, 2009; Shukla & Tripathi, 2009, Shukla & Vanlalfeli, 2014;

Shukla & Tripathi, 2014) has been mostly used by researchers in webometric studies.

Search engines like AltaVista (Almind & Ingwersen, 1997) and Yahoo Site Explorer use advanced programming through which webometric research data can be obtained in terms of counts of pages or linked pages. Due to this very facility included in search engines, webometrics developed very fast. For retrieving specific result from search engines, advanced search help pages and options can also be consulted. Search engines have a number of drawbacks. In a study conducted by Lawrence and Giles (1999) found that search engines cover only 16 percent of publicly available web. Search engines results are sometimes not reliable (Ingwersen, 1998; Rousseau, 1999; Snyder & Rosenbaum, 1999; Bar-Ilan, 1999; Mettrop & Nieuwenhuysen, 2001, Shukla & Vanlalfeli, 2014; Shukla & Tripathi, 2014) but there are no other options available. Despite that search engine AltaVista has been found to be more reliable (Thelwall, 2001c; Vaughan & Thelwall, 2003) and has given significant coverage to academic websites (Thelwall, 2001c).

REFERENCES

Aguillo, I. F. (1998). STM information on the web and the development of new Internet R & D databases and indicators. *Online Information 98: Proceedings* (pp. 239-243). Oxford: Learned Information.

Almind, T. C. & Ingwersen, P. (1996). Informetric analysis on the World Wide Web: a methodological approach to "internetometrics". Centre for Informetric Studies, Royal School of Library and Information Science [CIS Report 2].

Almind, T. C. & Ingwersen, P. (1997). Informetric analyses on the World Wide Web: methodological approaches to webometrics. *Journal of Documentation, 53*(4), 404-426.

Backlink Analyzer. (n.d.). [computer software]. Retrieved August 12, 2014, from SEOTOOLS. Available at http://tools.seobook.com/backlink-analyzer/

Backlink Watch!. (n.d.). [online software tool]. Retrieved August 12, 2014, from

BACKLINK WATCH! Available at http://www.backlinkwatch.com/

Bar-Ilan, J. (1997). The "mad cow disease", Usenet newsgroups and bibliometric laws. *Scientometrics, 39*(1), 29-55.

Bar-Ilan, J. (1999). Search engine results over time: a case study on search engine stability. *Cybermetrics, 2/3*(1), Paper 1. Available at http://www.cindoc.csic.es/cybermetrics/articles/v2i1p1.html

Bar-Ilan, J. (2000). Evaluating the stability of the search tools HotBot and Snap: a case study. *Online Information Review, 24*(6), 439-449.

Bar-Ilan, J. (2002). Methods for measuring search engine performance over time. *Journal of the American Society for Information Science and Technology, 53*(4), 308-319.

Bar-Ilan, J. (2004). A macroscopic link analysis of academic institutions within a country: the case of Israel. *Scientometrics, 59*(2), 391-403.

Barjak, F., Li, X. & Thelwall, M. (2007). Which factors explain the web impact of scientists' personal homepages? *Journal of the American Society for Information Science and Technology, 58*(2), 200-211.

Berners-Lee, T. & Cailliau, R. (1990). *World Wide Web: proposal for a hypertext project.* Available at http://www.w3.org/Proposal.html

Björneborn, L. (2001). Small-world linkage and co-linkage. *Proceedings of the 12th ACM Conference on Hypertext and Hypermedia* (pp. 133-134). New York: ACM.

Björneborn, L. (2004). *Small-world link structures across an academic web space: a library and information science approach (Doctoral Dissertation).* Copenhagen, Denmark: Royal School of Library and Information Science.

Björneborn, L. & Ingwersen, P. (2001). Perspectives of webometrics. *Scientometrics, 50*(1), 65-82.

Björneborn, L. & Ingwersen, P. (2004). Towards a basic framework for webometrics. *Journal of the American Society for Information Science and Technology, 55*(14), 1216-1227.

Bossy, M. J. (1995). *The last of the litter: "netometrics"*. *Solaris*, 2. Presses Universitaires de Rennes. Available at http://biblio-fr.info.unicaen.fr/bnum/jelec/Solaris/d02/2bossy.html

Bradford, S. C. (1934). Sources of information on specific subjects. *Engineering, 137*, 85–86.

Broder, A., Kumar, R., Maghoul, F., Raghavan, P., Rajagopalan, S., Stata, R., Wiener, J. (2000). Graph structure in the web. *Computer Networks, 33*(1-6), 309-320. Available at http://www.almaden.ibm.com/cs/k53/www9.final

Brookes, B. C. (1988). Comments on the scope of bibliometrics. *In* L. Egghe & R. Rousseau (Eds.), *Informetrics 87/88. Select Proceedings of the first International Conference on Bibliometrics and Theoretical Aspects of Information Retrieval* (pp. 29–41). Amsterdam: Elsevier Science.

Brookes, B. C. (1990). Biblio-, sciento-, infor- metrics? what are we talking about? *In* L. Egghe & R. Rousseau (Eds.), *Informetrics 89/90: selection of papers submitted for the Second International Conference on Bibliometrics, Scientometrics and Informetrics* (pp. 31-43). Amsterdam: Elsevier Science.

Chakrabarti, S., Dom, B. E., Kumar, S. R., ...Kleinberg, J. (1999). Mining the web's link structure. *IEEE Computer, 32*(8), 60-67.

Chen, C., Newman, J., Newman, R. & Rada, R. (1998). How did university departments interweave the web: a study of connectivity and underlying factors. *Interacting with Computers, 10*, 353-373.

Chu, H., He, S. & Thelwall, M. (2002). Library and information science schools in Canada and USA: a webometric perspective. *Journal of Education for Library and Information Science, 43*(2), 110-125.

Cole, F. J. & Eals, N. B. (1917). The history of comparative anatomy. Part I: a statistical analysis of the literature. *Science Progress, 11*, 578–596.

Cronin, B., Snyder, H. W., Rosenbaum, H., Martinson, A. & Callahan, E. (1998). Invoked in the web. *Journal of the American Society for Information Science, 49*(14), 1319-1328.

Data Doctor Backlink Checker (version 2.0.1.5). (n.d.). Retrieved June 17, 2009, from Pro Data Doctor. Available at http://www.softpedia.com/get/Internet/Other-Internet-Related/Data-Doctor-Back-Link-Checker.shtml

Derek J. de Solla Price. (n.d.). Retrieved June 17, 2009, from Wikipedia: http://en.wikipedia.org/wiki/Derek_J._de_Solla_Price

Domain Inbound Links Checker. (n.d.). [computer software]. Retrieved August 12, 2014, from Online Utility.org. Available at http://www.online-utility.org/webmaster/backlink_domain_analyzer.jsp

Dodge, M. (1999). The geography of cyberspace. *CASA Working Paper 8.* London: Centre for Advanced Spatial Analysis, University College London.

Egghe, L. & Rousseau, R. (1990). *Introduction to informetrics: quantitative methods in library, documentation and information science.* Amsterdam: Elsevier.

Etzioni, O. (1996). The World Wide Web: quagmire or gold mine? *Communications of the ACM, 39*(11), 65-68.

Fairthorne, R. A. (1969). Empirical hyperbolic distributions (Bradford-Zipf-Mandelbrot) for bibliometrics description and prediction. *Journal of Documentation, 25,* 319–343.

Fano, R. M. (1956). Information theory and the retrieval of recorded information. *In* Shera, J .H., Kent, A. & Perry, J. W. (Eds.), *Documentation in action* (pp. 238-244). New York: Rein-hold.

Garfield, E. (1972). Citation analysis as a tool in journal evaluation. *Science, 178*(4060), 471-479.

Girardin, L. (1996). Mapping the virtual geography of the World Wide Web. *Proceedings of the 5th WWW Conference.* Available at http://www.girardin.org/luc//cgv/www5/index.html

Glänzel, W. (2001). National characteristics in international scientific co-authorship relations. *Scientometrics, 51*(1), 69-115.

Glossary of Documentation Terms. (1976). London: British Standard Institution, 1976 (BS 5408:1976).

Gross, P. L. K. & Gross, F. M. (1927). College libraries and chemical education. *Science, 66,* 386-389.

Hawkins, D. T. (1977). Unconventional uses of on-line information retrieval systems: on-line bibliometrics studies. *Journal of the American Society for Information Science, 28*(1), 13–18.

Herring, S. C. (2002). Computer-mediated communication on the Internet. *In* B. Cronin (ed.), *Annual Review of Information Science and Technology* (pp. 109-168). Medford, NJ: Information Today.

Heydon, A. & Najork, M. (1999). Mercator: a scalable, extensible web crawler. *World Wide Web*, 2, 219-229.

Hulme, E. W. (1923). *Statistical bibliography in relation to the growth of modern civilization.* London: Butler & Grafton.

Ingwersen, P. (1998). The calculation of web impact factors. *Journal of Documentation, 54*(2), 236-243.

Ingwersen, P. & Christensen, F. H. (1997). Data set isolation for bibliometric online analyses of research publications: fundamental methodological issues. *Journal of the American Society for Information Science, 48*, 205–217.

Kessler, M. M. (1983). Bibliographic coupling between scientific papers. *American Documentation, 14*, 10-15.

Kim, H. J. (2000). Motivations for hyperlinking in scholarly electronic articles: a qualitative study. *Journal of the American Society for Information Science, 51*(10), 887-899.

Kosala, R. & Blockeel, H. (2000). Web mining research: a survey. *SIGKDD Explorations, 2*(1), 1-15.

Kousha, K. & Horri, A. (2004). The relationship between scholarly publishing and the counts of academic inlinks to Iranian university websites: exploring academic link creation motivations. *Journal of Information Management and Scientometrics, 1*(2), 13-22.

Larson, R. R. (1996). Bibliometrics of the World Wide Web: an exploratory analysis of the intellectual structure of cyberspace. *In* S. Hardin (Ed.), *Proceedings of the 59th Annual Meeting, ASIS 96, Baltimore, Maryland* (pp. 71-79).

Medford, NJ: Learned Information. Available at http://sherlock.berkley.edu/asis96/asis96.html

Lawrence, S. & Giles, C. L. (1999). Accessibility of information on the web. *Nature, 400*, 107-110.

Leydesdorff, L. & Curran, M. (2000). Mapping university-industry-government relations on the Internet: the construction of indicators for a knowledge-based economy.

Cybermetrics, 4(1). Available at http://www.cindoc.csic.es/cybermetrics/articles/v4i1p2.html

Li, X., Thelwall, M., Musgrove, P. & Wilkinson, D. (2003). The relationship between the WIFs or inlinks of computer science departments in UK and their RAE ratings or research productivities in 2001. *Scientometrics, 57*(2), 239-255.

Link Popularity. (n.d.). [online link popularity checker]. Retrieved June 17, 2009, from Add Me.com. Available at http://www.addme.com/popularity.htm

Link Popularity Check 3.0.3. (n.d.). [computer software]. Retrieved June 17, 2009, From Link Popularity Check. Available at http://www.checkyourlinkpopularity.com/

Marshakova, I. (1973). System of document connection based on references. *Nauchne-Tekumicheskala Informatsija* (Series 2). 3-8.

McKiernan, G. (1996). *CitedSites(sm): citation indexing of web resources.* Available at http://www.public.iastate.edu/~CYBERSTACKS/Cited.htm

Mettrop, W. & Nieuwenhuysen, P. (2001). Internet search engines - fluctuations in document accessibility. *Journal of Documentation, 57*(5), 623-651.

Molyneux, R. E. & Williams, R. V. (1999). Measuring the Internet. *Annual Review of Information Science and Technology, 34*, 287-339.

Nacke, O. (1979). Informetrie: eine neuer name für eine neue disziplin. *Nachrichten für Documentation, 30*(6), 219-226.

Nacke, O., Wehmeier, R. & Eisenhardt, O. H. (1980). Informetrie und scientometrie: cui bono? ein dialog, eine liste und ein programm. *Nachrichten für Dokumentation, 31*, 100–106.

Nalimov, V. V. & Mulchenko, Z. M. (1969). Scientometrics, study of the development of science as an information process. Moscow: Nauka.

Nelson, M. (2005). Academic homepages and Nobel laureates. *In* P. Ingwersen & B. Larson (Eds.), *Proceedings of ISSI 2005 - 10th International Conference of the International Society for Scientometrics and Informetrics* (Vol. 1, pp. 193-196). Stockhom: Karolinska University Press.

Noruzi, A. (2005). Web impact factors for Iranian universities. *Webology, 2*(1), Article 11. Retrieved from http://www.webology.ir/2005/v2n1/a11.html

Noruzi, A. (2006). The web impact factors: a critical review. *The Electronic Library, 24*(4), 490-500.

Otlet, P. (1934). Treatise on documentation. The book on the book. Theory and practice. Brussels: Van Keerberghen.

Pirolli, P., Pitkow, J. & Rao, R. (1996). Silk from a sow's ear: extracting usable structures from the web. *CHI 96 Electronic Proceedings*. Available at http://www.acm.org/sigchi/chi96/proceedings/papers/Pirolli_2/pp2.html

Potter, W. G. (1981). Introduction to bibliometrics. *Library Trends, 30*, 5.

Price, Derek de Solla (1970). Citation measures of hard science, soft science, technology and nonscience. *In* C. E. Nelson & D. K. Pollock (Eds.), *Communication among scientists and engineers* (pp. 3-22). Lexington: Heath Lexington Books.

Pritchard, A. (1969). Statistical bibliography or bibliometrics? *Journal of Documentation, 25*, 348–349.

PR Weaver. (n.d.). [computer software]. Retrieved August 12, 2014, from PR Weaver: PR tool for Search Engine Optimization. Available at http://www.prweaver.com/

Ravichandra Rao, I. K. (1983). *Quantitative methods in library and information science*. New Delhi: Wiley Eastern.

Rodríguez i Gairín, J. M. (1997). Impact assessment of information on the Internet: AltaVista, the citation index of the web. *Revista Española De Documentación Científica, 20*(2), 175-181.

Rousseau, R. (1997). Sitations: an exploratory study. *Cybermetrics*, 1(1), Available at http://www.cindoc.csic.es/cybermetrics/articles/v2i1p2.html

Rousseau, R. (1999). Daily time series of common single word searches in AltaVista and NorthernLight. *Cybermetrics, 2/3*(1), Paper 2. Available at http://www.cindoc.csic.es/cybermetrics/articles/v1i1p1.html

Scientometrics. (n.d.). Retrieved June 17, 2009, from Wikipedia: http://en.wikipedia.org/wiki/Scientometrics

Shukla, A. (2009). Measuring effectiveness of institutional websites: a case study of central universities of India. *Research Digest, 4* (3).

Shukla, A. & Tripathi, A. (2009). Webometric analysis of institutes of national importance in India. *IASLIC Bulletin, 54*(3), 165-180.

Shukla, A. & Tripathi, A. (2014). *Backlinks* analyses of institutes of national importance and premier management institutions library websites. *Journal of International Academic Research for Multidisciplinary, 2*(7), 560-575.

Shukla, A. & Vanlalfeli. (2014). Webometric analyses of library websites of Indian Institutes of Technology. *Journal of Advancements in Library Sciences, 1*(2), 34-48.

Small, H. (1937). Co-citation in the scientific literature: a new measure of relationship between two documents. *Journal of the American Society for Information Science and Technology, 24*(4), 265-269.

Smith, A. G. (1999). A tale of two web spaces: comparing sites using web impact factors. *Journal of Documentation, 55*(5), 577-592.

Smith, A. G. & Thelwall, M. (2002). Web impact factors for Australasian universities. *Scientometrics, 54*(3), 363-380.

Snyder, H. & Rosenbaum, H. (1999). Can search engines be used for web-link analysis? a critical review. *Journal of Documentation, 55*(4), 375-384.

Tague-Sutcliffe, J. (1992). An introduction to informetrics. *Information Processing & Management, 28*(1), 1-3.

Tang, R. & Thelwall, M. (2003). Disciplinary differences in US academic departmental website interlinking. *Library & Information Science Research, 25*(4), 437-458.

Tang, R. & Thelwall, M. (2004). Patterns of national and international web links to U.S. academic departments: an analysis of disciplinary variations. *Scientometrics, 60*, 475-485.

Thelwall, M. (2000). Web impact factors and search engine coverage. *Journal of Documentation, 56*(2), 185-189.

Thelwall, M. (2001a). A publicly accessible database of UK university website links and a discussion of the need for human intervention in web crawling. Available at http://www.scit.wlv.ac.uk/~cm1993/papers/a_publicly_accessible_database.pdf

Thelwall, M. (2001f). A web crawler design for data mining. *Journal of Information Science, 27*(5), 319-325.

Thelwall, M. (2001b). Exploring the link structure of the web with network diagrams. *Journal of Information Science, 27*(6), 393-402.

Thelwall, M. (2001c). Extracting macroscopic information from web links. *Journal of the American Society for Information Science and Technology, 52*(13), 1157-1168.

Thelwall, M. (2001d). Results from a web impact factor crawler. *Journal of Documentation, 57*(2), 177-191.

Thelwall, M. (2001e). The responsiveness of search engine indexes [Electronic version]. *Cybermetrics, 5*(1), Paper 1. Available at http://www.cindoc.csic.es/cybermetrics/articles/v5i1p1.html

Thelwall, M. (2002a). A comparison of sources of links for academic web impact factor calculations. *Journal of Documentation, 58*(1), 66-78.

Thelwall, M. (2002e). An initial exploration of the link relationship between UK university websites. *Aslib Proceedings, 54*(2), 118-126.

Thelwall, M. (2002b). Conceptualizing documentation on the web: an evaluation of different heuristic-based models for counting links between university websites. *Journal of the American Society for Information Science and Technology, 53*(12), 995-1005.

Thelwall, M. (2002c). Evidence for the existence of geographic trends in university website interlinking. *Journal of Documentation, 58*(5), 563-574.

Thelwall, M. (2002d). Methodologies for crawler based web surveys. *Internet Research: Electronic Networking and Applications, 12*(2), 124-138.

Thelwall, M. (2002f). The top 100 linked to pages on UK university websites: high inlink counts are not usually associated with quality scholarly content. *Journal of Information Science, 28*(6), 483.491.

Thelwall, M. (2003b). Can Google's PageRank be used to find the most important academic web pages? *Journal of Documentation, 59*(2), 205-217.

Thelwall, M. (2003a). Web use and peer interconnectivity metrics for academic websites. *Journal of Information Science, 29*(1), 1-10.

Thelwall, M. (2008). Extracting accurate and complete results from search engines: case study windows live. *Journal of the American Society for Information Science and Technology, 59(1), 38-50.*

Thelwall, M. & Harries, G. (2003). The connection between the research of a university and counts of links to its web pages: an investigation based upon a classification of the relationships of pages to the research of the host university. *Journal of the American Society for Information Science and Technology, 54*(7), 594-602. doi: 10.1002/asi.10161

Thelwall, M. & Harries, G. (2004). Do better scholars' web publications have significantly higher online impact? *Journal of the American Society for Information Science and Technology, 55*(2), 149-159.

Thelwall, M. & Smith, A. (2002). Interlinking between Asia-Pacific university websites. *Scientometrics, 55*(3), 363-376.

Thelwall, M. & Tang, R. (2003). Disciplinary and linguistic considerations for academic web linking: an exploratory hyperlink mediated study with Mainland China and Taiwan. *Scientometrics, 58*(1), 153-179.

Thelwall, M., Harries, G. & Wilkinson, D. (2003). Why do websites from different academic subjects interlink? *Journal of Information Science, 29*(6), 453-471.

Thelwall, M., Vaughan, L. & Björneborn, L. (2005). Webometrics. *Annual Review of Information Science and Technology, 39,* 81-135.

Thelwall, M., Vaughan, L., Cothey, V., Li, X. & Smith, A. (2003). Which academic subjects have more online impact? a pilot study and a new classification process. *Online Information Review, 27*(5), 333.343.

Thomas, O. & Willet, P. (2000). Webometric analysis of departments of librarianship and information science. *Journal of Information Science, 26*(6), 421-428. doi: 10.1177/016555150002600605

Vaughan, L. & Thelwall, M. (2003). Scholarly use of the web: what are the key inducers of links to journal websites?

Journal of the American Society for Information Science and Technology, 54(1), 29-38.

Vaughan, L. & Thelwall, M. (2004). Search engine coverage bias: evidence and possible causes. *Information Processing & Management, 40*(4), 693-707.

Vaughan, L. & Thelwall, M. (2005). A modeling approach to uncover hyperlink patterns: the case of Canadian universities. *Information Processing & Management, 41*(2), 347-359.

White, H. D. & McCain, K. W. (1989). Bibliometrics. *Annual Review of Information Science and Technology, 24*, 119-186.

Wilkinson, D., Harries, G., Thelwall, M. & Price, L. (2003). Motivations for academic website interlinking: evidence for the web as a novel source of information on informal scholarly communication. *Journal of Information Science. 29*(1), 59-66.

Wilson, C. S. (1999). Informetrics. *In* Williams, M. E. (Ed.), *Annual Review of Information Science and Technology, 34*, 107-247.

Wittig, G. R. (1978). Documentation note: statistical bibliography - a historical footnote. *Journal of Documentation, 34*, 240–241.

3

MEASURING CONTENT AWARENESS OF LIBRARY WEBSITES

3.1. INTRODUCTION

Evaluating the *content awareness* of web document is a tough task as it requires high degree of objectivity on the part of evaluator. The focus of the chapter is to provide a detailed account of *content awareness* and issues related to it. Libraries are considered to be "heart" of an academic institute. It plays a great role in academic development of an institute. Websites of libraries increase the reach of services and information to users. There is an attempt to evaluate the *content awareness* of Indian academic and research institute library websites.

3.2. CONTENT AWARENESS OF LIBRARY WEBSITES

Libraries are known as information resource centres which cater preservation, processing and dissemination of knowledge for decision making. Libraries have adopted information communication technology (ICT) tools to serve users' need in a better way. Websites are medium through which knowledge can be disseminated efficiently to every nook and corner of the world. It is believed that most of the libraries establish their websites for disseminating information among users and popularize their services. Richness of web content of library websites depends upon the respective library's collection, services, facilities, administrative support and updating policy etc. These features are collectively referred as *content awareness* of library websites. *Content awareness* indicates qualitative and quantitative aspects of information provided at the library websites. The criteria for evaluating library websites through *content awareness* is one method for measuring usefulness of websites, which is being least discussed so far. *Content awareness* evaluation criteria are developed to measure how effectively academic library websites share their knowledge, information, services and facilities with their users. An empirical approach is used in the development of *content awareness* evaluation criteria of academic library websites.

3.2.1. Content Awareness: A Perspective

The following section presents various perspectives related to *content awareness*:

- Works related to websites' usability;
- Works related to library websites' usability; and
- Works related to library websites' content evaluation.

3.2.1.1. Works Related to Websites' Usability

The web provides opportunity to the libraries to become disseminators of knowledge through websites. The most effective library website is that which has a clear sense of purpose as well as a clear sense of user needs. Therefore, an important aspect of planning and maintaining a website is to identify the likely users and review their needs (Clyde, 1996; Hightower et al., 1998). Rozic-Hristovski et al. (1999) started building the medical library website of University of Ljubljana,

Slovenia in which [they] included a guide for library services and resources. In the early 1990s Nielsen (1993) and Rubin (1994) pioneered the testing of websites to determine whether [websites] meet user needs. They adapted usability engineering techniques developed for computer software design and applied them to web design. Usability is a quality attribute that assesses user interfaces using five quality components, learnability, efficiency, memorability, errors, and satisfaction (Nielsen). In another way, web usability is an approach to make websites easy to use for an end-user, without requiring her/him to undergo any specialized training (Wikipedia). The usability is recognized as an important quality factor of any modern website. Usability testing has become the focus of considerable attention both for commercial and academic websites. Usability tests revealed that the way material is arranged, labeled, and presented on the web (the information architecture) has a major impact on users and their ability to operate a site effectively (Rosenfeld & Morville, 1998). In a study, Head (1999) and Fichter (2000) individually furnished a good synopsis of website usability testing. Norlin and Winters (2002) also provided an excellent "how to" guide aimed specifically at libraries and library staff who wish to conduct usability testing. Avouris et al. (2003) proposed the techniques for usability evaluation of a website and described its use. They discussed the applicability of the developed techniques in a wide area of web based applications and their importance in the context of today's web applications development.

Most notably, Rubin's *Handbook of Usability Testing* (1994) and *A Practical Guide to Usability Testing* (1993) of Dumas and Redish provide invaluable ideas and input in the process of instrument development. Rubin outlined the four types of usability tests (i.e. exploratory; assessment; validation/verification; and comparison). He further promotes the "user centered design" (UCD) philosophy, and described five attributes common to organizations practicing UCD:

(a) a phased approach that includes user input and feedback at all crucial points,

(b) a multidisciplinary team approach,

(c) concerned management,

(d) a "learn as you go" perspective; and

(e) usability goals and objectives.

Additionally, Rubin offered a detailed overview of the entire process including all aspects of planning, budgeting, test design and execution, as do Barnum (2002) and Dumas and Redish (1993). Dumas and Redish gave important insights into the interpersonal aspects of the testing process, such as the consideration given to "human computer interaction" (HCI) and the impact of certain behaviours on those giving and taking the tests. The said studies are much near to business process modules but application is also sought in web content development.

The effective website design guideline and extensive practical advice and hints are created and provided by Nielsen (1993) and Spool (1998). Nielsen developed "heuristic evaluation method[1]" for quick, cheap, and easy evaluation of a user interface design and provided a list of ten recommended heuristics for usable interface design. Constantine (1999), Morville (1999) and Rowlands (2000) also presented their viewpoints on good practices for design. McClements and Becker (1996) suggested that useful hints and design features must be included. Keevil (1998) developed "web usability index checklist" on the models provided by Ravden and Johnson (1989) and Chignell and Keevil (1996) which have a series of questions that

---

1 Heuristic evaluation method is most popular usability inspection methods and it also points out major and minor problems in a user interface.

could be answered with a "Yes" or "No". The HCI checklist of Ravden and Johnson had 120 detailed questions while Chignell and Keevil model had more than 180 questions. Fraser et al. (1998) supplemented the literature by providing an important reminder about accessibility in the interface design for users with disabilities, a feature curiously absent in many studies. Owen (2003) further emphasized that accessibility should not be ignored in visual design of a website. Ma (2002) applied reader-response criticism to examine the relationship between and among designers, text, and users of the Galter Health Sciences Library (GHSL) website. Cyr and Trevor-Smith (2004) explored issues related to user interface design with respect to culturally preferred design elements of German, Japanese and United States websites. Design elements considered are use of symbols and graphics, colour preferences, site features, language and content. Barber and Badre (1998) emphasized "culturability" in websites. Culturability is merging of culture and usability and represents a relationship between design elements and culture. Badre (2000) described culturability this way:

> *"Cultural usability is a term we use to emphasize the importance of the relationship between culture and usability in WWW design...Colour, spatial organisation, fonts, shapes, icons, and metaphors, geography, language, flags, sounds, and motion contribute to the design and content of a web page, which directly affects the way that a user interacts with the site".*

The culturability is described in various researches conducted by scholars. Sun (2001) in his exploratory study examined the cultural markers focused on language, pictures and graphics, colours, and page layout and found culture to be an important design consideration that increases usability of multilingual web pages. Del Galdo and Neilson (1996) demonstrated that colour and screen design directions have various psychological and social associations in different cultures, and diverse users have different concepts of screen usage. Language is distinctive aspect of culture. Accessible websites must be available in the language of users. Depmsey and Sussman (1999) suggested that to internationalize, web pages should have more than one language version. In a study (Robbins & Stylianou, 2003) in which global corporate websites were examined, 100 percent of Latin and Asian websites had translation capability, compared with only seven (7) percent of Anglo websites (including Canada and the United States). According to Yu and Roh (2002), layout and menu design has been central to research on information retrieval systems and appropriate design layout provides web visitors a contextual and structural model for understanding and accessing information, and provides a communication bridge between the user and the system. Specific orientations and page placement vary as per culture (Barber & Badre). For example, French websites have a centered orientation. Sun outlined that a user from a low context culture[2] such as Germany would prefer a logical and structured layout. Users from high context cultures are expected to have a strong preference for visuals. This work suggested that banner placement, menu placement, and other layout characteristics may differ across cultures. Marcus and Gould (2000) stated that symbols are an important element denoting culture and these vary and may represent a wide range of features from currency to time (Fernandes, 1995).

---

2 According to Hall & Hall (1990), "high context or low context refers to the amount of information that is in a given communication as a function of the context in which it occurs." In a high context culture, information is part of a contextual understanding and is implicit, while in low context cultures information is conveyed explicitly.

Symbols are "metaphors" denoting actions of the user (Barber & Badre). According to Huizingh (2000), content refers to information, features, and services offered in the website and represents form of communication between the user and the site. Hall and Hall's (1990) work on informational content may provide some clues for how communication operates in cyberspace across cultures. In Hall and Hall's framework, Germany is a very low-context culture in which messages are aimed to be complete, clear, and precise. In comparison, Japan is a high-context culture, and messages are multilevel and implicit. The United States is on the lower side of a mid-context culture (Beamer & Varner, 2001). Marcus and Gould contended that navigation has also cultural significance. Users from cultures who "feel anxiety about uncertain or unknown matters" prefer "navigation schemes intended to prevent users from becoming lost". Simon (2001) considered navigation and site interaction as part of the communication interface. Multimedia is another factor which researchers have examined related to culture. Marcus and Gould found site examples that suggest strong use of graphics and multimedia where the web designer is from a culture that values material goods and is more assertive. Importance of relationship between design and user perceptions was studied by Yoon (2002) and Simon individually and found that design issues are integral to user satisfaction of a website. Harley and Henke (2007) conducted an experimental analysis of two commonly used methods for exploring the use of university based web resources i.e. Transaction log analysis (TLA)[3] and online site surveys.

---

3 Transaction log analysis (TLA) takes advantage of the computerized log files that automatically record online access to any Web site. By analyzing these logs, one can determine a number of characteristics of the site's users and summarize total site use.

3.2.1.2. Works Related to Library Websites' Usability

The past works reveals that commendable researches have been made earlier concerning library website usability testing (Norlin & Winters, 2002). Letnikova (2003) prepared an excellent annotated bibliography of usability assessment sources whereas Chisman et al. (1999), Dickstein and Mills (2000), Battleson et al. (2001) and Augustine and Greene (2002) presented comprehensive case studies which included detailed descriptions of planning and implementation phases of usability testing at their institutes. Common website problems were discussed in the findings which included the excessive use of library terminology, an overabundance of information on opening pages, complicated or distracting graphics, poor website organization, and lack of breadcrumb trails[4].

A usability test has conducted for university library homepages in Sub-Saharan Africa which concluded that libraries are mainly providing general information about themselves and its services on their homepage (Chisenga, 1998). Battleson et al. have given comprehensive case study for usability tests of academic library website of University of Buffalo. Houghton (2000) shared his experience for designing and implementation process of developing an academic library website at De Montfort University (DMU) and gave practical guidance and advices. McMullen (2001) conducted an interview with users to find insight about user behaviour with library web interface for information seeking and revealed problems related to unclear terminology, proper use of colour, size, and

---

4 Web designers use the term "breadcrumbs" to describe navigational clues that show users where they are on a website. They trace the path the user has taken from the homepage to their present location.

location for navigational links, and the need for context sensitive help, built-in redundancy, and clear and consistent navigation. Rozic-Hristovski et al. (2002) built the Central Medical Library (CMK) website and evaluated the website by using web server log file data whereas Milunovich (2002) explored the design and maintenance of Law library websites and described various design principles and identified elements that are typically included in such sites. VandeCreek (2005) conducted a usability analysis using a trilateral approach i.e. usability testing, focus group sessions, and survey questionnaires for Northern Illinois University library website.

There is an effort for usability testing of virtual libraries by Allen (2002) for University of South Florida, for a new interface design. There are few studies found for redesigning of library websites by applying usability approach. George (2005) evaluated the usability studies conducted for redesign of website of Carnegie Mellon University library and found, key weaknesses with respect to navigation, screen design and labeling, leading to more revisions and the final release. During evaluation he found that coloured graphics attract attention; font, labels, and placement increase visibility; chunking and leading with keywords increase readability; and consistency increases usability. Fang (2007) conducted a survey for Rutgers-Newark Law library, to improve its design and content by using Google Analytics[5]. By analyzing the visitors' behaviour, he made changes to the library website and again compared web usage data from before and after the change, and found improvement in the library website

---

5 Google Analytics report provide information on where visitors came from, what pages they visited, how long they stayed on each page, how deep into the site they navigated, where their visits ended, and where they went from there.

in number of ways. Craven (2003) explored the awareness level of website developers in a supporting study for DISinHE (now TechDIS) between 1999 and 2000. Abels et al. (1997) identified user based design criteria for websites and found that content and ease of use is more important than appearance. Vasantha Raju and Harinarayana (2008) analysed the usability features of thirty (30) library websites of top science universities and institutes around the world (list of world's top science universities published by the Times Higher Education Supplement).

3.2.1.3. Works Related to Library Websites' Content Evaluation

From library and information science perspective, the number of such studies is relatively small (Clausen, 1999). Most of these studies are exclusively quantitative and have greater concentration on counting the number of pages, links, spelling mistakes, etc. An example of a study of this type has been carried out by Stover and Zink (1996) who dealt with forty (40) higher education libraries in North America. On the basis of quantitative data, the websites scored points and a top twenty (20) list was set up and some recommendations were formulated. A noteworthy study by Clyde, analyzed the contents of the websites of fifty (50) public libraries and fifty (50) school libraries from a number of different countries by applying quantitative method and concluded that "the most effective library websites or home pages appeared to be those that had a clear sense of purpose and a clear sense of the needs of users" (Clyde, p. 556). Despite this, Clyde has given ten advices for library website designers,

(a) The page should have a sensible title...that includes the keywords likely to be used by people searching for the page.

(b) Graphics and photographs can make a page very attractive. If they are too large or too complex, or there are too many of them, transmission may be too slow for the busy user.

(c) The page should clearly identify the library, its location and the organization of which it is part.

(d) The page should provide a good overview of library and its services.

(e) For foreign users, a short explanation in English would be helpful.

(f) The page should have features that will encourage first-time visitors to read on and then to return.

(g) People will be encouraged to use the page on an ongoing basis if they know that they will always find something new on it when they visit.

(h) Links to other Internet resources can be very useful to the users of a library homepage.

(i) The page should incorporate some means by which visitors to the page can contact the library staff.

(j) Other important features which should be used are, a "way out" of the page, last update, postal or street address for the library.

In a study, CSIR (1996) evaluated six websites that provide access to online reference materials at academic and public libraries while concentrating on their currency, accuracy, relevancy, structure, presentation, maintenance, and features. King (1998) examined the homepages of all 120 libraries in the Association of Research Libraries (ARL) to compare design similarities and differences. Clausen carried out an extensive pilot study and prepared thirty eight (38) evaluation criteria for high quality web pages with library and information centre specific criteria. Each of the evaluation criteria was rated on a scale from -2 to +2. Clausen had made an attempt for developing new methods of user oriented evaluation of library and information centre web pages because not many studies was reported dealing with the specific problems of library and information centre websites. The main areas investigated by Clausen includes, design and structure; information quality; links and navigation; visual quality; and updating. An appreciating effort was made by Abdullah (2001), where he conducted a research for the comparative study of eight (8) university library websites of Malaysia and designed extensive evaluation criteria and concluded that libraries of Malaysia are ready to provide online services to the users. Raward (2001) developed one hundred (100) questions based checklist for best practice design principles for academic library websites using a "usability index checklist" (UIC) with the help of HCI literature. He divided user's category into primary and secondary, based on their information needs. Hider and Ferguson (2006) evaluated the information architectural (Gullikson et al., 1999) qualities of twenty (20) Australian library websites by heuristic inspection which were compared with ten (10) retail websites and concluded the need of improvement and training. Holly (2005) deals the need, challenges, tools and methods for library web content management and provides several case studies of library websites. Jeffrey Schaffner (April 24, 2007 in unpublished white paper) emphasizes for good library web interface and Online Public Access Catalogs (OPAC). Dinkelman and Stacy-Bates (2007) examined the availability and access mechanism of electronic books available in the websites of academic libraries in the Association of Research Libraries and provide useful suggestions to improve it. Similar efforts have been made by Rich and Rabine (1999) for electronic serials in academic library websites and Ganski (2008) for e-resources in theological library websites. Krueger et al. (2004) adapted web usability techniques to assess student's awareness for their library websites by using a web browser. They categorized various approaches according to student's preferences and revealed that forty five percent (45%) of the students utilized the library website as first tool of choice.

Despite these studies in web user interface design and evaluation of library websites, the user oriented content awareness testing or theoretical model are still rare (Clausen) and extensive theory of *content awareness* is yet to come. The present work is focused on the design, development and establishment of user oriented *content awareness* evaluation criteria of academic library websites.

3.2.2. Methodology of Designing Content Awareness Evaluation Criteria

The evaluation criteria have been set to assess the *content awareness* of academic and research institute library websites. There are few library website evaluation criteria already available which evaluate accuracy, currency, authenticity, and usability etc. (Abdullah, 2001; George, 2005; Csir, 1996; VandeCreek, 2005; Sun, 2001, Krueger et al., 2004; Raward, 2001; Keevil, 1998). Abdullah has made a significant attempt to design qualitative criteria for evaluation of academic library websites of Malaysia. His study categorises the quality criteria into three categories with further sub-categories under each. He provided scores (1 and 0) for answers, which are structured in "Yes" (1) and "No" (0) format. The criteria those are not designed in this format are judged by a specific evaluation system adopted by him. Some quality criteria of website evaluation (developed by Abdullah) are similar to present *content awareness* evaluation criteria but the present evaluation criteria are more extensive than his quality criteria. Raward developed usability checklist for Australian academic library websites based on the Keevil's "web usability index checklist" which has one hundred (100) questions and divided into four sections. Clausen carried out an extensive pilot study and prepared thirty eight (38) evaluation criteria for high quality web pages with criteria specific to library and information centres. Each of the evaluation criteria is rated on a scale of -2 to +2. Jurkowski (2005) had made a code sheet for evaluation of colleges and university library websites, those serving distance education to their students.

The present evaluation criteria have impact of above mentioned evaluation criteria developed by many researchers. In the present work of *content awareness* evaluation criteria, following steps are taken:

Collection of Check Points

The features related to *content awareness* have been collected from various academic and research institutes library websites. Besides, ideas and views from library and information science professionals was also collected to know the other possible features that should be included in the study. Literature available in the journals, encyclopedias, library science handbooks, other library websites etc. was also consulted.

Matching, Removal and Grouping of Check Points

The tabulated features were matched with each other and duplicate features were removed from the tabulated data. Similar features (concepts) were grouped at one place.

Designing of Content Awareness Evaluation Criteria

On the basis of grouped similar features (concepts), the questionnaire was developed. For bias free and easy answering, two variables "Yes" and "No" have been chosen. For making the evaluation criteria more extensive, *conditional* and *additional scenarios* were added as per requirement. For example, a question has been asked,

Does the library website have?

(1) Multiple Web pages (...) [2 Point]

(2) Single Web page*

*If single, then

Does the library web page have the collection of library related content solely?

(1) Yes (...) [1 Point]

(2) No (...) [0 Point]

In the above mentioned evaluation criteria, first portion of this question is the main evaluation criteria which will be fulfilled by two answer options (1) and (2) where the option (2) will be further qualified by another *conditional* evaluation criterion. *Additional* evaluation points are added in evaluation criteria when the library website provides information regarding additional items, besides common items of the library website. The below mentioned items have been added as *additional* evaluation criteria which are not commonly found in library websites:

(1) Image Gallery of Library (...) [1/2 Point]

(2) Standards/Patents (...) [1/2 Point]

(3) Library Blog (...) [1/2 Point]

(4) Media Resource Centre (...) [1/2 Point]

For purposeful evaluation, scoring system was adopted. The scoring system details are as follows:

Answer variables	**Score allotted**
Yes (Normal)	+2
No (Normal)	0
Yes (Conditional)	+1
No (Conditional)	0
Yes (Additional)	+ ½

On the basis of scoring points, 108 point parameter based Website Performance Gradation System was devised. For assessing the academic library website content, two formulae Overall Website Performance Calculation (OWPC) and Criteria wise Website Performance Calculation (CWPC) were developed. The CWPC represents current status of *content awareness* of academic library websites. The *content awareness* criteria of academic library websites are provided with Appendix – I.

Addition of Definitions, Notes and Scope Notes

Definitions, explanations, notes and scope notes are given to the check-points wherever felt necessary.

Testing of Content Awareness Evaluation Criteria

The check points drafted for evaluation of *content awareness* of academic library websites was tested by pilot studies (twice) on academic and research institute libraries of India. The problems like inclusion and exclusion of check points, duplication in check points, information availability in multiple web pages and file formats, grouping of similar subjects etc. faced during first pilot testing was removed before the second pilot testing was initiated.

Features of Content Awareness Evaluation Criteria

Easy to understand : The evaluation criteria have been made very simple. Terminological difficulties have been resolved, with additional explanations.

Easy to answer : The evaluation criteria are very simple to answer. Attempt has been made to keep it two point scale.

Easy calculation : Overall score can be calculated easily.

Simple guidelines : Simple and very expressive guidelines i.e. definitions, notes, and scope notes are given wherever felt necessary.

Any additional item that cannot be categorized with any group has been added separately. For example,

If the library website/web page provide information regarding following additional items besides above mentioned then provide additional half (½) points for each of them.

(1) Library Archive	( )	[1/2 Point]
(2) Image Gallery	( )	[1/2 Point]
(3) Library Blog	( )	[1/2 Point]
(4) Media Resource Centre	( )	[1/2 Point]

(5) Book Fair ( ) [1/2 Point]

(6) Approved Vendors List ( ) [1/2 Point]

Limitations of Content Awareness Evaluation Criteria

Lengthy : The evaluation criterion has become very lengthy (in terms of number) due to its extensive as well as intensive nature.

Ambiguous : Sometimes evaluation criteria show ambiguous nature due to close relationship with other evaluation check points. Apart from that it is also observed that for one aspect there are different levels or methods of representation on the two different websites. Sometimes it is observed that detailed explanation or detailed insight is given for a particular aspect. In such situation it becomes very difficult for evaluator to assess the grading. For example, library website of Banaras Hindu University (BHU) provides an alphabetical list of acquired e-journals where as North-Eastern Hill University (NEHU) provides detailed explanation of each e-journal for the benefit of users. From an evaluator's point of view both the Universities do give information about the e-journals and grading wise both are given same points however it is clearly visible that NEHU carries an edge over BHU.

A sincere effort has been made to give a model of *content awareness* evaluation scale for assessing the user oriented *content awareness* for academic library websites.

3.2.3. Method of Calculation for *Content Awareness*

Suppose a university library website obtains 63 points on the basis of *content awareness* evaluation criteria. Then its OWPC is calculated as:

Overall Website Performance Calculation (OWPC)

$$\frac{\text{Total points obtained} \times 100}{108} = \frac{63 \times 100}{108} = 58.33\%$$

For instance, 63 points was scored on the basis of attempting 28 criterions out of total 41 criterions. Then the CWPC would be:

Criteria wise Website Performance Calculation (CWPC)

$$\frac{\text{Total points obtained} \times 100}{\text{Maximum points of attempted criteria}}$$

$$= \frac{63 \times 100}{77} = 81.81\ \%$$

3.3. INDIAN ACADEMIC AND RESEARCH INSTITUTES' LIBRARIES FOR *CONTENT AWARENESS*

India has a large educational system which is supported by 341 universities as listed in University Handbook and about 725 universities listed in the website of University Grants Commission (UGC), New Delhi. These are broadly categorized as Central Universities, State Universities, Deemed Universities, Institutes of National Importance and State Private Universities. For the evaluation of *content awareness* of libraries websites, twenty (20) Central Universities (CU) those are established before 2009, thirteen (13) Institutes of National Importance (INI), and six globally reputed management institutes known as Indian Institute of Management (IIM) have been considered. The detailed list of selected 20 Central Universities; and 13 Institutes of National Importance and 6 Indian Institutes of Management (with their website addresses) are given below:

Table 3.1: List of Central Universities of India (with website address)

SN	Name of Central University	Code Name	Website / URL
1	Aligarh Muslim University, Aligarh	AMU	http://www.amu.ac.in/

S N	Name of Central University	Code Name	Website / URL
2	Assam University, Silchar	AUS	http: / /assamuni versity.nic.in/
3	Babasaheb Bhimrao Ambedkar University, Lucknow	BBAU	http: / /www.bbau india.org/
4	Banaras Hindu University, Varanasi	BHU	http: / /www.bhu. ac.in/
5	Central Agricultural University, Imphal	CAUI	http: / /www.cic.n ic.in/cicmanipur /html/cau.asp
6	Indira Gandhi National Open University, New Delhi	IGNOU	http: / /www.igno u.ac.in/
7	Jamia Millia Islamia, New Delhi	JMI	http: / /www.jmi. nic.in/
8	Jawaharlal Nehru University, New Delhi	JNU	http: / /www.jnu. ac.in/
9	Mahatma Gandhi Antarrashtriya Hindi Vishwavidyalaya, Wardha	MGAHV	http: / /www.hind ivishwa.org/
10	Manipur University, Imphal	MU	http: / /manipuru niv.ac.in/
11	Maulana Azad National Urdu University, Hyderabad	MANUU	http: / /www.man uu.ac.in/
12	Mizoram University, Aizwal	MZU	http: / /www.mzu. edu.in/
13	Nagaland University, Kohima	NAGUN I	http: / /www.naga univ.org.in/
14	North-Eastern Hill University, Shillong	NEHU	http: / /www.neh u.ac.in/
15	Pondicherry University, Puducherry	PONDI	http: / /www.pond iuni.edu.in/
16	Tezpur University, Tezpur	TEZU	http: / /www.tezu. ernet.in/
17	University of Allahabad, Allahabad	UOA	http: / /www.alldu niv.ac.in/

S N	Name of Central University	Code Name	Website / URL
18	University of Delhi, Delhi	UOD	http://www.du.ac.in/
19	University of Hyderabad, Hyderabad	UOH	http://www.uohyd.ernet.in/
20	Visva-Bharati University, Santiniketan	VBU	http://www.visva-bharati.ac.in/

Table 3.2: List of Institute of National Importance and IIMs of India (with website address)

S N	Name of Institutes of National Importance	Code Name	Website / URL
1.	All India Institute of Medical Sciences, New Delhi	AIIMS	http://www.aiims.edu/
2.	Dakshina Bharat Hindi Prachar Sabha, Chennai	DBHPS	http://www.dbhps-chennai.com/
3.	Indian Institute of Management, Ahmedabad	IIMA	http://www.iimahd.ernet.in/
4.	Indian Institute of Management, Bangalore	IIMB	http://www.iimb.ernet.in/iimb/
5.	Indian Institute of Management, Calcutta	IIMC	http://www.iimcal.ac.in/
6.	Indian Institute of Management, Indore	IIMI	http://www.iimidr.ac.in/iimi/
7.	Indian Institute of Management, Kozhikode	IIMK	http://www.iimk.ac.in/
8.	Indian Institute of Management, Lucknow	IIML	http://www.iiml.ac.in/
9.	Indian Institute of Technology, Bombay	IITB	http://www.iitb.ac.in/
10.	Indian Institute of Technology, Delhi	IITD	http://www.iitd.ac.in/
11.	Indian Institute of Technology, Guwahati	IITG	http://www.iitg.ernet.in/
12.	Indian Institute of Technology, Kanpur	IITK	http://www.iitk.ac.in/

S N	Name of Institutes of National Importance	Code Name	Website / URL
13.	Indian Institute of Technology, Kharagpur	IITKGP	http://www.iitkgp.ac.in/
14.	Indian Institute of Technology, Madras	IITM	http://www.iitm.ac.in/
15.	Indian Institute of Technology, Roorkee	IITR	http://www.iitr.ac.in/
16.	Indian Statistical Institute, Kolkata	ISI	http://www.isical.ac.in/
17.	National Institute of Pharmaceutical Education and Research, Mohali	NIPER	http://www.niper.ac.in/
18.	Postgraduate Institute of Medical Education and Research, Chandigarh	PGIMER	http://pgimer.nic.in/
19.	Sree Chitra Tirunal Institute for Medical Sciences and Technology, Thiruvananthapuram	SCTIMST	http://www.sctimst.ac.in/

3.4. STATUS OF *CONTENT AWARENESS* OF LIBRARY WEBSITES

The *content awareness* of academic and research library websites of India was evaluated using the designed *content awareness* evaluation criteria. The evaluation process has been divided in two groups, first selected Central Universities (CU) library websites; and second selected Institutes of National Importance (INI) and Indian Institutes of Management library websites. The results are:

3.4.1. Central Universities (CU) Library Websites

Table 3.3: Data Representing Content Awareness of Central Universities Library Websites

SN	Central Universities Library Websites	OWPC Points (%)	CWPC (%)
1.	Aligarh Muslim University, Aligarh	13 (12.03)	59.09
2.	Assam University, Silchar	11.5 (10.64)	44.23
3.	Babasaheb Bhimrao Ambedkar University, Lucknow	23.5 (21.75)	58.75
4.	Banaras Hindu University, Varanasi	23.5 (21.75)	45.19
5.	Central Agricultural University, Imphal	N.A.	N.A.
6.	Indira Gandhi National Open University, New Delhi	48 (44.44)	70.58
7.	Jamia Millia Islamia, New Delhi	43.5 (40.27)	63.04
8.	Jawaharlal Nehru University, New Delhi	31 (28.70)	44.92
9.	Mahatma Gandhi Antarrashtriya Hindi Vishwavidyalaya, Wardha	N.A.	N.A.
10.	Manipur University, Imphal	18.5 (17.12)	40.21
11.	Maulana Azad National Urdu University, Hyderabad	26.5 (24.53)	40.76
12.	Mizoram University, Aizwal	11 (10.18)	68.75
13.	Nagaland University, Kohima	14 (12.96)	50
14.	North Eastern Hill University, Shillong	63 (58.33)	81.81
15.	Pondicherry University, Pondicherry	17 (15.74)	32.07
16.	Tezpur University, Tezpur	28 (25.92)	53.84
17.	University of Allahabad, Allahabad	11 (10.18)	34.37

SN	Central Universities Library Websites	OWPC Points (%)	CWPC (%)
18.	University of Delhi, Delhi	50.5 (46.75)	75.37
19.	University of Hyderabad, Hyderabad	53.5 (49.53)	66.04
20.	Visva-Bharati University, Santiniketan	10 (09.25)	41.66

Discussion : The 108 point scale has been divided in five grades each showing 20 percent of the total. Grades are labeled Excellent, Very Good, Good, Average and Unsatisfactory. On the basis of *content awareness* evaluation criteria, results are given in Table 3.3 and the analyzed results are given in Table 3.4.

Table 3.4: Status of Content Awareness of Central Universities Library Websites

Points Achieved (percentage)	Grading	Central Universities Library Websites (OWPC points)
≤ 108 (≤ 100%)	Excellent	None
≤ 86.4 (≤ 80%)	Very Good	None
≤ 64.8 (≤ 60%)	Good	North Eastern Hill University, Shillong (63) University of Hyderabad, Hyderabad (53.5) University of Delhi, Delhi (50.5) Indira Gandhi National Open Uni., New Delhi (48) Jamia Millia Islamia, New Delhi (43.5)
≤ 43.2	Average	Jawaharlal Nehru University, New Delhi (31)

Points Achieved (percentage)	Grading	Central Universities Library Websites (OWPC points)
(≤ 40%)		Tezpur University, Tezpur (28) Maulana Azad National Urdu Uni., Hyderabad (26.5) Babasaheb Bhimrao Ambedkar University, Lucknow (23.5) Banaras Hindu University, Varanasi (23.5)
≤ 21.6 (≤ 20%)	Unsatisfactory	Manipur University, Canchipur Imphal (18.5) Pondicherry University, Pondicherry (17) Nagaland University, Kohima (14) Aligarh Muslim University, Aligarh (13) Assam University, Silchar (11.5) Mizoram University, Aizwal (11) University of Allahabad, Allahabad (11) Visva-Bharati University, Santiniketan (10)

None of the Central University (CU) library websites fall in "Excellent" and "Very Good" status of *content awareness*. Among selected twenty (20) CU, two universities (i.e. 10%), Central Agricultural University, Imphal and Mahatma Gandhi Antarrashtriya Hindi Vishwavidyalaya, Wardha do not have separate library websites, though both of the universities have websites. Five of the CU library websites (i.e. 25%) have "Good" status of *content awareness*. Highest numbers of the CU library websites (i.e. 40%) have "Unsatisfactory" status of *content awareness* whereas five CU library websites (i.e. 25%) have "Average" status of *content awareness*. On analysing, it is found that highest number of CU library websites (i.e. 65%) have obtained OWPC points below 43.2 which indicates there is a big gap between information availability in the libraries and information dissemination through web media. However, a separate study can be done to get the detail insight. There are only 25% CU library websites which have obtained OWPC points above 43.2 and these library websites are disseminating sufficient knowledge and information (whatever available) to users via web media i.e. higher status of *content awareness*. The CWPC points indicate *content awareness* at individual level only. It shows information availability and their content management in web media individually. The CWPC is an indicator to librarians and webmasters to show how they have managed information earlier and how they have to manage. It also reveals level of interest of librarians and webmasters in dissemination of information available in the libraries to its users. On the basis of OWPC points, it is found that 65 percent CU libraries of India must improve their web *content awareness*.

3.4.2. Institutes of National Importance (INI) & IIMs Library Websites

Table 3.5: Data Representing Content Awareness of INI & IIMs Library Websites

SN	Institute of National Importance Library Websites	OWPC Points (%)	CWPC (%)
1.	All India Institute of Medical Sciences, New Delhi	25 (23.14)	43.85
2.	Dakshina Bharat Hindi Prachar Sabha, Chennai	N.A.	N.A.
3.	Indian Institute of Management, Ahmedabad	42.5 (39.35)	68.54

S N	Institute of National Importance Library Websites	OWPC Points (%)	CWPC (%)
4.	Indian Institute of Management, Bangalore	26 (24.07)	65
5.	Indian Institute of Management, Calcutta	40 (37.03)	55.55
6.	Indian Institute of Management, Indore	21 (19.44)	52.50
7.	Indian Institute of Management, Kozhikode	41 (37.96)	68.33
8.	Indian Institute of Management, Lucknow	59 (54.62)	76.62
9.	Indian Institute of Technology, Delhi	61 (56.48)	70.93
10.	Indian Institute of Technology, Guwahati	25.5 (23.61)	60.71
11.	Indian Institute of Technology, Kanpur	27 (25)	54
12.	Indian Institute of Technology, Kharagpur	46 (42.59)	71.87
13.	Indian Institute of Technology, Madras	60 (55.55)	74.07
14.	Indian Institute of Technology, Bombay	55 (50.92)	66.26
15.	Indian Institute of Technology, Roorkee	22 (20.37)	45.83
16.	Indian Statistical Institute, Kolkata	49.5 (45.83)	68.75
17.	National Institute of Pharmaceutical Education and Research, Mohali	N.A.	N.A.
18.	Postgraduate Institute of Medical Education and Research, Chandigarh	29 (26.85)	76.31
19.	Sree Chitra Tirunal Institute for Medical Sciences and Technology, Thiruvananthapuram	21 (19.44)	55.26

Discussion : The 108 point scale has been divided in five grades each showing 20 percent of the total is discussed in the section 3.4.1 of this Chapter. On the basis of *content awareness* evaluation criteria, results are given in Table 3.5 and analyzed results are given in Table 3.6.

Table 3.6: Status of Content Awareness of INI Library Websites

Points Achieved (Percentage)	Grading	Institutes of National Importance Library Websites (OWPC points)
≤ 108 (≤ 100%)	**Excellent**	None
≤ 86.4 (≤ 80%)	**Very Good**	None
≤ 64.8 (≤ 60%)	**Good**	Indian Institute of Technology, Delhi (61) Indian Institute of Technology, Madras (60) Indian Institute of Management, Lucknow (59) Indian Institute of Technology, Bombay (55) Indian Statistical Institute, Kolkata (49.5) Indian Institute of Technology, Kharagpur (46)
≤ 43.2 (≤ 40%)	**Average**	Indian Institute of Management, Ahmedabad (42.5) Indian Institute of Management, Kozhikode (41) Indian Institute of Management, Calcutta (40) Postgraduate Institute of Medical Education and Research, Chandigarh (29) Indian Institute of Technology,

Points Achieved (Percentage)	Grading	Institutes of National Importance Library Websites (OWPC points)
		Kanpur (27) Indian Institute of Management, Bangalore (26) Indian Institute of Technology, Guwahati (25.5) All India Institute of Medical Sciences, New Delhi (25) Indian Institute of Technology, Roorkee (22)
≤ 21.6 (≤ 20%)	**Unsatisfactory**	Indian Institute of Management, Indore (21) Sree Chitra Tirunal Institute For Medical Sciences and Technology, Thiruvananthapuram (21)

Again it is found that none of the Institutes of National Importance (INI) & IIMs library websites has the "Excellent" and "Very Good" status of *content awareness* according to the present study. Among nineteen (19) institutes, two institutes (i.e. 10.52%), Dakshina Bharat Hindi Prachar Sabha, Chennai and National Institute of Pharmaceutical Education and Research, Mohali have no separate library websites, though both of the institutes have websites. There are six INI library websites (i.e. 31.56%) have "Good" status of *content awareness* and two of the INI (i.e. 10.52%) library websites have "Unsatisfactory" status of *content awareness*. On analysing, it is found that about 31.56 percent INI library websites have obtained OWPC points above 43.2 which indicates their high status of *content awareness* whereas 47.36 percent of INI library websites have obtained OWPC points between 21.6 to 43.2 i.e. "Average" status of *content awareness*. Among seven Indian Institutes of Technology, four (i.e. 57.14%) have "Good" status of *content awareness*. However, among six Indian Institutes of Management, four Indian

Institutes of Management (i.e. 66.66%) have "Average" status of *content awareness*. Indian Institute of Technology, Delhi (61) and Indian Institute of Management, Lucknow (59) have highest OWPC points in their concerned categories.

REFERENCES

Abdullah, A. R. (2001). A comparative study of academic libraries websites in Malaysia (Master's Dissertation). Faculty of Information Studies, University Teknologi MARA.

Abels, E. G., White, M. D. & Hahn K. (1997). Identifying user-based criteria for web pages. Internet Research: Electronic Networking Applications and Policy, 7, 252–262.

Allen, M. (2002). A case study of the usability testing of the University of South Florida's virtual library interface design. Online Information Review, 26(1), 40-53.

Association of Indian Universities. (2006). University Handbook: India (31st ed.). New Delhi: Association of Indian Universities.

Augustine, A. & Greene, C. (2002). Discovering how students search a library website: a usability case study. *College & Research Libraries*, 63(4), 354-365.

Avouris, N., Tselios, N., Fidas, C. & Papachristos, E. (2003). Website evaluation: a usability-based perspective. Lecture Notes in Computer Science, 2563, 217-231.

Badre, A. N. (2000). The effecs of cross cultural interface design orientation on World Wide Web user performance. GVE Research Technical Reports. Retrieved April 24, 2001, from http://www.cc.gatech.edu/gvu/reports/2001/abstracts/01-03.html

Barber, W. & Badre, A. N. (1998). Culturability: the merging of culture and usability. In 4th Conference on Human Factors and the Web. Basking Ridge, NJ.

Barnum, C. (2002). Usability testing and research. New York: Longman.

Battleson, B., Booth, A. & Weintrop, S. (2001). Usability testing of an academic library website: a case study. *Journal of Academic Librarianship*, 27(3), 188-198.

Beamer, L. & Varner, I. (2001). *Intercultural communication in the global workplace*. Boston: McGraw-Hill.

Chignell, M. H. & Keevil, B. E. (1996). Developing usable online information for a web authoring tool. In SIGDOC96 Conference. New York: ACM.

Chisenga, J. (1998). A study of university libraries' home pages in Sub-Saharan Africa. *Libri*, 48(1), 49-57.

Chisman, J., Diller, K. & Walbridge, S. (1999). Usability testing: a case study. College & Research Libraries, 60(6), 552-569.

Clausen, H. (1999). User-oriented evaluation of library and information centre websites. New Library World, 100(1146), 5-10.

Clyde, L. A. (1996). The library as information provider: the home page. The Electronic Library, 14(6), 549–558.

Constantine, L. (1999). Usage-centered web design. Retrieved June 5, 2009, from http://web.archive.org/web/19991012141354/http://webreview.com/pub/1999/06/25/feature/constantine.html

Craven, J. (2003). Accessibility and usability of websites. Library & Information Update CILIP Magazine), May, 2003.

Csir, F. J. (1996). Evaluation and criteria of the World Wide Web: reference websites (Master's Dissertation). Kent State University.

Cyr, D. & Trevor-Smith, H. (2004). Localization of web design: an empirical comparison of German, Japanese, and United States website characteristics. Journal of the American Society for Information Science and Technology, 55(13), 1199-1208.

Del Galdo, E. & Neilson, J. (1996). International user interfaces. New York: Wiley.

Dempsey, G. & Sussman, R. (1999). A hands-on guide for multilingual websites. World Trade, 12(9), 68-70.

Dickstein, R. & Mills, V. (2000). Usability testing at the University of Arizona library: how to let users in on the design. Information Technology & Libraries, 19(3), 144-151.

Dinkelman, A. & Stacy-Bates, K. (2007). Accessing e-books through academic library websites. College & Research Libraries, 68(1), 45-58.

Dumas, J. S. & Redish, J. C. (1993). A practical guide to usability testing. [S.l.]: Intellect Books.

Fang, W. (2007). Using google analytics for improving library website content and design: a case study. Library

Philosophy and Practice 2007. Retrieved June, 2009, from http://www.webpages.uidaho.edu/~mbolin/fang.htm

Fernandes, T. (1995). Global user interface design. *Proceedings of the ACM Conference on Human Factors in Computing Systems - CHI '95, Mosaic of Creativity, May* (pp. 363-364). Denver: SIGCHI.

Fichter, D. (2000). Head start: usability testing up front. *Online,* 24(1), 79-81.

Fraser, B., Comden, D. & Bergstahler, S. (1998). Including users with disabilities: designing library websites for accessibility. CHOICE: Current Reviews for Academic Libraries, 35, 35-37.

Ganski, K. L. (2008). Accessibility of e-resources from theological library websites. Theological Librarianship, *1*(1), 38-45.

George, C. A. (2005). Usability testing and design of a library website: an iterative approach. OCLC Systems & Services, 21(3), 167-180.

Gullikson, S., Blades, R., Bragdon, M., McKibbon, S., Sparling, M. & Toms, E. G. (1999). The impact of information architecture on academic website usability. The Electronic Library, 17(5), 293-304.

Hall, E. & Hall, M. (1990). Understanding cultural differences. Yarmouth, ME: Intercultural Press.

Harley, D. & Henke, J. (2007). Toward an effective understanding of website users: advantages and pitfalls of linking transaction log analyses and online surveys. D-Lib Magazine, 13(3/4).

Head, A. J. (1999). Web redemption and the promise of usability. *Online,* 23(6), 20-23.

Hider, P. & Ferguson, S. (2006). An evaluation of the information architectural qualities of Australian library websites. In: ALIA 2006 Biennial Conference. Available at http://conferences.alia.org.au/alia2006/Papers/Philip_Hider.pdf

Hightower, C., Sih, J. & Tilghman, A. (1998). Recommendation for benchmarking website usage among academic libraries. College & Research Libraries, 59(1), 61-79.

Holly, Y. (2005). Content and workflow management for library websites: case studies. Hershey: Information Science Publishing.

Houghton, D. (2000). Building an academic library website: experiences at De Montfort University. Program, 34(3), 269-280.

Huizingh, E. (2000). The content and design of websites: an empirical study. Information and Management, 37(3), 123-134.

Jurkowski, O. L. (2005). An analysis of library web sites at colleges and universities serving distance education students. In E. D. Garten, D. E. Williams & J. M. Nyce (Eds.), Advances in Library Administration and Organization, 22 (pp. 23-77). [S.l.]: Emerald Group Publishing.

Keevil, B. E. (1998). Measuring the usability of your website: usability index checklist for websites. Retrieved June, 2009, from http://www3.sympatico.ca/bkeevil/sigdoc98/checklist/WebCheck_Sep13.html

King, D. L. (1998). Library home page design: a comparison of page layout for front-ends to ARL library websites. College & Research Libraries, 59, 458-465.

Krueger, J., Ray, R. L. & Knight, L. (2004). Applying web usability techniques to assess student awareness of library web resources. The Journal of Academic Librarianship, 30(4), 285-293.

Letnikova, G. (2003). Usability testing of academic library websites: a selective bibliography. *Internet Reference Services Quarterly*, 8(4), 53-68.

Ma, Y. (2002). A design analysis model for developing world wide web sites. Journal of the American Society for Information Science and Technology, 53(7), 531-535.

Marcus, A. & Gould, E. W. (2000). Cultural dimensions and global web user-interface design. Interactions, 7(4), 33-46.

McClements, N. & Becker, C. (1996). Writing web page standards. College & Research Libraries News, 57(1), 16-17.

McMullen, S. (2001). Usability testing in a library website redesign project. Reference Services Review, 29(1), 7-22.

Milunovich, K. (2002). Designing and maintaining Law library websites: some practical considerations. Law Library Journal, 94(3), 487-508. Retrieved June, 2009, from http://www.aallnet.org/products/pub_llj_v94n03/2002-29.pdf

Morville, P. (1999). Information, architecture, and usability. Web Architect. Retrieved June, 2009, from http://web.archive.org/web/19991013024942/http://webreview.com/pub/1999/03/12/arch/index.html

Nielsen, J. (1993). Usability engineering (ed. 13). Boston: Academic Press.

Nielsen, J. (n.d.). How to conduct a heuristic evaluation. Retrieved June, 2009, from http://www.useit.com/papers/heuristic/heuristic_evaluation.html

Nielsen, J. (n.d.). Usability 101: introduction to usability. Retrieved June, 2009, from http://www.useit.com/alertbox/20030825.html

Norlin, E. & Winters, C. M. (2002). Usability testing for library websites: a hands-on guide. Chicago: American Library Association.

Owen, J. (2003). Making your website accessible. Library & Information Update, (January 2003). Retrieved June, 2009, from http://www.cilip.org.uk/ publications/updatemagazine/archive/archive2003/january/update0301c.htm

Ravden, S. J. & Johnson, G. I. (1989). Evaluating the usability of human computer interfaces: a practical method. Chichester: E. Horwood.

Raward, R. (2001). Academic library website design principles: development of a checklist. Australian Academic & Research Libraries, 32(2). Available at http://www.alia.org.au/publishing/aarl/32.2/raward.html

Rich, L. A. & Rabine, J. L. (1999). How libraries are providing access to electronic serials: a survey of academic library websites. Serials Review, 25(2), 35-46.

Robbins, S. S. & Stylianou, A. C. (2003). Global corporate websites: an empirical investigation of content and design. Information and Management, 40(3), 205-212.

Rosenfeld, L. B. & Morville, P. (1998). Information architecture for the World Wide Web. Sebastopol, CA: O'Reilly.

Rowlands, C. (2000). Usability matters - what is good design? Retrieved June, 2009, from http://web.archive.org/web/20000815215258/www.webreview.com/pub/2000/03/10/feature/index3c.html

Rozic-Hristovski, A., Hristovski, D. & Todorovski, L. (2002). Users' information-seeking behavior on a medical library website. Journal of the Medical Library Association, *90*(2), 210-217.

Rozic-Hristovski, A., Todorovski, L. & Hristovski, D. (1999). Developing a medical library website at the University of Ljubljana, Slovenia. Program, 33(4), 313–325.

Rubin, J. (1994). Handbook of usability testing: how to plan, design and conduct effective tests. New York: John Wiley.

Schaffner, J. (2007). Good design for library websites and online public access catalogs [White paper, LIS 488]. Retrieved June, 2009, from http://web.simmons.edu/~schaffne/whitepaper.pdf

Simon, S. J. (2001). The impact of culture and gender on websites: an empirical study. The Data Base for Advances in Information Systems, 32(1), 18-37.

Spool, J. (1998). Website usability: the big picture. Retrieved June 5, 2009, from http://web.archive.org/web/19991013021157/http://webreview.com/pub/web98east/23/spoolx.html

Stover, M. & Zink, S. D. (1996). World Wide Web home page design: patterns and anomalies of higher education library home pages. *Reference Services Review*, 24(3), 7-20.

Sun, H. (2001). Building a culturally-competent corporate website: an explanatory study of cultural markers in multilingual web design. In: Proceedings of *ACM Special Interest Group for Design of Communication* (SIGDOC) 2001, 95-102. Available at http://faculty.gvsu.edu/sunh/resch/acm01.pdf

University Grants Commission. (n.d.). Retrieved April 27, 2006, from University Grants Commission (UGC): http://www.ugc.ac.in/

VandeCreek, L. M. (2005). Usability analysis of Northern Illinois University Libraries' website: a case study. OCLC Systems and Services, 21(3), 181-192.

Vasantha Raju, N. & Harinarayana, N. S. (2008). An analysis of usability features of library websites. Annals of Library and Information Studies, 55(2), 111-122.

Web usability. (n.d.). Retrieved June 4, 2009, from Wikipedia: http://en.wikipedia.org/wiki/Web_usability

Yoon, S. (2002). The antecedents and consequences of trust in online-purchase decisions. Journal of Interactive Marketing, 16(2), 47-63.

Yu, B. & Roh, S. (2002). The effects of menu design on information-seeking performance and user's attitude on the web. Journal of the American Society for Information Science and Technology, 53(11), 923-933.

4

MEASURING WEB IMPACT FACTOR OF LIBRARY WEBSITES

4.1. INTRODUCTION

The Web Impact Factor (WIF) data is collected for selected twenty (20) Central University (CU) library websites; and nineteen (19) Institutes of National Importance (INI) & Indian Institutes of Management (IIMs) library websites. For collection of data, web browser and search engines were used as tools. Initially each website was examined to find out number of active web pages and URL of each page was recorded. This was done for all thirty nine (39) selected library websites. Numbers of backlinks were recorded for each active web page for individual websites using Google. All the *backlinks* were added together and divided by total number of active web pages of individual websites to produce Web Impact Factor (WIF). Same exercise was done with search engines AlltheWeb, AltaVista and Yahoo Site Explorer. Hence, WIF of each website using each search engine was recorded. The data was collected in five rounds at the interval of five months. The collected data is presented in Tables 4.1, 4.2, 4.3, 4.4, 4.5, 4.6, 4.7, 4.8, 4.9 and 4.10. The analysis has been divided into five parts. They are:

- Web Impact Factor Calculation,
- Comparative Rankings,

- Breakdown of *Backlinks* of Library Websites,
- Size vs. WIF of Library Websites
- Domain wise Analysis of Library Websites

4.2. LIST OF EXCLUDED ITEMS FROM THE STUDY

Some of the website related issues have been excluded from the study. The details of such excluded items are as follows:

(a) Web OPAC pages / Catalogue Search / Online Search web pages

(b) Web pages that are not present in the website but links are alive

(c) Online directories of books of library (except index page of such directories)

(d) Links to other websites (outside the library website)

(e) Links / web pages of databases (search page)

(f) Links / web pages of departmental / campus / study centre libraries

(g) Email addresses

(h) Web pages that cannot be displayed

(i) Web mail login links / pages

(j) Live chat

(k) Under construction web pages and duplicate web pages

(l) Institutional repositories (except index pages)

(m) Digital library databases (except index pages)

(n) Software links

4.3. DATA PRESENTATION

The following Tables 4.1, 4.2, 4.3, 4.4 and 4.5 presents data of twenty (20) central university library websites and Tables 4.6, 4.7, 4.8, 4.9 and 4.10 presents data of nineteen (19) INIs & IIMs library websites collected in five rounds by using search engines Google, AlltheWeb, AltaVista and Yahoo Site Explorer.

Table 4.1: *Data of Backlinks for the CU Library Websites in Different Search Engines (Round 1, July, 2006)*

SEARCH ENGINES →	GOOGLE				ALLTHEWEB				ALTAVISTA				YAHOO SITE EXPLORER			
Universities (in Code) ↓	TNP	UNF	ANP	BACK	TNP	UNF	ANP	BACK	TNP	UNF	ANP	BACK	TNP	UNF	ANP	BACK
AMU	1	0	1	0	1	1	0	----	1	1	0	----	1	1	0	---
ASU	1	1	0	----	1	0	1	0	1	0	1	0	1	0	1	0
BBAU	No separate website exist for library															
BHU	10	5	5	0	10	1	9	8	10	1	9	10	10	1	9	12
CAUI	No separate website existfor library															
IGNOU	22	21	1	0	22	21	1	0	22	21	1	0	22	20	2	7
JMI	40	2	38	0	40	2	38	1	40	2	38	1	40	35	5	2
JNU	10	2	8	0	10	1	9	7	10	1	9	6	10	1	9	17
MGAHV	No website exist for library															
MANI	1	0	1	0	1	0	1	0	1	0	1	0	1	0	1	0
MANUU	2	0	2	0	2	0	2	0	2	0	2	0	2	0	2	1
MIZUNI	1	0	1	0	1	0	1	0	1	0	1	0	1	0	1	0
NAGUNI	No website exist for university															
NEHU	1	1	0	----	1	1	0	----	1	1	0	----	1	1	0	----
PONDI	1	1	0	----	1	1	0	----	1	1	0	----	1	1	0	----
TEZU	No separate website exist for library															
UOA	1	1	0	----	1	1	0	----	1	1	0	----	1	1	0	----
UOD	69	54	15	1	69	41	28	3	69	43	26	5	69	38	31	6
UOH	23	5	18	1	23	7	16	2	23	7	16	2	23	6	17	1
VBU	2	0	2	0	2	1	1	0	2	1	1	0	2	0	2	0

Legends: TNP = Total number of active URLs / web pages in website, UNF = URL / web page not found / indexed in search engines, ANP = Actual / indexed number of URLs / web pages in website, BACK = Total number of backlinks (inlinks) for a website.

Table 4.2: Data of Backlinks for the CU Library Websites in Different Search Engines (Round 2, January, 2007)

SEARCH ENGINES →	GOOGLE				ALLTHEWEB				ALTAVISTA				YAHOO SITE EXPLORER			
Universities (in Code) ↓	TNP	UNF	ANP	BACK	TNP	UNF	ANP	BACK	TNP	UNF	ANP	BACK	TNP	UNF	ANP	BACK
AMU	1	0	1	0	1	0	1	0	1	0	1	0	1	0	1	0
ASU	1	0	1	0	1	0	1	0	1	0	1	0	1	0	1	0
BBAU	No separate website exist for library															
BHU	10	3	7	0	10	0	10	10	10	0	10	12	10	0	10	16
CAUI	No separate website exist for library															
IGNOU	22	21	1	0	22	21	1	0	22	21	1	0	22	20	2	2
JMI	38	3	35	1	38	2	36	1	38	2	36	1	38	18	20	2
JNU	4	0	4	0	4	0	4	7	4	0	4	7	4	0	4	18
MGAHV	No website exist for library															
MANI	1	0	1	0	1	0	1	0	1	0	1	0	1	0	1	0
MANUU	2	0	2	0	2	0	2	1	2	0	2	1	2	0	2	2
MIZUNI	1	0	1	0	1	0	1	0	1	0	1	0	1	0	1	0
NAGUNI	No website exist for university															
NEHU	8	3	5	0	8	1	7	2	8	1	7	2	8	1	7	1
PONDI	1	1	0	----	1	1	0	----	1	1	0	----	1	1	0	----
TEZU	No separate website exist for library															
UOA	1	1	0	----	1	1	0	----	1	1	0	----	1	1	0	----
UOD	64	29	35	4	64	22	42	4	64	23	41	5	64	20	44	9
UOH	23	2	21	3	23	4	19	5	23	5	18	5	23	3	20	6
VBU	2	0	2	0	2	0	2	0	2	0	2	0	2	0	2	0

Legends: TNP = Total number of active URLs / web pages in website, UNF = URL / web page not found / indexed in search engines, ANP = Actual / indexed number of URLs / web pages in website, BACK = Total number of backlinks (inlinks) for a website.

Table 4.3: Data of Backlinks for the CU Library Websites in Different Search Engines (Round 3, July, 2007)

SEARCH ENGINES →	GOOGLE				ALLTHEWEB				ALTAVISTA				YAHOO SITE EXPLORER			
Universities (in Code) ↓	TNP	UNF	ANP	BACK	TNP	UNF	ANP	BACK	TNP	UNF	ANP	BACK	TNP	UNF	ANP	BACK
AMU	1	0	1	0	1	1	0	----	1	1	0	----	1	0	1	0
ASU	1	0	1	0	1	0	1	0	1	0	1	0	1	0	1	1
BBAU	No separate website exist for library															
BHU	10	0	10	3	10	0	10	13	10	0	10	15	10	0	10	22
CAUI	No separate website exist for library															
IGNOU	19	18	1	0	19	18	1	0	19	18	1	0	19	17	2	2
JMI	41	5	36	1	41	4	37	2	41	4	37	2	41	11	30	3
JNU	3	0	3	1	3	0	3	7	3	0	3	7	3	0	3	20
MGAHV	No website exist for library															
MANI	1	0	1	0	1	0	1	0	1	0	1	0	1	0	1	0
MANUU	2	0	2	3	2	0	2	3	2	0	2	3	2	0	2	4
MIZUNI	1	0	1	0	1	0	1	0	1	0	1	0	1	0	1	0
NAGUNI	No separate website exist for library															
NEHU	18	8	10	0	18	6	12	1	18	6	12	1	18	6	12	1
PONDI	1	1	0	----	1	1	0	----	1	1	0	----	1	1	0	----
TEZU	9	2	7	0	9	3	6	0	9	3	6	0	9	3	6	0
UOA	1	1	0	----	1	1	0	----	1	1	0	----	1	1	0	----
UOD	62	13	49	7	62	13	49	6	62	14	48	7	62	12	50	11
UOH	16	8	8	1	16	11	5	1	16	12	4	1	16	10	6	1
VBU	2	0	2	0	2	0	2	0	2	0	2	0	2	0	2	0

Legends: TNP = Total number of active URLs / web pages in website, UNF = URL / web page not found / indexed in search engines, ANP = Actual / indexed number of URLs / web pages inwebsite, BACK = Total number of backlinks(inlinks) for a website.

Table 4.4: Data of Backlinks for the CU Library Websites in Different Search Engines (Round 4, January, 2008)

SEARCH ENGINES →	GOOGLE				ALLTHEWEB				ALTAVISTA				YAHOO SITE EXPLORER			
Universities (in Code) ↓	TNP	UNF	ANP	BACK	TNP	UNF	ANP	BACK	TNP	UNF	ANP	BACK	TNP	UNF	ANP	BACK
AMU	1	0	1	0	1	1	0	----	1	1	0	----	1	0	1	0
ASU	1	0	1	0	1	0	1	0	1	0	1	0	1	0	1	1
BBAU	No separate website exist for library															
BHU	10	0	10	4	10	0	10	15	10	0	10	15	10	0	10	23
CAUI	No separate website exist for library															
IGNOU	20	19	1	0	20	19	1	0	20	19	1	0	20	18	2	2
JMI	42	3	39	2	42	2	40	3	42	2	40	3	42	8	34	5
JNU	3	0	3	1	3	0	3	9	3	0	3	9	3	0	3	20
MGAHV	No website exist for library															
MANI	1	0	1	0	1	0	1	0	1	0	1	0	1	0	1	0
MANUU	2	0	2	2	2	0	2	4	2	0	2	4	2	0	2	4
MIZUNI	1	0	1	0	1	0	1	0	1	0	1	0	1	0	1	0
NAGUNI	Library website exists but URLs are not extractable															
NEHU	17	9	8	0	17	8	9	1	17	8	9	1	17	4	13	1
PONDI	1	1	0	----	1	1	0	----	1	1	0	----	1	1	0	----
TEZU	13	5	8	0	13	4	9	0	13	4	9	0	13	4	9	0
UOA	1	1	0	----	1	1	0	----	1	1	0	----	1	1	0	----
UOD	130	111	19	2	130	111	19	3	130	111	19	3	130	109	21	4
UOH	170	156	14	4	170	160	10	5	170	160	10	5	170	158	12	4
VBU	2	0	2	0	2	0	2	0	2	0	2	0	2	0	2	0

Legends: TNP = Total number of active URLs / webpages in website, UNF = URL / web page not found / indexed in search engines, ANP = Actual / indexed number of URLs / web pages in website, BACK = Total number of backlinks (inlinks) for a website.

Table 4.5: Data of Backlinks for the CU Library Websites in Different Search Engines (Round 5, July, 2008)

SEARCH ENGINES→	GOOGLE				ALLTHEWEB				ALTAVISTA				YAHOO SITE EXPLORER			
Universities (in Code) ↓	TNP	UNF	ANP	BACK	TNP	UNF	ANP	BACK	TNP	UNF	ANP	BACK	TNP	UNF	ANP	BACK
AMU	1	0	1	0	1	1	0	----	1	1	0	----	1	1	0	----
ASU	1	1	0	----	1	0	1	0	1	0	1	0	1	0	1	0
BBAU	No separate website exist for library															
BHU	11	5	6	2	11	0	11	16	11	0	11	16	11	1	10	21
CAUI	No separate website exist for library															
IGNOU	37	37	0	----	37	35	2	1	37	35	2	1	37	35	2	1
JMI	52	0	52	0	52	2	50	3	52	2	50	3	52	46	6	4
JNU	4	1	3	0	4	0	4	11	4	0	4	11	4	0	4	22
MGAHV	No website exist for library															
MANI	1	0	1	0	1	0	1	0	1	0	1	0	1	0	1	0
MANUU	2	0	2	0	2	0	2	1	2	0	2	1	2	0	2	3
MIZUNI	1	0	1	0	1	0	1	0	1	0	1	0	1	0	1	0
NAGUNI	Library website exists but URLs are not extractable															
NEHU	39	39	0	----	39	39	0	----	39	39	0	----	39	39	0	----
PONDI	1	0	1	0	1	0	1	1	1	0	1	1	1	0	1	1
TEZU	11	4	7	0	11	7	4	1	11	7	4	1	11	3	8	2
UOA	1	1	0	----	1	1	0	----	1	1	0	----	1	1	0	----
UOD	230	96	134	2	230	11	219	15	230	7	223	24	230	4	226	17
UOH	173	125	48	1	173	167	6	1	173	167	6	1	173	168	5	1
VBU	2	0	2	0	2	0	2	0	2	0	2	0	2	0	2	0

Legends: TNP = Total number of active URLs / web pages in website, UNF = URL / web page not found / indexed in search engines, ANP = Actual / indexed number of URLs/ web pages in website, BACK = Total number of backlinks (inlinks) for a website.

Table 4.6: Data of Backlinks for the INIs & IIMs Library Websites in Different Search Engines (Round 1, July, 2006)

SEARCH ENGINES→	GOOGLE				ALLTHEWEB				ALTAVISTA				YAHOO SITE EXPLORER			
Institutes (in Code) ↓	TNP	UNF	ANP	BACK	TNP	UNF	ANP	BACK	TNP	UNF	ANP	BACK	TNP	UNF	ANP	BACK
AIIMS	27	24	3	0	27	3	24	2	27	3	24	2	27	2	25	8
DBHPS	No website exist for library															
IIMA	64	42	22	0	64	28	36	14	64	28	36	13	64	28	36	11
IIMB	24	19	5	0	24	12	12	1	24	12	12	1	24	13	11	1
IIMC	48	42	6	1	48	9	39	6	48	9	39	7	48	34	14	12
IIMI	4	3	1	0	4	0	4	0	4	0	4	0	4	0	4	0
IIMK	39	27	12	3	39	16	23	15	39	16	23	15	39	20	19	40
IIML	92	84	8	0	92	37	55	3	92	34	58	3	92	32	60	3
IITB	110	44	66	6	110	26	84	34	110	26	84	35	110	50	60	72
IITD	102	54	48	12	102	51	51	24	102	49	53	26	102	46	56	55
IITG	40	35	5	1	40	22	18	13	40	22	18	14	40	20	20	19
IITK	6	2	4	1	6	0	6	9	6	0	6	10	6	0	6	24
IITKGP	315	210	105	3	315	115	200	16	315	114	201	17	315	124	191	39
IITM	156	101	55	5	156	102	54	25	156	101	55	26	156	97	59	52
IITR	1	0	1	0	1	0	1	1	1	0	1	1	1	0	1	1
ISIK	82	59	23	1	82	14	68	43	82	14	68	46	82	7	75	58
NIPER	No separate website exist for library															
PGIMER	No separate website exist for library															
SCTIMST	5	5	0	----	5	5	0	----	5	5	0	----	5	5	0	----

Legends: TNP = Total number of active URLs / web pages in website, UNF = URL / web page not found / indexed in search engines, ANP = Actual / indexed number of URLs / web pages in website, BACK = Totla number of backlinks (inlinks) for a website.

Table 4.7: Data of Backlinks for the INIs & IIMs Library Websites in Different Search Engines (Round 2, January, 2007)

SEARCH ENGINES →	GOOGLE				ALLTHEWEB				ALTAVISTA				YAHOO SITE EXPLORER			
Institutes (in Code) ↓	TNP	UNF	ANP	BACK	TNP	UNF	ANP	BACK	TNP	UNF	ANP	BACK	TNP	UNF	ANP	BACK
AIIMS	27	21	6	0	27	2	25	2	27	2	25	2	27	1	26	8
DBHPS	No website exist for library															
IIMA	62	32	30	0	62	23	39	12	62	23	39	13	62	23	39	12
IIMB	24	12	12	0	24	7	17	1	24	7	17	1	24	11	13	1
IIMC	44	33	11	2	44	4	40	8	44	5	39	8	44	30	14	10
IIMI	4	4	0	---	4	0	4	0	4	0	4	0	4	0	4	0
IIMK	46	23	23	6	46	21	25	20	46	21	25	20	46	19	27	56
IIML	86	76	10	0	86	35	51	4	86	31	55	4	86	32	54	3
IITB	139	81	58	9	139	62	77	41	139	60	79	43	139	60	79	80
IITD	101	51	50	20	101	49	52	31	101	48	53	32	101	44	57	65
IITG	40	31	9	1	40	22	18	14	40	22	18	15	40	20	20	20
IITK	6	2	4	2	6	0	6	10	6	0	6	11	6	0	6	26
IITKGP	353	241	112	4	353	153	200	19	353	152	201	22	353	161	192	42
IITM	140	85	55	9	140	86	54	30	140	84	56	32	140	77	63	55
IITR	2	1	1	1	2	1	1	1	2	1	1	1	2	1	1	1
ISIK	48	30	18	1	48	6	42	45	48	7	41	47	48	2	46	60
NIPER	No separate website exist for library															
PGIMER	15	6	9	0	15	6	9	0	15	6	9	0	15	2	13	0
SCTIMST	5	3	2	0	5	5	0	----	5	5	0	----	5	5	0	----

Legends: TNP = Total number of active URLs / web pages in website, UNF = URL / web page not found / indexed in search engines, ANP = Actual / indexed number of URLs / web pages in website, BACK = Totla number of backlinks (inlinks) for a website.

Table 4.8: Data of Backlinks for the INIs & IIMs Library Websites in Different Search Engines (Round 3, July, 2007)

SEARCH ENGINES→	GOOGLE				ALLTHEWEB				ALTAVISTA				YAHOO SITE EXPLORER			
Institutes (in Code) ↓	TNP	UNF	ANP	BACK	TNP	UNF	ANP	BACK	TNP	UNF	ANP	BACK	TNP	UNF	ANP	BACK
AIIMS	28	3	25	0	28	1	27	3	28	1	27	3	28	1	27	12
DBHPS	No website exist for library															
IIMA	48	15	33	0	48	9	39	14	48	9	39	15	48	11	37	16
IIMB	25	5	20	0	25	5	20	1	25	5	20	1	25	5	20	1
IIMC	47	33	14	2	47	32	15	8	47	32	15	8	47	33	14	11
IIMI	4	4	0	----	4	0	4	2	4	0	4	2	4	0	4	3
IIMK	42	19	23	8	42	15	27	38	42	15	27	40	42	13	29	66
IIML	96	81	15	0	96	14	82	5	96	14	82	5	96	16	80	3
IITB	102	88	14	4	102	66	36	71	102	66	36	71	102	62	40	84
IITD	140	103	37	20	140	102	38	55	140	102	38	57	140	98	42	61
IITG	55	30	25	1	55	22	33	19	55	22	33	19	55	20	35	26
IITK	6	2	4	2	6	0	6	18	6	0	6	18	6	0	6	30
IITKGP	172	145	27	3	172	139	33	26	172	139	33	27	172	146	26	47
IITM	137	76	61	11	137	77	60	35	137	77	60	36	137	75	62	51
IITR	2	2	0	----	2	1	1	3	2	1	1	3	2	1	1	2
ISIK	75	24	51	2	75	15	60	54	75	15	60	54	75	14	61	66
NIPER	No separate website exist for library															
PGIMER	15	3	12	0	15	3	12	0	15	3	12	0	15	0	15	0
SCTIMST	5	5	0	----	5	5	0	----	5	5	0	----	5	5	0	----

Legends: TNP = Total number of active URLs / web pages in website, UNF = URL / web page not found / indexed in search engines, ANP = Actual / indexed number of URLs / web pags in website, BACK = Total number of backlinks (inlinks) for a website.

Table 4.9: Data of Backlinks for the INIs & IIMs Library Websites in Different Search Engines (Round 4, January, 2008)

SEARCH ENGINES →	**GOOGLE**				**ALLTHEWEB**				**ALTAVISTA**				**YAHOO SITE EXPLORER**			
Institutes (in Code) ↓	TNP	UNF	ANP	BACK	TNP	UNF	ANP	BACK	TNP	UNF	ANP	BACK	TNP	UNF	ANP	BACK
AIIMS	27	6	21	0	27	5	22	3	27	5	22	3	27	3	24	12
DBHPS	No website exist for library															
IIMA	55	21	34	0	55	12	43	15	55	12	43	15	55	16	39	16
IIMB	25	10	15	0	25	8	17	1	25	8	17	1	25	12	13	1
IIMC	93	74	19	2	93	71	22	6	93	71	22	6	93	70	23	9
IIMI	4	3	1	0	4	0	4	1	4	0	4	1	4	0	4	2
IIMK	47	18	29	9	47	21	26	36	47	21	26	36	47	18	29	71
IIML	84	65	19	0	84	7	77	2	84	7	77	2	84	7	77	2
IITB	86	67	19	3	86	18	68	67	86	18	68	67	86	24	62	82
IITD	162	133	29	14	162	104	58	47	162	104	58	49	162	108	54	56
IITG	54	26	28	1	54	25	29	20	54	25	29	20	54	19	35	27
IITK	6	0	6	1	6	0	6	16	6	0	6	17	6	0	6	26
IITKGP	206	191	15	2	206	169	37	27	206	169	37	28	206	176	30	40
IITM	139	91	48	13	139	75	64	36	139	75	64	37	139	72	67	49
IITR	11	5	6	0	11	3	8	2	11	3	8	2	11	4	7	2
ISIK	55	19	36	4	55	11	44	56	55	11	44	57	55	7	48	64
NIPER	No separate website exist for library															
PGIMER	15	3	12	0	15	3	12	0	15	3	12	0	15	0	15	0
SCTIMST	5	4	1	0	5	5	0	----	5	5	0	----	5	5	0	----

Legends: TNP = Total number of active URLs / web pages in website, UNF = URL / web page not found / indexed in search engines, ANP = Actual / indexed number of URLs / web pages in website, BACK = Totla number of backlinks(inlinks) for a website.

Table 4.10: Data of Backlinks for the INIs & IIMs Library Websites in Different Search Engines (Round 5, July, 2008)

SEARCH ENGINES →	GOOGLE				ALLTHEWEB				ALTAVISTA				YAHOO SITE EXPLORER			
Institutes (in Code) ↓	TNP	UNF	ANP	BACK	TNP	UNF	ANP	BACK	TNP	UNF	ANP	BACK	TNP	UNF	ANP	BACK
AIIMS	27	22	5	0	27	1	26	3	27	2	25	3	27	0	27	12
DBHPS	No website exist for library															
IIMA	160	114	46	0	160	44	116	18	160	44	116	18	160	42	118	21
IIMB	25	15	10	0	25	5	20	1	25	5	20	1	25	2	23	1
IIMC	105	95	10	1	105	3	102	12	105	3	102	12	105	2	103	28
IIMI	4	3	1	0	4	0	4	0	4	0	4	0	4	0	4	0
IIMK	44	28	16	6	44	21	23	30	44	21	23	33	44	21	23	79
IIML	102	85	17	0	102	1	101	3	102	1	101	3	102	0	102	3
IITB	240	112	128	6	240	23	217	81	240	8	232	83	240	12	228	99
IITD	800	665	135	7	800	658	142	27	800	656	144	27	800	651	149	57
IITG	55	47	8	1	55	29	26	19	55	29	26	18	55	29	26	25
IITK	12	3	9	2	12	2	10	17	12	2	10	18	12	2	10	37
IITKGP	132	10	122	1	132	48	84	55	132	47	85	56	132	79	53	41
IITM	165	69	96	12	165	60	105	42	165	58	107	39	165	57	108	78
IITR	10	0	10	0	10	0	10	2	10	0	10	2	10	0	10	4
ISIK	91	63	28	1	91	11	80	55	91	13	78	59	91	2	89	72
NIPER	No separate website exist for library															
PGIMER	22	3	19	0	22	5	17	0	22	3	19	0	22	4	18	0
SCTIMST	5	4	1	0	5	5	0	----	5	5	0	----	5	5	0	----

Legends: TNP = Total number of active URLs / web pages in website, UNF = URL / web page not found / indexed in search engines, ANP = Actual / indexed number of URLs / web pages in website, BACK = Totla number of backlinks(inlinks) for a website.

4.4. WEB IMPACT FACTOR (WIF) CALCULATION

The following legends are used in calculation of WIF:

R1 = Round 1 (July, 2006)

R2 = Round 2 (January, 2007)

R3 = Round 3 (July, 2007)

R4 = Round 4 (January, 2008)

R5 = Round 5 (July, 2008)

TNP = Total number of active URLs / web pages in a website

UNF = URL / web page not found / not indexed in search engine

ANP = Actual / indexed number of URLs / web pages in a website

BACK = Total number of *backlinks* (*inlinks*) for a website

WIF = Web Impact Factor

YSE = Yahoo Site Explorer

In the graphs, black line, green line, red line and blue line represent Google, AlltheWeb, AltaVista and Yahoo Site Explorer respectively.

WIF Calculation Method

Suppose there are ten (10) web pages in the library website of BHU in 1st round. One web page is not indexed by the Yahoo Site Explorer which results total nine (9) web pages for WIF data retrieval. For these nine web pages, Yahoo Site Explorer has yielded twelve (12) *backlinks* in total. The WIF is calculated for BHU library website by using the formula:

$$\text{WIF} = \frac{\text{Total backlinks (inlinks)}}{\text{Total number of indexed web pages of the website at a time}}$$

Thus, WIF for BHU library website will be:

$$WIF = \frac{12}{9} = 1.3333$$

Likewise, WIF is calculated for all five rounds using four search engines individually for each of the library website.

4.4.1. Central Universities (CU) Library Websites

The WIF data and graphs are more or less similar to each other amongst central universities library websites. So, WIF data and graphs of some central universities library websites have been given below as illustration.

A. Library, Banaras Hindu University, Varanasi (BHU)

There are 10 web pages in BHU library website. The data was collected using all the search engines. Google did not retrieve *backlinks* in two rounds of data collection (1st and 2nd) hence; WIF using Google could not be collected for these rounds.

Table 4.11: Web Impact Factor of Library, BHU

Round↓	Search Engine			
	Google	All the Web	AltaVista	Yahoo Site Explorer
R1	--	0.8888	1.1111	1.3333
R2	--	1	1.2	1.6
R3	0.3	1.3	1.5	2.2
R4	0.4	1.5	1.5	2.3
R5	0.3333	1.4545	1.4545	2.1

The graph plotted for BHU library website (Fig. 4.1) demonstrates curves for WIF of the library website using all four search engines. The curves show a continuous increase in WIF of library website. However, in last round all the curves plotted using all search engines show decreasing trend in WIF. In 3rd and 4th round of data collection using AltaVista, the WIF was constant. During the study period, there was no change in website size (number of web pages) of the BHU library websites.

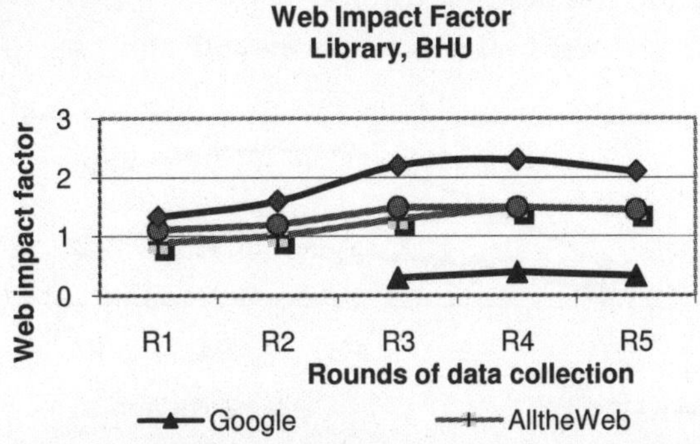

Fig. 4.1: Web Impact Factor of Library, BHU

B. *Library, Jawaharlal Nehru University, New Delhi (JNU)*

JNU library website is very well referred by *backlinks*. The data of *backlinks* was not retrieved for 1st, 2nd 5th round when Google is used. The calculated WIFs of JNU library website in all the rounds using all the search engines is presented in Table 4.12.

Table 4.12: Web Impact Factor of Library, JNU

Round↓	Search Engine			
	Google	All the Web	AltaVista	Yahoo Site Explorer
R1	--	0.7777	0.6666	1.8888
R2	--	1.75	1.75	4.5
R3	0.3333	2.3333	2.3333	6.6666
R4	0.3333	3	3	6.6666
R5	--	2.75	2.75	5.5

The graph plot of WIFs of all the five rounds using search engines is presented in Fig. 4.2. The curve for AlltheWeb and AltaVista is same and hence overlaps. Highest WIF values were achieved only when Yahoo Site

Explorer was used. There was no *backlinks* for JNU library website in 1st, 2nd and 3rd rounds when Google is employed for data collection, hence WIF could not be calculated for the said rounds.

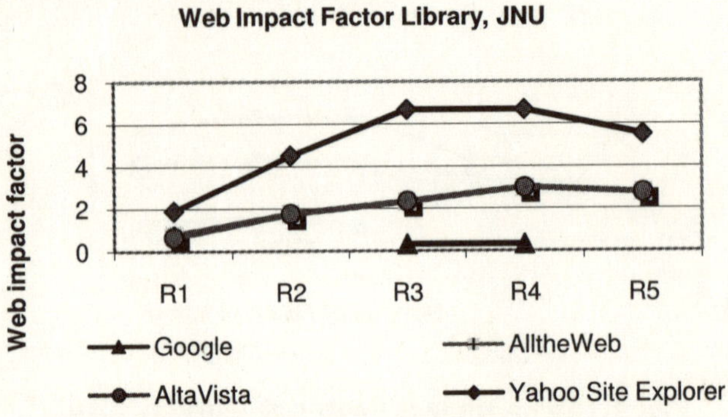

Fig. 4.2: Web Impact Factor of Library, JNU

C. Library, University of Delhi, Delhi (UOD)

UOD has separate website for its university library. The website receives *backlinks* from other websites which is reflected in the *backlink* data collected by all of the four search engines. The WIF values are different in different rounds. Yahoo Site Explorer has given lower WIF values than AltaVista in 5th round. However, WIF is higher by Yahoo Site Explorer for UOD compare to the WIF given by other search engines in 1st to 4th round. The WIF data of UOD was not similar for AlltheWeb and AltaVista.

Table 4.13: Web Impact Factor of Library, UOD

Round↓	Search Engine			
	Google	**AlltheWeb**	**AltaVista**	**Yahoo Site Explorer**
R1	0.0666	0.1071	0.1923	0.1935
R2	0.1142	0.0952	0.1219	0.2045
R3	0.1428	0.1224	0.1458	0.22
R4	0.1052	0.1578	0.1578	0.1904
R5	0.0149	0.0684	0.1076	0.0752

A clear plot for WIFs of UOD library website is seen by different search engines in Fig. 4.3. The black curve of Google show increase of WIF from 1st to 3rd round and further decrease from 3rd to 5th round. The curve of AlltheWeb and AltaVista does not overlap except in 4th round. The blue curve appears above other three curves indicating Yahoo Site Explorer has given again higher WIF values for UOD library website except 5th round.

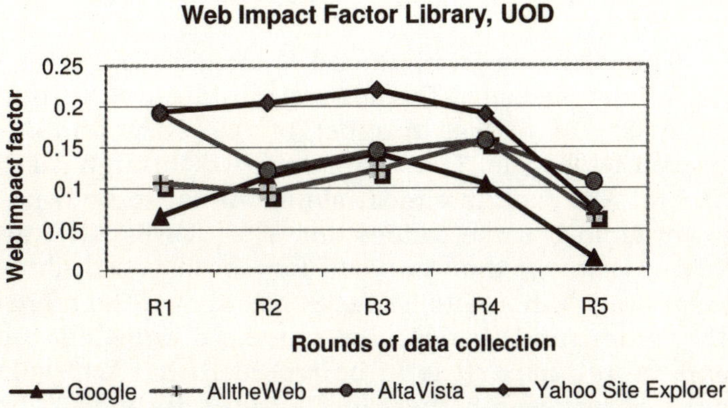

Fig. 4.3: Web Impact Factor of Library, UOD

4.4.2. Institutes of National Importance (INI) & IIMs Library Websites

The WIF data and graphs are more or less similar to each other amongst Institutes of National Importance and Indian Institutes of Management library websites. So, WIF data and graphs of some institutes library websites have been given below as illustration.

A. Library, Indian Institute of Management, Kozhikode (IIMK)

IIMK has website for its library and it is covered by all the search engines and hence *backlinks* are recorded for all the rounds. The WIF values for IIMI library website are presented in the Table 4.14.

Table 4.14: Web Impact Factor of Library, IIMK

Round↓	Search Engine			
	Google	**All the Web**	**AltaVista**	**Yahoo Site Explorer**
R1	0.25	0.6521	0.6521	2.1052
R2	0.2608	0.8	0.8	2.074
R3	0.3478	1.4074	1.4814	2.2758
R4	0.3103	1.3846	1.3846	2.4482
R5	0.375	1.3043	1.4347	3.4347

The following graph (Fig. 4.4) shows WIF curves of IIMK library website. The lowest strata curve through Google is due to less number of *backlinks* and ANP retrieved by Google. The WIF calculated through All the Web and AltaVista is almost similar because both have shown almost same values for TNP, UNF, ANP and BACK. Hence, the curves for both are almost overlapping. Yahoo Site Explorer has shown the highest WIF values and hence the curve is crawling high compare to others. It is to be recorded that WIF value for the library was highest in 5th round through Yahoo Site Explorer. This is due to increase in *backlinks* and decrease in ANP in the data of Yahoo Site Explorer.

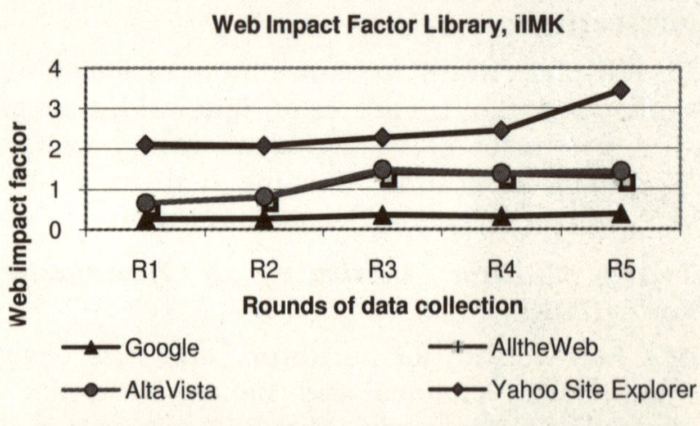

Fig. 4.4: Web Impact Factor of Library, IIMK

B. Library, Indian Institute of Technology, Bombay (IITB)

IITB has separate website for its library and it is well covered by all the search engines. The WIF data is presented in the following table (Table 4.15).

Table 4.15: Web Impact Factor of Library, IITB

Round↓	Search Engine			
	Google	**All the Web**	**AltaVista**	**Yahoo Site Explorer**
R1	0.0909	0.4047	0.4166	1.2
R2	0.1551	0.5324	0.5443	1.0126
R3	0.2857	1.9722	1.9722	2.1
R4	0.1578	0.9852	0.9852	1.3225
R5	0.0468	0.3732	0.3577	0.4342

The plotted graph (Fig. 4.5) shows WIF curves of IITB library website calculated through the *backlinks* data collected by all search engines in all five rounds. The Google curve for IITB library website lies lowest as it had retrieved less number of *backlinks* and ANP than others. The WIF values of the library website through AlltheWeb and AltaVista were very close and were same in 3rd and 4th rounds. This was due to the closeness of data of TNP, UNF, ANP and BACK. Yahoo Site Explorer had retrieved more *backlinks* which resulted in the highest WIF values for the library website and hence the Yahoo Site Explorer curve crawls highest in the plotted graph.

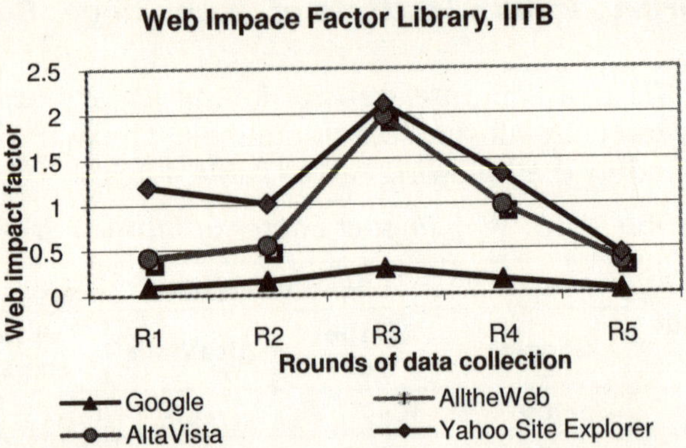

Fig. 4.5: Web Impact Factor of Library, IITB

C. Library, Indian Statistical Institute, Kolkata (ISIK)

ISIK has website for its library. All of the search engines have indexed the web pages of library website. The Table 4.16 presents the WIF values collected in five rounds.

Table 4.16: Web Impact Factor of Library, ISIK

Round↓	Search Engine			
	Google	**All the Web**	**AltaVista**	**Yahoo Site Explorer**
R1	0.0434	0.6323	0.6764	0.7733
R2	0.0555	1.0714	1.1463	1.3043
R3	0.0392	0.9	0.9	1.0819
R4	0.1111	1.2727	1.2954	1.3333
R5	0.0357	0.6875	0.7564	0.8089

The graph (Fig. 4.6) shows WIF curves of ISIK library. The Google curve lies the lowest due to less number of *backlinks*. Yahoo Site Explorer had shown the highest WIF values for each round for the library website. The WIF values of library website as per the *backlink* data of AlltheWeb, AltaVista and Yahoo Site Explorer were found very close.

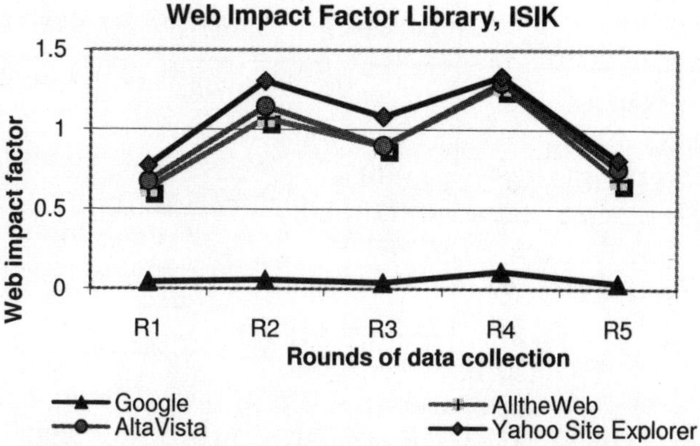

Fig. 4.6: Web Impact Factor of Library, ISIK

4.5. COMPARATIVE RANKINGS BASED ON WEB IMPACT FACTOR (WIF)

4.5.1. List of Excluded CU and INI Library Websites

The following table presents a list of CU and INI libraries which are excluded from the WIF study. The reasons for exclusion are also mentioned against each of them.

Table 4.17: List of Excluded Library Websites

SN	University / Institute	Category	Reason for Exclusion
1	BBAU	Central Universities	University has no website for library
2	CAUI		University has no website for library
3	MGAHV		University has no website for library
4	NAGUNI		Library website URL is not extractable
5	TEZU		Lack of data for first two rounds [Library website appears since 3rd round (R3) of data collection]

SN	University / Institute	Category	Reason for Exclusion
6	DBHPS	Institutes of National Importance	Institute has no website for library
7	NIPER		Institute has no website for library
8	PGIMER		Lack of data for 1st round [Library website appears since 2nd round (R2) of data collection]

Five CU libraries (i.e. 25%) out of twenty (20) and three INI libraries (i.e. 15.78%) out of nineteen (19), are excluded from the present study.

4.5.2. Central Universities (CU) Library Websites

Google WIF Analysis:

Table 4.18 represents ranking of CU library websites according to their respective Average WIF[1].

Table 4.18: Category Ranking of CU Library Websites based on Google

SN	Central University	GR1	GR2	GR3	GR4	GR5	Google Average	Category Ranking
1.	MANUU	Nil	Nil	1.5	1	Nil	0.5	1
2.	BHU	Nil	Nil	0.3	0.4	0.3333	0.20666	2
3.	JNU	Nil	Nil	0.3333	0.3333	Nil	0.13332	3
4.	UOH	0.0555	0.1428	0.125	0.2857	0.0208	0.12596	4
5.	UOD	0.0666	0.1142	0.1428	0.1052	0.0149	0.08874	5
6.	JMI	Nil	0.0285	0.0277	0.0512	Nil	0.02148	6
7.	MANI	Nil	Nil	Nil	Nil	Nil	Nil	7

1 Average WIF is an average of WIF values achieved in five rounds through a search engine for a library website.

SN	Central University	GR1	GR2	GR3	GR4	GR5	Google Average	Category Ranking
8.	AMU	Nil	Nil	Nil	Nil	Nil	Nil	7
9.	ASU	Nil	Nil	Nil	Nil	Nil	Nil	7
10.	IGNOU	Nil	Nil	Nil	Nil	Nil	Nil	7
11.	MIZUNI	Nil	Nil	Nil	Nil	Nil	Nil	7
12.	NEHU	Nil	Nil	Nil	Nil	Nil	Nil	7
13.	PONDI	Nil	Nil	Nil	Nil	Nil	Nil	7
14.	UOA	Nil	Nil	Nil	Nil	Nil	Nil	7
15.	VBU	Nil	Nil	Nil	Nil	Nil	Nil	7

Legends: GR1 = Google 1st round, GR2 = Google 2nd round, GR3 = Google 3rd round, GR4 = Google 4th round, GR5 = Google 5th round

AlltheWeb WIF Analysis:

Table 4.19 represents AlltheWeb ranking of CU library websites according to their respective Average WIF.

Table 4.19 : Category Ranking of CU Library Websites based on AlltheWeb

SN	Central University	AWR1	AWR2	AWR3	AWR4	AWR5	AlltheWeb Average	Category Ranking
1.	JNU	0.7777	1.75	2.3333	3	2.75	2.1222	1
2.	BHU	0.8888	1	1.3	1.5	1.4545	1.22866	2
3.	MANUU	Nil	0.5	1.5	2	0.5	0.9	3
4.	UOH	0.125	0.2631	0.2	0.5	0.1666	0.25094	4
5.	PONDI	Nil	Nil	Nil	Nil	1	0.2	5
6.	UOD	0.1071	0.0952	0.1224	0.1578	0.0684	0.11018	6
7.	IGNOU	Nil	Nil	Nil	Nil	0.5	0.1	7
8.	NEHU	Nil	0.2857	0.0833	0.1111	Nil	0.09602	8

SN	Central University	AWR1	AWR2	AWR3	AWR4	AWR5	AlltheWeb Average	Category Ranking
9.	JMI	0.0263	0.0277	0.054	0.075	0.06	0.0486	9
10.	AMU	Nil	Nil	Nil	Nil	Nil	Nil	10
11.	ASU	Nil	Nil	Nil	Nil	Nil	Nil	10
12.	MANI	Nil	Nil	Nil	Nil	Nil	Nil	10
13.	MIZUNI	Nil	Nil	Nil	Nil	Nil	Nil	10
14.	UOA	Nil	Nil	Nil	Nil	Nil	Nil	10
15.	VBU	Nil	Nil	Nil	Nil	Nil	Nil	10

Legends: AWR1 = AlltheWeb 1st round, AWR2 = AlltheWeb 2nd round, AWR3 = AlltheWeb 3rd round, AWR4 = AlltheWeb 4th round, AWR5 = AlltheWeb 5th round

AltaVista WIF Analysis:

Table 4.20 represents AltaVista ranking of CU library websites according to their respective Average WIF.

Table 4.20: Category Ranking of CU Library Websites based on AltaVista

SN	Central University	AVR1	AVR2	AVR3	AVR4	AVR5	AltaVista Average	Category Ranking
16.	JNU	0.6666	1.75	2.3333	3	2.75	2.09998	1
17.	BHU	1.1111	1.2	1.5	1.5	1.4545	1.35312	2
18.	MANUU	Nil	0.5	1.5	2	0.5	0.9	3
19.	UOH	0.125	0.2777	0.25	0.5	0.1666	0.26386	4
20.	PONDI	Nil	Nil	Nil	Nil	1	0.2	5
21.	UOD	0.1923	0.1219	0.1458	0.1578	0.1076	0.14508	6
22.	IGNOU	Nil	Nil	Nil	Nil	0.5	0.1	7
23.	NEHU	Nil	0.2857	0.0833	0.1111	Nil	0.09602	8

SN	Central University	AVR1	AVR2	AVR3	AVR4	AVR5	AltaVista Average	Category Ranking
24.	JMI	0.0263	0.0277	0.054	0.075	0.06	0.0486	9
25.	AMU	Nil	Nil	Nil	Nil	Nil	Nil	10
26.	ASU	Nil	Nil	Nil	Nil	Nil	Nil	10
27.	MANI	Nil	Nil	Nil	Nil	Nil	Nil	10
28.	MIZUNI	Nil	Nil	Nil	Nil	Nil	Nil	10
29.	UOA	Nil	Nil	Nil	Nil	Nil	Nil	10
30.	VBU	Nil	Nil	Nil	Nil	Nil	Nil	10

Legends: AVR1 = AltaVista 1st round, AVR2 = AltaVista 2nd round, AVR3 = AltaVista 3rd round, AVR4 = AltaVista 4th round, AVR5 = AltaVista 5th round

Yahoo Site Explorer WIF Analysis:

Table 4.21 represents Yahoo Site Explorer ranking of CU library websites based on their respective Average WIF.

Table 4.21: Category Ranking of CU Library Websites based on Yahoo Site Explorer

SN	Central University	YSER1	YSER2	YSER3	YSER4	YSER5	YSE Average	Category Ranking
1.	JNU	1.8888	4.5	6.6666	6.6666	5.5	5.0444	1
2.	BHU	1.3333	1.6	2.2	2.3	2.1	1.90666	2
3.	IGNOU	3.5	1	1	1	0.5	1.4	3
4.	MANUU	0.5	1	2	2	1.5	1.4	3
5.	ASU	Nil	Nil	1	1	Nil	0.4	4
6.	JMI	0.4	0.1	0.1	0.147	0.6666	0.28272	5
7.	UOH	0.0588	0.3	0.1666	0.3333	0.2	0.21174	6
8.	PONDI	Nil	Nil	Nil	Nil	1	0.2	7
9.	UOD	0.1935	0.2045	0.22	0.1904	0.0752	0.17672	8
10.	NEHU	Nil	0.1428	0.0833	0.0769	Nil	0.0606	9
11.	AMU	Nil	Nil	Nil	Nil	Nil	Nil	10
12.	MANI	Nil	Nil	Nil	Nil	Nil	Nil	10

SN	Central University	YSER1	YSER2	YSER3	YSER4	YSER5	YSE Average	Category Ranking
13.	MIZUNI	Nil	Nil	Nil	Nil	Nil	Nil	10
14.	UOA	Nil	Nil	Nil	Nil	Nil	Nil	10
15.	VBU	Nil	Nil	Nil	Nil	Nil	Nil	10

Legends: YSER1 = Yahoo Site Explorer 1st round, YSER2 = Yahoo Site Explorer 2nd round, YSER3 = Yahoo Site Explorer 3rd round, YSER4 = Yahoo Site Explorer 4th round, YSER5 = Yahoo Site Explorer 5th round

4.5.3. Institutes of National Importance (INI) & IIMs Library Websites

Google WIF Analysis

Table 4.22 represents Google ranking of INI library websites based on their respective Average WIF.

Table 4.22: Category Ranking of INI Library Websites based on Google

SN	Institute of National Importance	GR1	GR2	GR3	GR4	GR5	Google Average	Category Ranking
1.	IITD	0.25	0.4	0.5405	0.4827	0.0518	0.345	1
2.	IITK	0.25	0.5	0.5	0.1666	0.2222	0.32776	2
3.	IIMK	0.25	0.2608	0.3478	0.3103	0.375	0.30878	3
4.	IITR	Nil	1	Nil	Nil	Nil	0.2	4
5.	IITM	0.0909	0.1636	0.1803	0.2708	0.125	0.16612	5
6.	IITB	0.0909	0.1551	0.2857	0.1578	0.0468	0.14726	6
7.	IIMC	0.1666	0.1818	0.1428	0.1052	0.1	0.13928	7
8.	IITG	0.2	0.1111	0.04	0.0357	0.125	0.10236	8
9.	IITKGP	0.0285	0.0357	0.1111	0.1333	0.0081	0.06334	9
10.	ISIK	0.0434	0.0555	0.0392	0.1111	0.0357	0.05698	10
11.	AIIMS	Nil	Nil	Nil	Nil	Nil	Nil	11
12.	IIMA	Nil	Nil	Nil	Nil	Nil	Nil	11

SN	Institute of National Importance	GR1	GR2	GR3	GR4	GR5	Google Average	Category Ranking
13.	IIMB	Nil	Nil	Nil	Nil	Nil	Nil	11
14.	IIMI	Nil	Nil	Nil	Nil	Nil	Nil	11
15.	IIML	Nil	Nil	Nil	Nil	Nil	Nil	11
16.	SCTIMST	Nil	Nil	Nil	Nil	Nil	Nil	11

Legends: GR1 = Google 1st round, GR2 = Google 2nd round, GR3 = Google 3rd round, GR4 = Google 4th round, GR5 = Google 5th round

AlltheWeb WIF Analysis:

Table 4.23 represents AlltheWeb rankings of INI library websites based on their respective Average WIF.

Table 4.23: Category Ranking of INI Library Websites based on AlltheWeb

SN	Institute of National Importance	AWR1	AWR2	AWR3	AWR4	AWR5	AlltheWeb Average	Category Ranking
1.	IITK	1.5	1.6666	3	2.6666	1.7	2.10664	1
2.	IIMK	0.6521	0.8	1.4074	1.3846	1.3043	1.10968	2
3.	IITR	1	1	3	0.25	0.2	1.09	3
4.	ISIK	0.6323	1.0714	0.9	1.2727	0.6875	0.91278	4
5.	IITB	0.4047	0.5324	1.9722	0.9852	0.3732	0.85354	5
6.	IITD	0.4705	0.5961	1.4473	0.8103	0.1901	0.70286	6
7.	IITG	0.7222	0.7777	0.5757	0.6896	0.7307	0.69918	7
8.	IITM	0.4629	0.5555	0.5833	0.5625	0.4	0.51284	8
9.	IITKGP	0.08	0.095	0.7878	0.7297	0.6547	0.46944	9
10.	IIMA	0.3888	0.3076	0.3589	0.3488	0.1551	0.31184	10
11.	IIMC	0.1538	0.2	0.5333	0.2727	0.1176	0.25548	11
12.	IIMI	Nil	Nil	0.5	0.25	Nil	0.15	12

SN	Institute of National Importance	AWR1	AWR2	AWR3	AWR4	AWR5	AlltheWeb Average	Category Ranking
13.	AIIMS	0.0833	0.08	0.1111	0.1363	0.1153	0.1052	13
14.	IIMB	0.0833	0.0588	0.05	0.0588	0.05	0.06018	14
15.	IIML	0.0545	0.0784	0.0609	0.0259	0.0297	0.04988	15
16.	SCTIMST	Nil	Nil	Nil	Nil	Nil	Nil	16

Legends: AWR1 = AlltheWeb 1st round, AWR2 = AlltheWeb 2nd round, AWR3 = AlltheWeb 3rd round, AWR4 = AlltheWeb 4th round, AWR5 = AlltheWeb 5th round

AltaVista WIF Analysis:

Table 4.24 represents AltaVista ranking of INI library websites based on their Average WIF.

Table 4.24: Category Ranking of INI Library Websites based on AltaVista

SN	Institute of National Importance	AVR1	AVR2	AVR3	AVR4	AVR5	AltaVista Average	Category Ranking
1.	IITK	1.6666	1.8333	3	2.8333	1.8	2.22664	1
2.	IIMK	0.6521	0.8	1.4814	1.3846	1.4347	1.15056	2
3.	IITR	1	1	3	0.25	0.2	1.09	3
4.	ISIK	0.6764	1.1463	0.9	1.2954	0.7564	0.9549	4
5.	IITB	0.4166	0.5443	1.9722	0.9852	0.3577	0.8552	5
6.	IITD	0.4905	0.6037	1.5	0.8448	0.1875	0.7253	6
7.	IITG	0.7777	0.8333	0.5757	0.6896	0.6923	0.71372	7
8.	IITM	0.4727	0.5714	0.6	0.5781	0.3644	0.51732	8
9.	IITKGP	0.0845	0.1094	0.8181	0.7567	0.6588	0.4855	9
10.	IIMA	0.3611	0.3333	0.3846	0.3488	0.1551	0.31658	10
11.	IIMC	0.1794	0.2051	0.5333	0.2727	0.1176	0.26162	11

SN	Institute of National Importance	AVR1	AVR2	AVR3	AVR4	AVR5	AltaVista Average	Category Ranking
12.	IIMI	Nil	Nil	0.5	0.25	Nil	0.15	12
13.	AIIMS	0.0833	0.08	0.1111	0.1363	0.12	0.10614	13
14.	IIMB	0.0833	0.0588	0.05	0.0588	0.05	0.06018	14
15.	IIML	0.0517	0.0727	0.0609	0.0259	0.0297	0.04818	15
16.	SCTIMST	Nil	Nil	Nil	Nil	Nil	Nil	16

Legends: AVR1 = AltaVista 1st round, AVR2 = AltaVista 2nd round, AVR3 = AltaVista 3rd round, AVR4 = AltaVista 4th round, AVR5 = AltaVista 5th round

Yahoo Site Explorer WIF Analysis:

Table 4.25 represents Yahoo Site Explorer ranking of INI library websites according to their respective Average WIF.

Table 4.25: Category Ranking of INI Library Websites based on Yahoo Site Explorer

SN	Institute of National Importance	YSER1	YSER2	YSER3	YSER4	YSER5	YSE Average	Category Ranking
1.	IITK	4	4.3333	5	4.3333	3.7	4.27332	1
2.	IIMK	2.1052	2.074	2.2758	2.4482	3.4347	2.46758	2
3.	IITB	1.2	1.0126	2.1	1.3225	0.4342	1.21386	3
4.	ISIK	0.7733	1.3043	1.0819	1.3333	0.8089	1.06034	4
5.	IITD	0.9821	1.1403	1.4523	1.037	0.3825	0.99884	5
6.	IITR	1	1	2	0.2857	0.4	0.93714	6
7.	IITG	0.95	1	0.7428	0.7714	0.9615	0.88514	7
8.	IITKGP	0.2041	0.2187	1.8076	1.3333	0.7735	0.86744	8
9.	IITM	0.8813	0.873	0.8225	0.7313	0.7222	0.80606	9

SN	Institute of National Importance	YSER1	YSER2	YSER3	YSER4	YSER5	YSE Average	Category Ranking
10.	IIMC	0.8571	0.7142	0.7857	0.3913	0.2718	0.60402	10
11.	AIIMS	0.32	0.3076	0.4444	0.5	0.4444	0.40328	11
12.	IIMA	0.3055	0.3076	0.4324	0.4102	0.1779	0.32672	12
13.	IIMI	Nil	Nil	0.75	0.5	Nil	0.25	13
14.	IIMB	0.0909	0.0769	0.05	0.0769	0.0434	0.06762	14
15.	IIML	0.05	0.0555	0.0375	0.0259	0.0294	0.03966	15
16.	SCTIMST	Nil	Nil	Nil	Nil	Nil	Nil	16

Legends: YSER1 = Yahoo Site Explorer 1st round, YSER2 = Yahoo Site Explorer 2nd round, YSER3 = Yahoo Site Explorer 3rd round, YSER4 = Yahoo Site Explorer 4th round, YSER5 = Yahoo Site Explorer 5th round

4.5.4. Overall Category Ranking of Library Websites

4.5.4.1. Central Universities Library Websites

Average WIF of CU library websites through different search engines (i.e. Google, AlltheWeb, AltaVista and Yahoo Site Explorer) is collated within the Table 4.26. Also, an Overall Average WIF is calculated for each of the CU library websites. An Overall Average WIF is calculated on the basis of Average WIF calculated from the data retrieved through each search engine for a library website. The main objective for Overall Average WIF calculation was to find out the Overall Category Ranking for CU library websites.

$$\text{Overall Average WIF} = \frac{\text{Average WIF of (Google + AlltheWeb + AltaVista + Yahoo Site Explorer) for CU Library Websites}}{4}$$

Giving a glance through the Table 4.26, it was observed that Google has the lowest Average WIF for CU library websites among all search engines. AlltheWeb and AltaVista both have demonstrated more or less similar Average WIF whereas Yahoo Site Explorer has shown the highest Average WIF among all four search engines.

On the basis of Overall Average WIF, it was observed there are only two CU library websites (i.e. JNU and BHU) which have shown Overall Average WIF above 1.0 and seven CU library websites (i.e. 46.66%) have Overall Average WIF between 0.1 to 0.925. Since, Average WIF for AMU, MANI, MIZUNI, UOA and VBU library websites was zero; their Overall Average WIF is also zero. There is one CU library website (i.e. NEHU) which has Overall Average WIF below 0.1 (i.e. 0.063155).

On the basis of Overall Average WIF, an Overall Category Ranking for CU library websites is done. JNU, BHU, MANUU, IGNOU and UOH library websites occupies top five positions in Overall Category Rankings, respectively.

Table 4.26: Overall Category Ranking of CU Library Websites

SN	Central University	Google Average	AlltheWeb Average	AltaVista Average	YSE Average	Overall Average WIF	Overall Category Ranking
1.	JNU	0.13332	2.1222	2.09998	5.0444	2.349975	1
2.	BHU	0.20666	1.22866	1.35312	1.90666	1.173775	2
3.	MANUU	0.5	0.9	0.9	1.4	0.925	3
4.	IGNOU	Nil	0.1	0.1	1.4	0.4	4
5.	UOH	0.12596	0.25094	0.26386	0.21174	0.213125	5
6.	PONDI	Nil	0.2	0.2	0.2	0.15	6
7.	UOD	0.08874	0.11018	0.14508	0.17672	0.13018	7
8.	JMI	0.02148	0.0486	0.0486	0.28272	0.10035	8
9.	ASU	Nil	Nil	Nil	0.4	0.1	9

SN	Central University	Google Average	AlltheWeb Average	AltaVista Average	YSE Average	Overall Average WIF	Overall Category Ranking
10	NEHU	Nil	0.096	0.09602	0.0606	0.063155	10
11	AMU	Nil	Nil	Nil	Nil	Nil	11
12	MANI	Nil	Nil	Nil	Nil	Nil	11
31	MIZUNI	Nil	Nil	Nil	Nil	Nil	11
14	UOA	Nil	Nil	Nil	Nil	Nil	11
15	VBU	Nil	Nil	Nil	Nil	Nil	11

Legends: YSE = Yahoo Site Explorer

4.5.4.2. Institutes of National Importance & IIMs Library Websites

Average WIF of INI & IIMs library websites through different search engines (i.e. Google, AlltheWeb, AltaVista and Yahoo Site Explorer) is collated within the Table 4.27. Also, an Overall Average WIF is calculated for each of the INI & IIMs library websites. An Overall Average WIF is calculated on the basis of Average WIF calculated from the data retrieved through each search engine for a library website. The main objective for Overall Average WIF calculation was to find out the Overall Category Ranking for INI & IIMs library websites.

$$\text{Overall Average WIF} = \frac{\text{Average WIF of (Google + AlltheWeb + AltaVista + Yahoo Site Explorer) for INI Library Websites}}{4}$$

On the basis of this study, it is observed that Google has shown the lowest Average WIF values for INI library websites among all search engines. However, AlltheWeb and AltaVista both have shown almost similar Average WIF for INI library websites. Comparatively, Yahoo Site Explorer has shown the highest Average WIF among all search engines. Five (i.e. 31.25%) INI library websites have shown Average WIF through all search engines except Google. SCTIMST library website has not shown Average WIF values through any of the search engines.

Table 4.27: Overall Category Ranking of INI & IIMs Library Websites

SN	Institute of National Importance	Google Average	AlltheWeb Average	AltaVista Average	YSE Average	Overall Average WIF	Overall Category Ranking
1.	IITK	0.32776	2.10664	2.22664	4.27332	2.23359	1
2.	IIMK	0.30878	1.10968	1.15056	2.46758	1.25915	2
3.	IITR	0.2	1.09	1.09	0.93714	0.829285	3
4.	IITB	0.14726	0.85354	0.8552	1.21386	0.767465	4
5.	ISIK	0.05698	0.91278	0.9549	1.06034	0.74625	5
6.	IITD	0.345	0.70286	0.7253	0.99884	0.693	6
7.	IITG	0.10236	0.69918	0.71372	0.88514	0.6001	7
8.	IITM	0.16612	0.51284	0.51732	0.80606	0.500585	8
9.	IITKGP	0.06334	0.46944	0.4855	0.86744	0.47143	9
10	IIMC	0.13928	0.25548	0.26162	0.60402	0.3151	10
11	IIMA	Nil	0.31184	0.31658	0.32672	0.238785	11
12	AIIMS	Nil	0.1052	0.10614	0.40328	0.153655	12
31	IIMI	Nil	0.15	0.15	0.25	0.1375	13
14	IIMB	Nil	0.06018	0.06018	0.06762	0.046995	14
15	IIML	Nil	0.04988	0.04818	0.03966	0.03443	15
16	SCTIMST	Nil	Nil	Nil	Nil	Nil	16

Legends : YSE = Yahoo Site Explorer

On the basis of Overall Average WIF, it is found that all INI & IIMs library websites have shown Overall

Average WIF values except SCTIMST library website. There are two INI & IIMs library websites (i.e. IITK and IIMK) which have Overall Average WIF above 1.0 and eleven INI library websites (i.e. 68.75%) having Overall Average WIF in between 0.1 to 0.9. On the basis of Overall Average WIF, Overall Category Rankings have been done for INI & IIMs library websites. IITK, IIMK, IITR, IITB and ISIK library websites holds top five Overall Category Rankings, respectively. The IIM library websites have achieved Overall Category Rankings in between 10th to 15th, except IIMK library website which stands 2nd in the list from top. Among library websites of IIMs, IIM Kozhikode has achieved first rank over IIM Calcutta (2nd), IIM Ahmedabad (3rd), IIM Indore (4th), IIM Bangalore (5th) and IIM Lucknow (6th). AIIMS (All India Institute for Medical Sciences, New Delhi) library website has achieved 12th overall category rank whereas Sree Chitra Tirunal Institute for Medical Sciences and Technology, Thiruvananthapuram (SCTIMST) library website has achieved 16th overall category rank because of zero WIF. Indian Statistical Institute, Kolkata (ISIK) library website has achieved 5th overall category rank among sixteen INI library websites.

4.5.4.3. Comparison of Overall Average WIF of CU and INI Library Websites

The Table 4.28 demonstrates summary and conclusion of overall categorized rankings of library websites of CU and INI of India. It indicates that INI & IIMs library websites have quite higher WIF in comparison to CU library websites. INI & IIMs library websites are well indexed by search engines and have retrieved more *backlinks* compared to CU library websites. The average of Overall Average WIF of all CU library websites is 0.373704 and INI library websites is 0.564207. This demonstrates that INI library websites have higher Overall Average WIF over CU library websites.

Table 4.28: Summary of Overall Category Ranking of Library Websites

SN	Central University	Overall Average WIF	Overall Category Ranking	Institute of National Importance	Overall Average WIF	Overall Category Ranking
1.	JNU	2.349975	1	IITK	2.23359	1
2.	BHU	1.173775	2	IIMK	1.25915	2
3.	MANUU	0.925	3	IITR	0.829285	3
4.	IGNOU	0.4	4	IITB	0.767465	4
5.	UOH	0.213125	5	ISIK	0.74625	5
6.	PONDI	0.15	6	IITD	0.693	6
7.	UOD	0.13018	7	IITG	0.6001	7
8.	JMI	0.10035	8	IITM	0.500585	8
9.	ASU	0.1	9	IITKGP	0.47143	9
10.	NEHU	0.063155	10	IIMC	0.3151	10
11.	AMU	Nil	11	IIMA	0.238785	11
12.	MANI	Nil	11	AIIMS	0.153655	12
13.	MIZUNI	Nil	11	IIMI	0.1375	13
14.	UOA	Nil	11	IIMB	0.046995	14
15.	VBU	Nil	11	IIML	0.03443	15
16.	--	--	--	SCTIMST	Nil	16
Average WIF		0.373704			0.564207	

4.6. BREAKDOWN OF BACKLINKS POINTING TO LIBRARY WEBSITES

In order to study the pointing behaviour of *backlinks* to a library website, seven categories of library web pages have been identified which are given in Table 4.29.

Table 4.29: Categories of Library Web pages

SN	Library Web Pages Categories	Code
1	Index page / homepage	IP
2	Library databases / e-journals / journals web pages	JP
3	Institutional repository / digital library web pages	DL
4	E-resources (including e-books, e-reference sources, e-standards, etc.)	ER
5	Library OPAC	OP
6	Theses / e-theses	ET
7	Other web pages[2]	OL

Note : The websites which are without any backlink is indicated by symbol "N" and websites which are not indexed by search engines are indicates by symbol "W" wherever applicable.

Further, all web pages available within a library website is categorized based on these features.

The *backlinks* received by library websites of CU and INI & IIMs are assessed on the basis of these seven (7) categories. This analysis is important to study the pointing behaviour of *backlinks* on library web pages including the categories to which it is pointing. Pointing behaviour of *backlinks* indicate usefulness of library web pages for library users.

4.6.1. Central Universities (CU) Library Websites

Google Distribution of Backlinks:

The following table presents Google distribution of *backlinks* over CU library websites:

2 Category of "Other web pages" includes web pages of library collection, library services, library sections, library facilities, library rules, library history / introduction etc.

Table 4.30: Distribution of Backlinks over Web pages of CU Library Websites

Central Universities	Search Engine – Google					
	GR1	**GR2**	**GR3**	**GR4**	**GR5**	**TOTAL**
AMU	N	N	N	N	N	--
ASU	W	N	N	N	W	--
BBAU	Not included due to lack of library website					
BHU	N	N	2 IP, 1 OL	2 IP, 1 OL, 1 JP	2 IP	6 IP, 2 OL, 1 JP
CAUI	Not included due to lack of library website					
IGNOU	N	N	N	N	N	--
JMI	N	1 IP	1 IP	1 IP, 1 JP	N	3 IP, 1 JP
JNU	N	N	1 IP	1 IP	N	2 IP
MGAHV	Not included due to lack of library website					
MANI	N	N	N	N	N	--
MANUU	N	N	3 IP	2 IP	N	5 IP
MIZUNI	N	N	N	N	N	--
NAGUNI	Not included due to non extraction of library website					
NEHU	W	N	N	N	W	--
PONDI	W	W	W	W	N	--
TEZU	Not included due to lack of library website during two rounds					
UOA	W	W	W	N	N	--
UOD	1 IP	3 IP, 1 ER	5 IP, 1 ER, 1 OP	2 IP	1 IP, 1 OP	12 IP, 2 ER, 2 OP
UOH	1 IP	2 IP, 1 JP	1 IP	4 IP	1 IP	9 IP, 1 JP
VBU	N	N	N	N	N	--

Legends: IP = Index page / homepage, JP = Library databases / e-journals / journals web pages, DL = Institutional repository / digital library web pages, ER = E-resources (including e-books, e-reference sources, e-standards, etc.), OP = Library OPAC, ET = Theses / e-theses, OL = Other web pages, N = No *backlinks*, W = Website not indexed

AlltheWeb Distribution of Backlinks:

The following table presents AlltheWeb distribution of *backlinks* over CU library websites:

Table 4.31: Distribution of Backlinks over Web pages of CU Library Websites

Central Universities	Search Engine – AlltheWeb					
	AWR1	AWR2	AWR3	AWR4	AWR5	TOTAL
AMU	W	N	W	W	W	--
ASU	N	N	N	N	N	--
BBAU	Not included due to lack of library website					
BHU	5 IP, 1 OL, 2 JP	6 IP, 1 OL, 3 JP	7 IP, 2 OL, 4 JP	8 IP, 2 OL, 5 JP	9 IP, 4 OL, 3 JP	35 IP, 10 OL, 17 JP
CAUI	Not included due to lack of library website					
IGNOU	N	N	N	N	1 IP	1 IP
JMI	1 IP	1 IP	2 IP	2 IP, 1 JP	2 IP, 1 JP	8 IP, 2 JP
JNU	7 IP	7 IP	7 IP	9 IP	11 IP	41 IP
MGAHV	Not included due to lack of library website					
MANI	N	N	N	N	N	--
MANUU	N	1 IP	3 IP	4 IP	1 IP	9 IP
MIZUNI	N	N	N	N	N	--
NAGUNI	Not included due to non extraction of library website					
NEHU	W	1 IP, 1 OL	1 IP	1 IP	W	3 IP, 1 OL
PONDI	W	W	W	W	1 IP	1 IP
TEZU	Not included due to lack of library website during two rounds					
UOA	W	W	W	N	N	--
UOD	3 IP	4 IP	5 IP, 1 OP	3 IP	13 IP, 2 OL	28 IP, 1 OP, 2 OL
UOH	1 IP, 1 JP	2 IP, 1 OL, 1 JP, 1 DL	1 IP	5 IP	1 IP	10 IP, 1 OL, 1 JP, 1 DL
VBU	N	N	N	N	N	--

Legends: IP = Index page / homepage, JP = Library databases / e-journals / journals web pages, DL = Institutional repository / digital library web pages, ER = E-resources (including e-books, e-reference sources, e-standards, etc.), OP = Library OPAC, ET = Theses / e-theses, OL = Other web pages, N = No *backlinks*, W = Website not indexed

AltaVista Distribution of Backlinks:

The following table presents AltaVista distribution of *backlinks* over CU library websites:

Table 4.32: Distribution of Backlinks over Web pages of CU Library Websites

Central Universities	Search Engine – AltaVista					
	AVR1	AVR2	AVR3	AVR4	AVR5	TOTAL
AMU	W	N	W	W	W	--
ASU	N	N	N	N	N	--
BBAU	Not included due to lack of library website					
BHU	6 IP, 1 OL, 3 JP	7 IP, 1 OL, 4 JP	8 IP, 2 OL, 5 JP	8 IP, 2 OL, 5 JP	9 IP, 4 OL, 3 JP	38 IP, 10 OL, 20 JP
CAUI	Not included due to lack of library website					
IGNOU	N	N	N	N	1 IP	1 IP
JMI	1 IP	1 IP	2 IP	2 IP, 1 JP	2 IP, 1 JP	8 IP, 2 JP
JNU	6 IP	7 IP	7 IP	9 IP	11 IP	40 IP
MGAHV	Not included due to lack of library website					
MANI	N	N	N	N	N	--
MANUU	N	1 IP	3 IP	4 IP	1 IP	9 IP
MIZUNI	N	N	N	N	N	--
NAGUNI	Not included due to non extraction of library website					
NEHU	W	1 IP, 1 OL	1 IP	1 IP	W	3 IP, 1 OL
PONDI	W	W	W	W	1 IP	1 IP
TEZU	Not included due to lack of library website during two rounds					
UOA	W	W	W	N	N	--
UOD	5 IP	5 IP	6 IP, 1 OP	3 IP	18 IP, 2 ER, 4 OL	37 IP, 1 OP, 2 ER, 4 OL

Central Universities	Search Engine - AltaVista					
	AVR1	AVR2	AVR3	AVR4	AVR5	TOTAL
UOH	1 IP, 1 JP	2 IP, 1 OL, 1 JP, 1 DL	1 IP	5 IP	1 IP	10 IP, 2 JP, 1 OL, 1 DL
VBU	N	N	N	N	N	--

Legends: IP = Index page / homepage, JP = Library databases / e-journals / journals web pages, DL = Institutional repository / digital library web pages, ER = E-resources (including e-books, e-reference sources, e-standards, etc.), OP = Library OPAC, ET = Theses / e-theses, OL = Other web pages, N = No *backlinks*, W = Website not indexed

Yahoo Site Explorer Distribution of Backlinks:

The following table presents Yahoo Site Explorer distribution of *backlinks* over CU library websites:

Table 4.33: Distribution of Backlinks over Web pages of CU Library Websites

Central Universities	Search Engine – Yahoo Site Explorer					
	YSER1	YSER2	YSER3	YSER4	YSER5	TOTAL
AMU	W	N	N	N	W	--
ASU	N	N	1 IP	1 IP	N	2 IP
BBAU	Not included due to lack of library website					
BHU	5 IP, 4 OL, 3 JP	6 IP, 5 OL, 5 JP	8 IP, 7 OL, 7 JP	8 IP, 7 OL, 8 JP	10 IP, 8 OL, 3 JP	37 IP, 31 OL, 26 JP
CAUI	Not included due to lack of library website					
IGNOU	7 IP	2 IP	2 IP	2 IP	1 ER	13 IP, 1 ER
JMI	2 IP	2 IP	3 IP	4 IP, 1 JP	2 IP, 2 JP	13 IP, 3 JP
JNU	17 IP	18 IP	20 IP	20 IP	22 IP	97 IP
MGAHV	Not included due to lack of library website					
MANI	N	N	N	N	N	--
MANUU	1 IP	2 IP	4 IP	4 IP	2 IP, 1 OL	13 IP, 1 OL
MIZUNI	N	N	N	N	N	--
NAGUNI	Not included due to non extraction of library website					

Central Universities	Search Engine – Yahoo Site Explorer					
	YSER1	YSER2	YSER3	YSER4	YSER5	TOTAL
NEHU	W	1 IP	1 IP	1 IP	W	3 IP
PONDI	W	W	W	W	1 IP	1 IP
TEZU	Not included due to lack of library website during two rounds					
UOA	W	W	W	N	N	--
UOD	5 IP, 1 OL	7 IP, 1 OL, 1 ER	9 IP, 1 OL, 1 ER	4 IP	13 IP, 1 ER, 3 OL	38 IP, 6 OL, 3 ER
UOH	1 IP	3 IP, 1 OL, 1 JP, 1 DL	1 IP	4 IP	1 IP	10 IP, 1 OL, 1 JP, 1 DL
VBU	N	N	N	N	N	--

Legends: IP = Index page / homepage, JP = Library databases / e-journals / journals web pages, DL = Institutional repository / digital library web pages, ER = E-resources (including e-books, e-reference sources, e-standards, etc.), OP = Library OPAC, ET = Theses / e-theses, OL = Other web pages, N = No *backlinks*, W = Website not indexed

Discussion : The *backlinks* retrieved by Google, AlltheWeb, AltaVista and Yahoo Site Explorer for CU library websites are analyzed and it is observed that index page / homepage of library websites have attracted the highest *backlinks* than any other web pages of library websites. Few of the *backlinks* are attracted at journals, e-resources and web OPAC pages of library websites. *Backlinks* to "Other web pages" are also witnessed. This indicates that index page / homepage of library websites contains useful information for users. Journals, e-resources and OPAC pages are also important. This analysis indicates that if library websites have provided useful information on pages, then it attracts more *backlinks*.

4.6.2. Institutes of National Importance (INI) & IIMs Library Websites

Google Distribution of Backlinks:

The following table presents Google distribution of *backlinks* over INI library websites:

Table 4.34: Distribution of Backlinks over Web pages of INI Library Websites

Institutes of National Importance	Search Engine – Google					
	GR1	GR2	GR3	GR4	GR5	Total
AIIMS	N	N	N	N	N	--
DBHPS	Not included due to lack of institute's library website					
IIMA	N	N	N	N	N	--
IIMB	N	N	N	N	N	--
IIMC	1 IP	2 IP	2 IP	2 IP	1 IP	8 IP
IIMI	N	W	W	N	N	--
IIMK	3 DL	1 IP, 5 DL	1 IP, 7 DL	1 IP, 8 DL	6 DL	3 IP, 29 DL
IIML	N	N	N	N	N	--
IITB	4 IP, 2 DL	6 IP, 3 DL	4 IP	3 IP	6 IP	23 IP, 5 DL
IITD	8 IP, 4 DL	11 IP, 7 DL, 2 OL	11 IP, 1 OL, 8 DL	7 IP, 1 OL, 6 DL	2 IP, 5 DL	39 IP, 30 DL, 4 OL
IITG	1 IP	1 IP	1 IP	1 IP	1 IP	5 IP
IITK	1 OL	1 IP, 1 OL	1 IP, 1 OL	1 IP	2 OL	3 IP, 5 OL
IITKGP	2 IP, 1 DL	3 IP, 1 DL	2 IP, 1 DL	2 IP	1 IP	10 IP, 3 DL
IITM	5 IP	6 IP, 1 ER, 1 ET, 1 OP	8 IP, 1 ER, 2 ET	10 IP, 1 ER, 2 ET	11 IP, 1 OL	40 IP, 3 ER, 5 ET, 1 OP, 1OL

Institutes of National Importance	Search Engine – Google					
	GR1	GR2	GR3	GR4	GR5	Total
IITR	N	1 IP	W	N	N	1 IP
ISIK	1 IP	1 IP	2 IP	3 IP, 1 OP	1 IP	8 IP, 1 OP
NIPER	Not included due to lack of institute's library website					
PGIMER	Not included due to lack of institute's library website during first round					
SCTIMST	W	N	W	N	N	--

Legends: IP = Index page / homepage, JP = Library databases / e-journals / journals web pages, DL = Institutional repository / digital library web pages, ER = E-resources (including e-books, e-reference sources, e-standards, etc.), OP = Library OPAC, ET = Theses / e-theses, OL = Other web pages, N = No *backlinks*, W = Website not indexed

AlltheWeb Distribution of Backlinks:

The following table presents AlltheWeb distribution of *backlinks* over INI library websites:

Table 4.35: Distribution of Backlinks over Web pages of INI Library Websites

Institutes of National Importance	Search Engine – AlltheWeb					
	AWR1	AWR2	AWR3	AWR4	AWR5	TOTAL
AIIMS	2 IP	2 IP	3 IP	3 IP	3 IP	13 IP
DBHPS	Not included due to lack of institute's library website					
IIMA	14 IP	12 IP	14 IP	15 IP	18 IP	73 IP
IIMB	1 OL	1 OL	1 OL	1 OL	1 OL	5 OL
IIMC	6 IP	8 IP	8 IP	6 IP	9 IP, 1 JP, 2 OL	37 IP, 1 JP, 2 OL
IIMI	N	N	2 IP	1 IP	N	3 IP
IIMK	2 IP, 13 DL	3 IP, 17 DL	3 IP, 35 DL	3 IP, 33 DL	6 IP, 24 DL	17 IP, 122 DL
IIML	2 OL, 1 JP,	1 IP, 2 OL, 1 JP	1 IP, 2 JP, 2 OL	1 JP, 1 OL	2 OL, 1 JP	2 IP, 9 OL, 6 JP
IITB	31 IP, 1 ET, 2 DL	35 IP, 2ET, 4 DL	57 IP, 11DL, 3JP	57 IP, 10 DL	66 IP, 1 OL, 12 DL,	246 IP, 3 ET, 39 DL,

Institutes of National Importance	Search Engine – AlltheWeb					
	AWR1	AWR2	AWR3	AWR4	AWR5	TOTAL
					2 JP	5 JP, 1 OL
IITD	16 IP, 8 DL	20 IP, 1 OL, 10 DL	24 IP, 1 OL, 30 DL	19 IP, 1 OL, 27 DL	25 DL, 2 OL	79 IP, 100 DL, 5 OL
IITG	12 IP, 1 OP	13 IP, 1OP	18 IP,1OP	19 IP, 1OP	18 IP, 1 OP	80 IP, 5 OP
IITK	8 IP, 1 OL	9 IP, 1 OL	16 IP,2OL	14 IP,2OL	15 IP, 2 OL	62 IP, 8 OL
IITKGP	14 IP, 2 DL	17 IP, 2DL	23 IP, 2DL, 1ER	25 IP, 1DL, 1 ER	53 IP, 2 ER	132 IP, 7 DL, 4 ER
IITM	18 IP, 3ER, 2 OL, 1 JP	20 IP, 1 JP 3 ER,2OL, 2 ET, 2 OP	23 IP, 2 P, 4 OL,1OP 3ER, 2ET	26 IP,1OP 4OL,1JP 3 ER,1ET,	25 IP, 1JP, 8 OL, 5ER, 3 OP,1 JP	112 IP, 17 ER, 20 OL, 6 JP, 5 ET, 7 OP
IITR	1 IP	1 IP	3 IP	2 IP	2 IP	9 IP
ISIK	41 IP, 2 OP	44 IP, 1 OP	51 IP, 1 OP, 2 JP	55 IP, 1 OP	52 IP, 2OP, 1 JP	243 IP, 7 OP, 3 JP
NIPER	Not included due to lack of institute's library website					
PGIMER	Not included due to lack of institute's library website during one round					
SCTIMST	W	W	W	W	W	--

Legends: IP = Index page / homepage, JP = Library databases / e-journals / journals web pages, DL = Institutional repository / digital library web pages, ER = E-resources (including e-books, e-reference sources, e-standards, etc.), OP = Library OPAC, ET = Theses / e-theses, OL = Other web pages, N = No *backlinks*, W = Website not indexed

AltaVista Distribution of Backlinks:

The following table presents AltaVista distribution of *backlinks* over INI library websites:

Table 4.36: Distribution of Backlinks over Web pages of INI Library Websites

Institutes of National Importance	Search Engine – AltaVista					
	AVR1	AVR2	AVR3	AVR4	AVR5	Total
AIIMS	2 IP	2 IP	3 IP	3 IP	3 IP	13 IP
DBHPS	Not included due to lack of institute's library website					
IIMA	13 IP	13 IP	15 IP	15 IP	18 IP	74 IP
IIMB	1 OL	1 OL	1 OL	1 OL	1 OL	5 OL
IIMC	7 IP	8 IP	8 IP	6 IP	9 IP, 1 JP, 2 OL	38 IP, 1 JP, 2 OL
IIMI	N	N	2 IP	1 IP	N	3 IP
IIMK	2 IP, 13DL	3 IP, 17DL	3 IP, 37 DL	3 IP, 33 DL	6 IP, 27DL	17 IP, 127 DL
IIML	2 OL,1JP	1 IP, 2OL,1 JP	1 IP, 2 JP, 2 OL	1 JP, 1 OL	2 OL, 1 JP	2 IP, 9 OL, 6 JP
IITB	31 IP, 2ET,2DL	36 IP, 3ET,4DL	57 IP, 3JP,11DL	57 IP, 10 DL	66 IP,4JP, 1OL,12DL	247 IP, 5 ET, 39 DL, 7 JP, 1 OL
IITD	16 IP, 10 DL	21 IP, 1OL,10DL	24 IP, 1OL,32DL	19 IP, 1OL,29DL	2 OL, 25 DL	80 IP, 106 DL, 5 OL
IITG	13IP,1OP	14IP,1OP	18 IP,1 OP	19 IP, 1OP	17 IP, 1OP	81 IP, 5 OP
IITK	9 IP,1OL	10 IP,1OL	16 IP,2OL	15 IP,2OL	16 IP,2OL	66 IP, 8 OL
IITKGP	15IP,2DL	19IP,3 DL	23IP, 3DL, 1 ER	26 IP, 1 DL, 1ER	54 IP, 2ER	137 IP, 9 DL, 4 ER
IITM	18IP,3ER, 4OL, 1JP	21IP, 1 JP, 3 ER,3OL, 2 ET, 2OP	23IP, 2 JP, 3 ER,4OL, 2 ET, 2OP	26IP, 1 JP, 3 ER,1ET, 2 OP, 4OL	24IP, 1 JP, 6 OL,5ER, 3 OP	112 IP, 6 JP, 17 ER, 5 ET, 9 OP, 21 OL,
IITR	1 IP	1 IP	3 IP	2 IP	2 IP	9 IP

ISIK	42 IP, 2OP,2 JP	44 IP, 2JP, 1 OP	51 IP, 2 JP, 1 OP	56 IP, 1 OP	53 IP, 3 OP, 3 JP	246 IP, 8 OP, 9 JP
NIPER	Not included due to lack of institute's library website					
PGIMER	Not included due to lack of institute's library website during one round					
SCTIMST	W	W	W	W	W	--

Legends: IP = Index page / homepage, JP = Library databases / e-journals / journals web pages, DL = Institutional repository / digital library web pages, ER = E-resources (including e-books, e-reference sources, e-standards, etc.), OP = Library OPAC, ET = Theses / e-theses, OL = Other web pages, N = No *backlinks*, W = Website not indexed

Yahoo Site Explorer Distribution of Backlinks:

The following table presents Yahoo Site Explorer distribution of *backlinks* over INI library websites:

Table 4.37: Distribution of Backlinks over Web pages of INI Library Websites

Institutes of National Importance	Search Engine – Yahoo Site Explorer					
	YSER1	**YSER2**	**YSER3**	**YSER4**	**YSER5**	**Total**
AIIMS	8 IP	8 IP	12 IP	12 IP	12 IP	52 IP
DBHPS	Not included due to lack of institute's library website					
IIMA	11 IP	12 IP	16 IP	16 IP	21 IP	76 IP
IIMB	1 OL	1 OL	1 OL	1 OL	1 OL	5 OL
IIMC	12 IP	10 IP	11 IP	9 IP	17 IP, 1 JP, 10 OL	59 IP, 1 JP, 10 OL
IIMI	N	N	3 IP	2 IP	N	5 IP
IIMK	8 IP, 32 DL	10 IP, 46 DL	11 IP, 55 DL	12 IP, 59 DL	13 IP, 66 DL	54 IP, 258 DL
IIML	2 OL, 1 JP	2 OL, 1 JP	2 JP, 1 OL	2 JP	2 OL, 1 JP	7 OL, 7 JP
IITB	64 IP, 1	68 IP, 3	69 IP,	69 IP,	83 IP, 4	353

Institutes of National Importance	Search Engine – Yahoo Site Explorer					
	YSER1	YSER2	YSER3	YSER4	YSER5	Total
	ET, 7 DL	ET, 9 DL	15 DL	13 DL	JP, 11 DL, 1 OL	IP, 4 JP, 4 ET, 55 DL, 1 OL
IITD	13 IP, 41 DL, 1 OL	16 IP, 4 OL, 45 DL	16 IP, 1 OL, 44 DL	15 IP, 40 DL	3 OL, 54 DL	60 IP, 224 DL, 9 OL
IITG	18 IP, 1 OP	19 IP, 1 OP	24 IP, 2 OP	25 IP, 2 OP	24 IP, 1 OP	110 IP, 7 OP
IITK	22 IP, 2 OL	24 IP, 2 OL	27 IP, 3 OL	23 IP, 3 OL	32 IP, 5 OL	128 IP, 15 OL
IITKGP	36 IP, 1 JP, 2 DL	37 IP, 1 JP, 4 DL	42 IP, 5 DL	38 IP, 2 DL	40 IP, 1 ER	193 IP, 2 JP, 13 DL, 1 ER
IITM	21 IP, 5 JP, 9 ER, 4 OP, 3 ET, 10 OL	32 IP, 1 JP, 5 ER, 4 ET, 9 OL, 4 OP	27 IP, 3 JP, 6 ER, 4 ET, 9 OL, 2 OP	30 IP, 2 JP, 6 ER, 2 ET, 7 OL, 2 OP	37 IP, 4 JP, 17 OL, 12 ER, 3 ET, 5 OP	147 IP, 15 JP, 38 ER, 17 OP, 16 ET, 52 OL
IITR	1 IP	1 IP	2 IP	2 IP	4 IP	10 IP
ISIK	55 IP, 2 OP, 1 JP	57 IP, 1 JP, 2 OP	63 IP, 2 JP, 1 OP	63 IP, 1 OP	66 IP, 3 JP, 3 OP	304 IP, 7 JP, 9 OP
NIPER	Not included due to lack of institute's library website					
PGIMER	Not included due to lack of institute's library website during one round					

Institutes of National Importance	Search Engine – Yahoo Site Explorer					
	YSER1	YSER2	YSER3	YSER4	YSER5	Total
SCTIMST	W	W	W	W	W	--

Legends: IP = Index page / homepage, JP = Library databases / e-journals / journals web pages, DL = Institutional repository / digital library web pages, ER = E-resources (including e-books, e-reference sources, e-standards, etc.), OP = Library OPAC, ET = Theses / e-theses, OL = Other web pages, N = No *backlinks*, W = Website not indexed

Discussion : The *backlinks* retrieved by Google, AlltheWeb, AltaVista and Yahoo Site Explorer for INI library websites are analyzed and it is observed that index page / homepage of library websites attract the highest *backlinks* than other pages of library websites. There are quite good number of *backlinks* available for digital libraries, journals, e-resources, theses and web OPAC pages. The "Other web pages" have also received few *backlinks*. This indicates that index page / homepage of library websites contain valuable information for library users in case of INI library websites. Digital library have also received quite good number of *backlinks* which shows that these pages are also important and contain information which mostly a user will look for.

4.6.3. Summary of Backlinks Breakdown of Library Websites

The *backlinks* received by CU and INI & IIMs library websites are summarized individually. The total *backlinks* received through all four search engines by each of the library websites are separated as per seven categories mentioned in Table 4.29.

4.6.3.1. Central Universities (CU) Library Websites

The Table 4.38 represents summary of distribution of overall *backlinks* according to seven categories of library web pages for CU library websites. The summary table clearly indicates that majority of *backlinks* (76.93%) pointed to index page / homepage of library websites. The index page / homepage is a web page which is connected with each web pages available in the website and functions as starting point for the whole website. The web pages which have information regarding electronic journals, online databases etc. have also received *backlinks* (10.97%) which clearly indicates the importance of these pages. About 2.11% of *backlinks* points towards digital library, e-resources, library OPAC, theses web pages of library websites. About 9.99% of *backlinks* connects to "Other web pages" which includes library collection, library facilities and other services of the library etc.

Table 4.38: Summary of Distribution of Backlinks over Web pages of CU Library Websites

Central Universities	Library Web pages Categories							
	IP	JP	DL	ER	OP	ET	OL	Total
AMU	--	--	--	--	--	--	--	--
ASU	2	--	--	--	--	--	--	2
BBAU	Not included due to lack of library website							--
BHU	116	64	--	--	--	--	53	233
CAUI	Not included due to lack of library website							--
IGNOU	15	--	--	1	--	--	--	16
JMI	32	8	--	--	--	--	--	40
JNU	180	--	--	--	--	--	--	180
MGAHV	Not included due to lack of library website							--
MANI	--	--	--	--	--	--	--	--
MANUU	36	--	--	--	--	--	1	37
MIZUNI	--	--	--	--	--	--	--	--
NAGUNI	Not included due to non extraction of library website							--
NEHU	9	--	--	--	--	--	2	11
PONDI	3	--	--	--	--	--	--	3
TEZU	Not included due to lack of library website during two rounds							--
UOA	--	--	--	--	--	--	--	--
UOD	115	--	--	7	4	--	12	138
UOH	39	6	3	--	--	--	3	51

Central Universities	Library Web pages Categories							
	IP	JP	DL	ER	OP	ET	OL	Total
VBU	--	--	--	--	--	--	--	--
Total	547	78	3	8	4	0	71	711
Percentage	76.93	10.97	0.42	1.13	0.56	0	9.99	100

Legends: IP = Index page / homepage, JP = Library databases / e-journals / journals web pages, DL = Institutional repository / digital library web pages, ER = E-resources (including e-books, e-reference sources, e-standards, etc.), OP = Library OPAC, ET = Theses / e-theses, OL = Other web pages

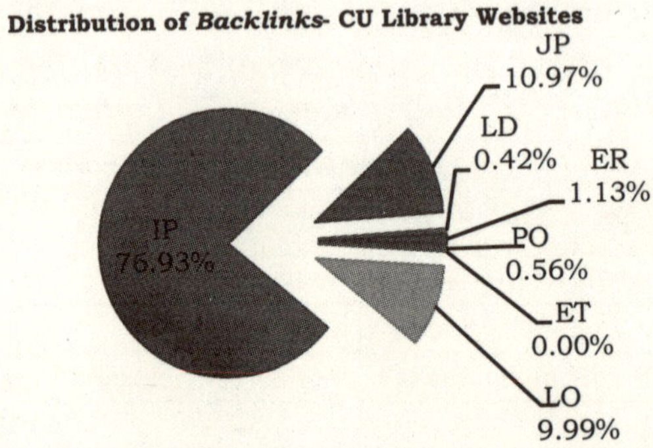

Fig. 4.7: Distribution of *Backlinks* over Web pages of CU Library Websites

4.6.3.2. Institutes of National Importance (INI) & IIMs Library Websites

The Table 4.39 represents summary of distribution of overall *backlinks* as per seven categories for INI library websites. The summary table indicates that majority of *backlinks* (70.21%) again points to index page / homepage of library websites. The web pages which have information regarding electronic journals and online databases etc. have received 1.54% *backlinks*. Digital library pages (20.86%), e-resources pages (1.5%), web OPAC (1.36%), theses pages (0.77%) etc. have also received *backlinks*. However, unlike Central Universities, "Other web pages" of library websites have received only 3.76% *backlinks*.

Table 4.39: Summary of Distribution of Backlinks over Web pages of INI Library Websites

Institutes of National Importance	Library Web pages Categories							
	IP	JP	DL	ER	OP	ET	OL	Total
AIIMS	78	--	--	--	--	--	--	78
DBHPS	Not included due to lack of institute's library website							--
IIMA	223	--	--	--	--	--	--	223
IIMB	--	--	--	--	--	--	15	15
IIMC	142	3	--	--	--	--	14	159
IIMI	11	--	--	--	--	--	--	11
IIMK	91	--	536	--	--	--	--	627
IIML	4	19	--	--	--	--	25	48
IITB	869	16	138	--	--	12	3	1038
IITD	258	--	460	--	--	--	23	741
IITG	276	--	--	--	17	--	--	293
IITK	259	--	--	--	--	--	36	295
IITKGP	472	2	32	9	--	--	--	515
IITM	411	27	--	75	34	31	94	672
IITR	29	--	--	--	--	--	--	29
ISIK	801	19	--	--	25	--	--	845
NIPER	Not included due to lack of institute's library website							--
PGIMER	Not included due to lack of institute's library website during one round							--
SCTIMST	--	--	--	--	--	--	--	--
Total	3924	86	1166	84	76	43	210	5589

Institutes of National Importance	Library Web pages Categories							
	IP	JP	DL	ER	OP	ET	OL	Total
Percentage	70.21	1.54	20.86	1.50	1.36	0.77	3.76	100

Legends: IP = Index page / homepage, JP = Library databases / e-journals / journals web pages, DL = Institutional repository / digital library web pages, ER = E-resources (including e-books, e-reference sources, e-standards, etc.), OP = Library OPAC, ET = Theses / e-theses, OL = Other web pages

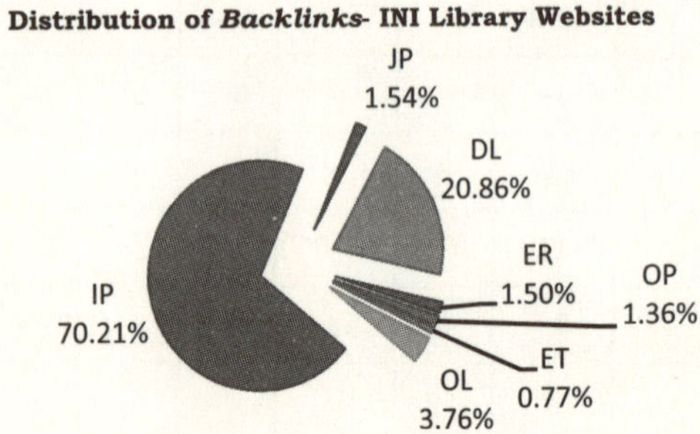

Fig. 4.8: Distribution of *Backlinks* over Web pages of INI Library Websites

4.7. SIZE OF LIBRARY WEBSITES

The size of a library website is one aspect which is assumed to play a key role in calculating WIF. The size of websites varies with time due to addition and deletion of web pages on WWW. The present study is outcome of long term observation of CU; and INI & IIMs library websites. The study is conducted in five rounds giving a gap of five months between each round. In this study, it was observed that 21 websites have changes in their number of web pages. The analysis of 21 library websites have been done and there graph is plotted against the number of pages and corresponding WIF. In the study, numbers of TNPs are taken as size of the website. Table 4.40 represents those CU; and INI & IIMs library websites which have observed change in number of pages over different rounds of data collection.

Table 4.40: Data Representing Change in Website Size for CU and INI Library Websites

SN	University / Institute	WSZ R1	Avg. WIF R1	WSZ R2	Avg. WIF R2	WSZ R3	Avg. WIF R3	WSZ R4	Avg. WIF R4	WSZ R5	Avg. WIF R5
1.	BHU	10	0.8333	10	0.95	10	1.325	10	1.425	11	1.335575
2.	IGNOU	22	0.875	22	0.25	19	0.25	20	0.25	37	0.375
3.	JMI	40	0.11315	38	0.045975	41	0.058925	42	0.08705	52	0.19665
4.	JNU	10	0.833275	4	2	3	2.916625	3	3.249975	4	2.75
5.	NEHU	1	0	8	0.17855	18	0.062475	17	0.074775	39	0
6.	UOD	69	0.139875	64	0.13395	62	0.15775	130	0.1528	230	0.066525
7.	UOH	23	0.091075	23	0.2459	16	0.1854	170	0.40475	173	0.1385
8.	AIIMS	27	0.12165	27	0.1169	28	0.16665	27	0.19315	27	0.169925
9.	IIMA	64	0.26385	62	0.237125	48	0.293975	55	0.27695	160	0.122025
10.	IIMB	24	0.064375	24	0.048625	25	0.0375	25	0.048625	25	0.03585
11.	IIMC	48	0.339225	44	0.325275	47	0.498775	93	0.260475	105	0.15175
12.	IIMK	39	0.91485	46	0.9837	42	1.3781	47	1.381925	44	1.637175
13.	IIML	92	0.03905	86	0.05165	96	0.039825	84	0.019425	102	0.0222
14.	IITB	110	0.52805	139	0.5611	102	1.582525	86	0.862675	240	0.302975
15.	IITD	102	0.548275	101	0.685025	140	1.235025	162	0.7937	800	0.202975
16.	IITG	40	0.662475	40	0.680525	55	0.48355	54	0.546575	55	0.627375
17.	IITK	6	1.85415	6	2.0833	6	2.875	6	2.49995	12	1.85555
18.	IITKGP	315	0.099275	353	0.1147	172	0.88115	206	0.73825	132	0.523775
19.	IITM	156	0.47695	140	0.540875	137	0.546525	139	0.535675	165	0.4029
20.	IITR	1	0.75	2	1	2	2	11	0.196425	10	0.2
21.	ISIK	82	0.53135	48	0.894375	75	0.730275	55	1.003125	91	0.572125

Legends: WSZ = Website Size, Avg. WIF = Average WIF of all search engines, R1 = Round 1, R2 = Round 2, R3 = Round 3, R4 = Round 4, R5 = Round 5

A detailed analysis of website size and their corresponding WIFs for some of the CU; and INI & IIMs library websites, as mentioned in Table 4.40, is given below:

Library Website, UOD

As per Fig. 4.9, size of website is different in all of the rounds. With almost constant website size WIF initially decreases and then increases and further, with increase in website size, decreases. Once again no relationship is traced between size and WIF.

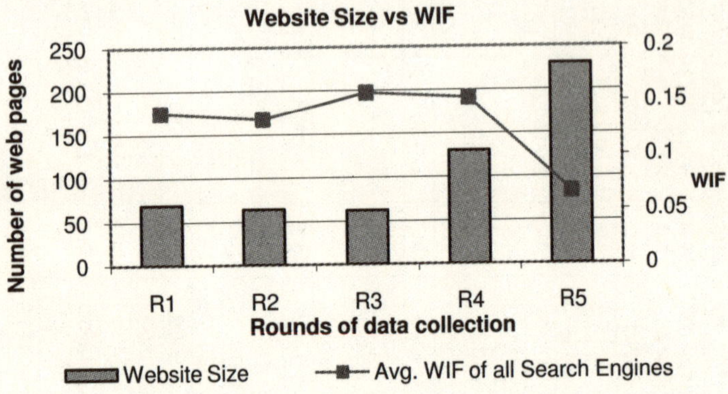

Fig. 4.9: Website Size vs WIF of Library Website, UOD

Library Website, UOH

As per Fig. 4.10, with the constant website size for R1 and R2, WIF increases but decreases with decrease in website size for R3. Again WIF increases with increased website size for R4 but decreases for R5 when the size is increasing.

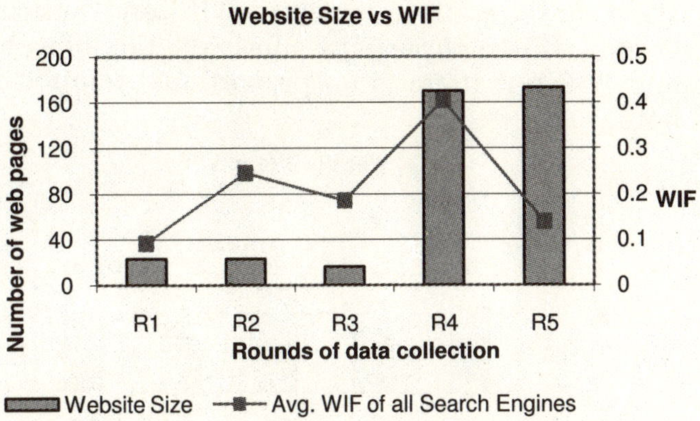

Fig. 4.10: Website Size vs WIF of Library Website, UOH

Library Website, IIMA

In Fig. 4.11, with decrease in website size, WIF decreases for R2 but increases for R3 with further decrease in website size. For R4 and R5, WIF decreases with the increase of website size. The plot does not follow any relation between size of the website and WIF.

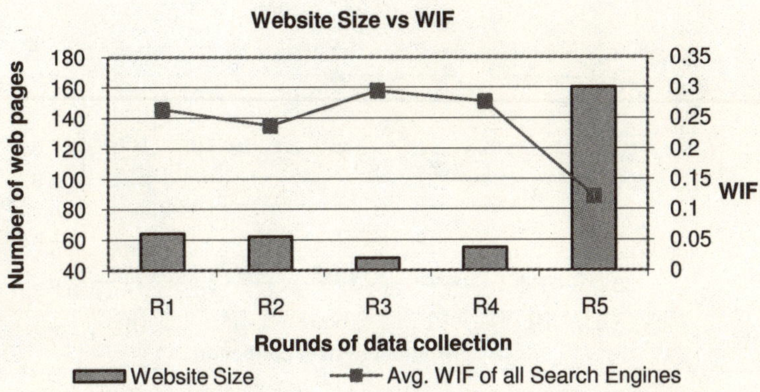

Fig. 4.11: Website Size vs WIF of Library Website, IIMA

Library Website, IIML

In the Fig. 4.12, from R3 to R4, WIF decreases with decrease in website size and further with increase in website size, it increases for R5. Initial rounds do not show any relation between WIF and website size. Overall, this plot partially shows relation of website size and WIF but there is no proportional relation between both.

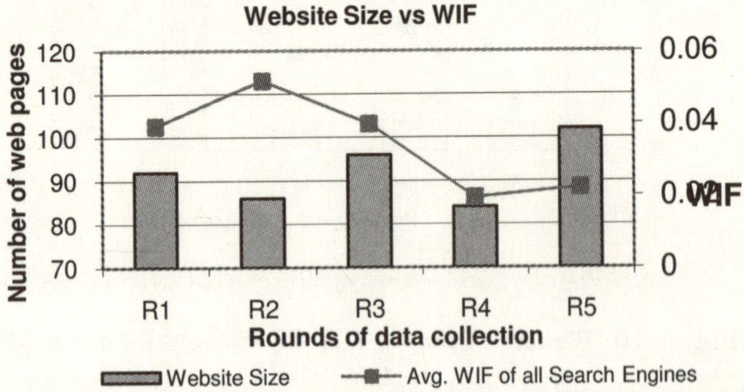

Fig. 4.12: Website Size vs WIF of Library Website, IIML

Library Website, IITD

In the Fig. 4.13, with the increased website size till R3, WIF increases. Further, WIF decreases for R4 and R5 with increase in the website size.

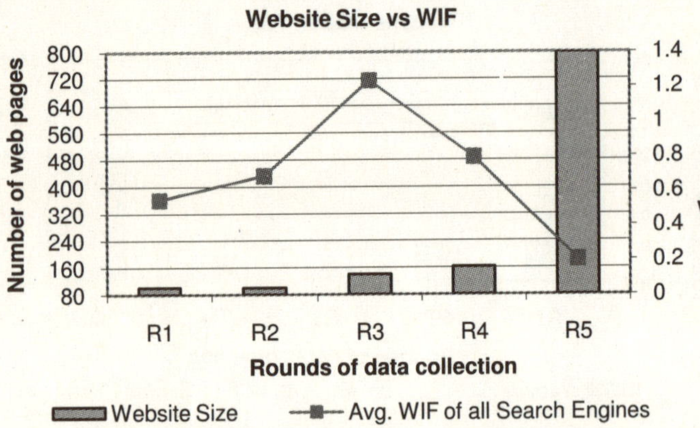

Fig. 4.13: Website Size vs WIF of Library Website, IITD

Library Website, IITKGP

In Fig. 4.14, with increased website size, WIF is slightly increasing for R2 and with decrease in website size for R3, WIF shows steep increase. WIF again decreases for R4 and R5, in spite of increase of website size in R4. Overall there is no relation between size and WIF.

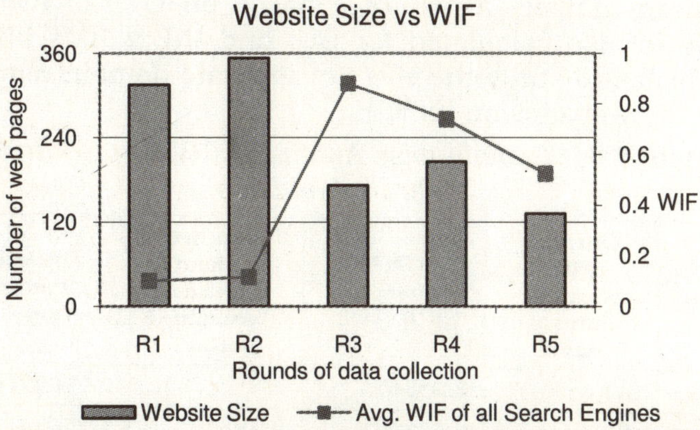

Fig. 4.14: Website Size vs WIF of Library Website, IITKGP

Discussion : On the observation of Table 4.40 and 6 samples of graphs of different library websites shows that there is no relation between size of the library websites / number of pages of library website and their corresponding WIF. It is not necessary that if there is increase in number of pages in website, the corresponding *backlinks* to website must also increase. The *backlinks* solely depends on the indexing policy of search engine. *Backlinks* are completely a subjective phenomenon and depends on the quality of information available in the web page. Apart from this, the periodicity of indexing by the search engine plays a decisive role in recording or indexing the page.

4.8. DOMAIN WISE ANALYSIS OF LIBRARY WEBSITES

The present study also analyses availability of separate domain names for library websites and effect of separate domain names on WIF. There are only seven libraries which have separate domain name for their websites whereas twenty four libraries do not have separate domain name for their websites. Table 4.41 represents the Overall Average WIF of libraries with separate domain names and libraries without separate domain names. An average based on Overall Average WIF is also calculated for CU; and INI & IIMs library websites to study the effect of separate domain name of library websites on its WIF.

Table 4.41: Domain wise Analysis of WIF of CU and INI Library Websites

SN	Libraries with separate domain name	Overall Average WIF	Libraries without separate domain name	Overall Average WIF
	IITK	**2.23359**	JNU	**2.349975**
	IITB	**0.767465**	IIMK	**1.25915**
	IITM	**0.500585**	BHU	**1.173775**
	IITKGP	**0.47143**	MANUU	**0.925**
	UOH	**0.213125**	IITR	**0.829285**
	UOD	**0.13018**	ISIK	**0.74625**
	IIML	**0.03443**	IITD	**0.693**
			IITG	**0.6001**
			IGNOU	**0.4**
			IIMC	**0.3151**
			IIMA	**0.238785**
			AIIMS	**0.153655**
			PONDI	**0.15**
			IIMI	**0.1375**
			JMI	**0.10035**
			ASU	**0.1**
			NEHU	**0.063155**
			IIMB	**0.046995**
			SCTIMST	**Nil**
			AMU	**Nil**
			MANI	**Nil**

SN	Libraries with separate domain name	Overall Average WIF	Libraries without separate domain name	Overall Average WIF
			MIZUNI	**Nil**
			UOA	**Nil**
			VBU	**Nil**
Average WIF		**0.621543**		**0.428419**

After analyzing Table 4.41, it is observed that library websites which have separate domain name have higher Average WIF than the library websites which do not have separate domain name. Thus, it can be inference that libraries which have separate domain name may attract more *backlinks*, causing higher WIF.

4.9. SOLUTIONS FOR INCREASING THE WEB IMPACT FACTOR OF LIBRARY WEBSITES

Since the web has dynamic nature, everything (hypertext documents and websites, in our context) available in the web is temporary. Appearance and disappearance of hypertext documents is the main activity of the dynamic web. The half life of web documents are less than two years and that of websites are more than two years as measured by Koehler (1999, 2002). The web impact factor (WIF) is one aspect which is measured by link analysis techniques. Link analysis studies link creation, link destruction, in other words link behaviour. For higher WIF, website has to have higher number of *backlinks*. It is a known fact that WIF reflects international visibility of websites. Generally, link creation is not a simple task. The websites link each other on the basis of subject or context relativity. In an academic environment, link creation is less prevalent than business environment (business organizations build links for their business promotion). Link building is prevalent marketing strategy of business organizations over the web.

Link building is phenomenon of creating *backlinks* from other websites to own website. This is also known as link popularity. Link building can be reciprocal or one way link. Reciprocal linking is the process where two websites establish links between each other. One way linking is the process where one website links to other website but other website doesn't link to previous one. Link building is also important to achieve top search ranking in search engines based on PageRank[3] calculation (Admin Zone Forum).

4.9.1. Advantages of Link Building

Link building helps in getting quality traffic from other relevant sites which increases importance of website. High quality *backlinks* proves that a site has valuable resource. It helps in creating awareness, visibility and credibility as well as wider search engine exposure and hence higher web impact factor.

4.9.2. How to Increase Web Impact Factor

As earlier alluded (cf. Section 4.9), higher WIF increases international visibility of a website. WIF depends on *backlinks* (*incoming links* or *inlinks*). In an academic environment, webmasters link relative or contextual websites. In present study, it was found that *backlinks* have more tendencies to link homepages (index pages) of library websites. Some *backlinks* tend to link internal web pages or other web pages of library websites. Majority of such links are towards digital library web pages, institutional repository web pages, and e-journals and e-databases web pages. This reveals

---

3 PageRank is the measure of importance, Google assigns to a web page in which the algorithm counts the number of sites that link to a page and then assigns the page an importance score on a scale of 1-10. The higher the number and importance of sites that link to a page, the higher the PageRank of that very web site. (http://en.wikipedia.org/wiki/PageRank)

that *backlinks* are targeting only those web pages which have something meaningful or useful for users. In contrary, business organizations have *backlinks* to any web page of the website. This is due to distinct nature of profession. Link building, nowadays, is not a natural phenomenon. Many of business organizations / firms are involved in creation of link building. Anyone can get more *backlinks* by paying these business firms.

There are many software tools and programming techniques available which helps in link building. Some business organizations are also involved in reciprocal link building without any economic spending. Westergren (2006) has given suggestions to build more *backlinks*. Kent (2006) has explored ways to get more *backlinks* by applying search engine optimization techniques. Here are listings of best practices by which academic library websites can increase their web impact factor.

4.9.3. Best Practices for Getting More Backlinks

Register with search directories

The web directories are collections of web pages with similar subject and content. These directories help in many ways as they are extremely popular among Internet users as they are considered as a source of valuable information. Listings in directories improve the chances of page ranking as well. If a library website is listed in a directory, the search engines are more likely to find it and add it in their listings for free. There are few directories which provide featured links, regular links and free reciprocal links, examples are as follows:

- http://www.a1weblinks.net
- http://www.addurl-free.com/
- http://www.bzzu.com/
- http://www.cbravo.com/
- http://www.ccislinks.com
- http://www.cell-search.com/

- http://www.centraldirectory.net/

Popularize through friends, family and employees

Many people now have their own websites and blogs. Ask people to mention the library website in their website. Just prepare a HTML code and send it to them for this purpose. It can also be included in the signature of e-mails. Whenever they send messages via e-mail to discussion groups, search engines may pick up the link. Libraries can make it compulsory for employees to insert library website in their e-mail signatures, blog posts, visiting cards and personal websites.

Contact association sites

There are number of associations in every field. Libraries may contact with such associations to build reciprocal links. By this both will get incoming links. In library and information science perspective, ILA, IASLIC, OCLC, IFLA, FID, Library of Congress, CILIP are the reputed associations which can be contacted.

Contact publishers and vendors websites

Libraries are spending lots of money on collection development. Publishers of books and journals as well as suppliers / vendors can be contacted easily by one way linking to library website in their customers list, if they have their own blog or website.

Submit to announcement sites and newsletters

These are less popular but influential service because it is read by many people. URLwire (http://www.urlwire.com/) is a site announcement website which posts website advertisements in their news announcements. Libraries can submit a request to publish their website in advertisements of new announced sites and online newsletters.

Promote something on your site

This is a free technique to build links for library

websites. Libraries can promote some programs like conferences / workshops / book fair / exhibitions, book reviews and special services etc. on their websites. This promotes more *backlinks.*

Ask other sites for links (city guides)

There are a lot of visitors coming to visit historical places, monuments, art galleries, museums etc. There are number of other websites which provide information to visitors, the libraries may approach the authorities of such websites to provide link to the library websites with the aim of promoting the use of libraries website. District web portal may also be contacted for this very purpose. The district web portal of Varanasi (http://varanasi.nic.in/) has listing of educational institutes in which Banaras Hindu University and other educational institutes are mentioned with brief.

Make reciprocal link requests with other libraries

Libraries share documents and expertise via inter library loan (ILL) or resource sharing. This indicates strong collaboration among them. For the purpose of link building, libraries can again share links to each other i.e. reciprocal links. Hence, they would get more relevant *backlinks* than any other.

Use of link building software(s)

Link building software creates links to websites. There are various link building software available which can be used to build *backlinks* automatically. Some link building tools are also available for this purpose. Link Machine[4], ARELIS 4.3.1[5], Auto Link Exchange Software

---

4 Link Machine (Software). Available at http://linkmachine.net/

5 ARELIS 4.3.1 (Software). Available at http://www.freedownloadscenter.com/Web_Authoring/Web_Site_Promotion_Tools/ARELIS.html

5.1[6] are few examples of these tools. These are very powerful tools to build links.

Mention your site in discussion groups

There are a lot of discussion groups running where participants are posting their views on certain topic / subject. Libraries can become member and participate in discussion groups. During participation libraries may post website address with message. Search engines will fetch the link from discussion group. This creates more links to the library websites.

Respond to blogs[7]

Since the inception of blogging, it is used more by general public, academic institutions, business organizations, professional associations, libraries etc. Some of the blogs are running by technical experts through which one can find solutions to his problems. Some blogs are running to share ideas about certain topic / subject. By responding to these blogs, libraries can build *backlinks*. Blog posts are indexed by search engines, which may increase *backlinks*. Examples of blogs are:

- http://www.jimwestergren.com/link-building-guide/
- http://thelinkspiel.blogspot.com/

---

6 Auto Link Exchange Software 5.1 (Software). Available at http://www.rocketdownload.com/scripts/program/web-site-developers-link-automate-software-11199.html

7 A blog is a website where entries are made in journal style and displayed in a reverse chronological order. Blogs often provide commentary or news on a particular subject, such as food, politics, or local news; some function as more personal online diaries. A typical blog combines text, images, and links to other blogs, Web pages, and other media related to its topic. On a blog readers can leave comments in an interactive format. (http://www.sussex learningnetwork.org.uk/glossary/B)

- http://www.dreamsubmitting.tk/
- http://dlisnews.blogspot.com/
- Libraries can initiate their own blogs.

Article submission

Writing articles for online journals and mentioning library website address in resource section of an article, makes valuable and permanent *backlinks*. Librarians and other library staff can mention their library website address in authority area of an online article or reference or acknowledgement area. This may successfully build *backlinks*.

Use a service or buy links

There are a lot of business firms available which may build *backlinks* to library on payment basis. Libraries can buy services of these very firms. The firms will run link acquisition campaign for library websites. One Way Text Links sells 100 quality links for $24.95 per month. There are some businesses firms which offer this type of services are:

- http://www.onewaytextlinks.com/index.aspx
- http://www.linkadage.com/
- http://www.textlinkbrokers.com/
- http://www.livecustomer.com/

However, this is not ethical and advisable to use such services.

Link baiting

Link baiting (or linkbaiting) is the latest buzz word in the search engine optimization (SEO) world and has come to be the preferred way to natural link building. It creates something that naturally attract *backlinks* for a website by getting people to talk about it, discussing it on forums, blogging about it and linking to it from their sites. It also attracts a lot of visitors. Some examples of link baiting are:

- Interview (e-mail / phone) prominent people and publish it.
- Write an interesting article
- Test something new that has not been done before
- Be the first in doing something on the Internet
- Write something controversial
- Disagree with an authority
- Write some funny humor
- Make an interesting picture
- Make a theme, plug-in or piece of software
- Make a tool that others can put on their sites but that links to you
- Make a joke about a known person
- Write an outrageous theory and back it up with logics
- Write useful comments on something that is happening
- Coin a new acronym in your niche and get people to talk about it
- Become an expert in a given subject and write valuable information

However, many of these are non advicable but are being practiced by webmasters.

Libraries and information centers can increase their web impact factor by applying the above mentioned best practices and techniques. There are many business organizations which are applying these techniques to build more *backlinks* for their business promotion. In academic environment, applications of these best practices (however some used practices cannot be said well) are rarely found. Any academic institute can increase its web impact factor by using these methods, however it is more significant if *backlinks* come from academic environment or similar domain. Libraries can look for building *backlinks* from their relative domains like other libraries, referral centers, library and information science departments, library associations, publishers, vendors, library automation software vendors, academic and research institutes and so on.

REFERENCES

Kent, P. (2006). *Search engine optimization for dummies* (2nd ed.). Hoboken, NJ: Wiley.

Koehler, W. (1999). Digital libraries and World Wide Web sites and page persistence. *Information Research, 4*(4). Available at: http://informationr.net/ ir/4-4/paper60.html

Koehler, W. (2002). Web page change and persistence: a four year longitudinal study. *Journal of the American Society for Information Science and Technology, 53*(2), 162-171.

Westergren, J. (2006). *Link building guide*. Retrieved June 4, 2009, from http://www.jimwestergren.com/link-building-guide/

What is link building. (n.d.). Retrieved June 7, 2009, from Admin Zone Forum: http://www.theadminzone.com/forums/showthread.php?t=25021

5

IMPLICATIONS OF WEBOMETRIC STUDIES AND FUTURE

5.1. INTRODUCTION

Webometric studies have opened a new area of research and applications for those who are involved with Internet in one way or the other. Such studies started with the novel idea of measuring the growth of web due to increased tendency of keeping web presence in the form of institutional and personal web profile. A search in the Google with the term "webometrics" resulted into nearly 12, 10, 000 search results (query was shot on 17.08.2014). This reflects the extent to which the subject has grown. There are now several emerging related areas which includes,

- Impact Factor
- PageRank
- Network Mapping
- Search Engine Optimization
- Ranking of World Universities

In order to facilitate webometric studies, laws of bibliometrics, scientometrics, informetrics and other statistical techniques serve as guiding principles. There are online and offline tools for webometric studies which includes search engines and customized web crawlers. However, the completeness of the collected data is always questionable if one is using a single tool. Apart from that, the logic used in the tool for data collection can be also questioned. Whatever one has in support or against but fact cannot be denied that such studies present a good understanding to scientific community about the growth and development of Internet as an important source of information.

5.2. WEB GROWTH

Since the evolution of World Wide Web (WWW), there has been many efforts to investigate its' nature and properties by applying modern informetrics methodologies to its contents, link structures and search engines (Björneborn & Ingwersen, 2001). The WWW has emerged as a new research area in library and information science because the WWW has now become one of the main sources of information for academic and research community. Web is a system of interconnected hypertext documents available over the Internet. Web is growing in multi-dimensions: as service, as techniques; as tools; as social networking etc. Internet users are globally increasing day by day. The global penetration of web usage reached up to 39 percent in the world. In web usage, India has 11.4 percent penetration rate of its total population. Western countries have much higher web usage penetration rate than Eastern part of the world. Internet Systems Consortium surveyed the host counts about 1,010,251,829 till January, 2014 which reveals the tremendous growth in domain host counts. Google leads in number of searches and popularity in the web search done worldwide. The web has been measured by various dimensions and methods. Some illustrations in this regard are search engine performance, recall and precision of search engines, query analysis, indexing of search engine databases, behaviour of search engines, website usage analysis, website content analysis, URL analysis, depth of the web, qualitative analysis of web documents and so on.

5.3. WEBOMETRICS IN ACADEMIC WEB SPACES

The scientific study of web is known as "webometrics" which is the combination of informetrics, scientometrics and bibliometrics. The main area of webometric researches are search engines' coverage and quality analysis, web page property analysis and web impact factor (WIF) analysis, domain and sub-domain analysis, and TLDs analysis. There are many researches conducted on the area of webometrics. The field of webometrics in broad sense including the researches from disciplines outside of information science such as communication studies, statistical physics and computer science. *"Bibliometrics of the World Wide Web: an exploratory analysis of the intellectual structure of Cyberspace"* was the first effort in academic web spaces by Larson (1996). Web Impact Factor (WIF) has been conceptualized from ISI's "journal impact factor" (JIF) which has close analogy with citation analysis. Webometric investigations of academic web spaces have been deployed by personal web crawlers and various search engines. In academic web spaces, interlinking studies of *backlinks* within academic departments of scientific domain have been carried out successfully. The international linking patterns between universities of UK, Australia, New Zealand, Japan, and Asia-Pacific Region have been also focused. Besides this, countrywide universities' network has been the focus for *backlink* analysis to analyze the interlinking pattern among all of the universities and institutes of a single country domain. Academic web spaces and their scholarly productivity have much influence on the web which has been assessed by number of studies conducted for universities of UK, Australia, and Taiwan. In academic web spaces, it has been proved that scholars' personal and institutional characteristics are the significant reasons for higher impact on the web.

5.4. CONTENT AWARENESS IN ACADEMIC WEB SPACES

Websites are medium through which knowledge can be disseminated efficiently to every nook and corner of the world. Richness of web content of websites depends upon their information content, services, facilities, feedback, administrative support and updating policy etc. These features are collectively referred as *content awareness* of websites. *Content awareness* indicates qualitative and quantitative aspects of information provided on the websites. *Content awareness* is one of the methods for measuring usefulness of websites. *Content awareness* evaluation criteria have been developed with 41 check points to measure how effectively academic library websites share their knowledge, information, services and facilities with their users. A website's *content awareness* performance can be assessed on the basis of 108 point scale as *website performance grade table* (see Appendix – III). The two formulae *Overall Website Performance Calculation (OWPC)* and *Criteria wise Website Performance Calculation (CWPC)* (see Appendix – II) can be used for calculating the performance of library websites. The total 108 points are divided in five (5) grades i.e. *excellent, very good, good, average and unsatisfactory*. As an experiment, evaluation of Indian academic & research library websites is presented in the preceding chapter. Librarians and webmasters should use the evaluation criteria to evaluate time to time their existing library website and improve upon the content awareness by further improving the score of library website.

5.5. WEB IMPACT FACTOR OF ACADEMIC WEB SPACES

Web Impact Factor is an important tool for

measuring the reputation and the content of the library website. The author conducted a survey of two groups, one group consisting of Central Universities (CU) which represented Indian academic community and other group represented Institutes of National Importance (INI) & Indian Institutes of Management (IIMs) which were de-facto considered as reputed institutes. The Institutes of National Importance are outstanding academic and research institutes in India for imparting education and research. The libraries of these academic and research institutes as per their collection, services and facilities have wide range of information to be included in their websites. In the study, web impact factor (WIF) was the one of the parameter for evaluation of library websites and it was found that Institutes of National Importance library websites have higher overall average web impact factor. This leads to the conclusion that library websites of Institutes of National Importance are more viewed and popular as compared to CU library websites; and established that library websites of reputed institutes have high web impact factor. The following Table 5.1 presents a summary of the study conducted.

Table 5.1: Category wise Ranking of CU and INI Library Websites

SN	Central University	Overall Average WIF	Overall Category Ranking	Institute of National Importance	Overall Average WIF	Overall Category Ranking
1.	JNU	2.349975	1	IITK	2.23359	1
2.	BHU	1.173775	2	IIMK	1.25915	2
3.	MANUU	0.925	3	IITR	0.829285	3
4.	IGNOU	0.4	4	IITB	0.767465	4
5.	UOH	0.213125	5	ISIK	0.74625	5
6.	PONDI	0.15	6	IITD	0.693	6
7.	UOD	0.13018	7	IITG	0.6001	7
8.	JMI	0.10035	8	IITM	0.500585	8
9.	ASU	0.1	9	IITKGP	0.47143	9

SN	Central University	Overall Average WIF	Overall Category Ranking	Institute of National Importance	Overall Average WIF	Overall Category Ranking
10.	NEHU	0.063155	10	IIMC	0.3151	10
11.	AMU	Nil	11	IIMA	0.238785	11
12.	MANI	Nil	11	AIIMS	0.153655	12
13.	MIZUNI	Nil	11	IIMI	0.1375	13
14.	UOA	Nil	11	IIMB	0.046995	14
15.	VBU	Nil	11	IIML	0.03443	15
16.				SCTIMST	Nil	16
Average WIF		0.373704			0.564207	

For the study of pointing behaviour of *backlinks* to a library website, seven categories of library web pages have been identified; and all web pages available within a library website have been categorized based on seven categories of library web pages. The *backlinks* received by library websites of CU; and INI & IIMs are assessed on the basis of these seven (7) categories. The pointing behaviour of *backlinks* indicates usefulness of library web pages for library users. On the analysis of CU library websites, it has been observed that majority of *backlinks* (76.93%) pointed to index page / homepage of library websites followed by journals related web pages (10.97%). Similarly on the analysis of INIs & IIMs library websites, it has been inference that index pages (70.21%) attracts more *backlinks* than any other. In case of INIs and IIMs, digital library pages (20.86%) have received significant number of *backlinks* than CU library websites.

The size (number of web pages) of library website is one of the important criteria to measure its' effect on WIF value. The study conducted for twenty one (21) library websites where there was change in the Total Number of Pages (TNP) in different rounds. Though it was hypothesized that size matters for improving WIF but it was found true only in case of JMI. In majority of the cases there was fluctuation in the WIF even if the numbers of pages were same and hence the size of the website has no direct correlation with the WIF. Often, it has been seen that if there is increase in the number of web pages then WIF goes down. In such cases it was observed that though there was increase in *backlinks* with the size increase of site but the increase was not in the proportion to the size. Apart from that, the indexing policy of search engines and time of data collection may also affect the results. Hence, it can be concluded that there is no relation of size of the website to the WIF. Finally, study of individual library websites suggests that size really does not play much role in attracting *backlinks* and hence it does not significantly affect the WIF.

The domain based web impact factor analysis of library websites concluded that libraries with separate domain name have higher web impact factor. The study reveals that only seven (7) academic universities / institutes had separate domain names. The average WIF of all such universities / institutes was found to be higher than the one which do not have separate domain name (Table 5.2).

Table 5.2: Domain wise Analysis of WIF of CU and INI Library Websites

SN	Libraries with separate domain name	Overall Average WIF	Libraries without separate domain name	Overall Average WIF
1.	IITK	2.23359	JNU	2.349975
2.	IITB	0.767465	IIMK	1.25915
3.	IITM	0.500585	BHU	1.173775
4.	IITKGP	0.47143	MANUU	0.925
5.	UOH	0.213125	IITR	0.829285
6.	UOD	0.13018	ISIK	0.74625
7.	IIML	0.03443	IITD	0.693
8.			IITG	0.6001
9.			IGNOU	0.4

SN	Libraries with separate domain name	Overall Average WIF	Libraries without separate domain name	Overall Average WIF
10.			IIMC*	0.3151
11.			IIMA	0.238785
12.			AIIMS	0.153655
13.			PONDI	0.15
14.			IIMI	0.1375
15.			JMI	0.10035
16.			ASU	0.1
17.			NEHU	0.063155
18.			IIMB	0.046995
19.			SCTIMST	Nil
20.			AMU	Nil
21.			MANI	Nil
22.			MIZUNI	Nil
23.			UOA	Nil
24.			VBU	Nil
Average WIF		0.621543		0.428419

- IIMC showed separate domain name in the fifth round of data collection only, so it was included in the list of "libraries without separate domain name".

5.6. SOLUTIONS FOR INCREASING WEB IMPACT FACTOR

WIF is taken as measure for quantifying the importance of library's web content. It can also be set as parameter to measure the quality of library website. Website usability techniques and *content awareness* evaluation criteria jointly become very effective guidelines for designing academic library websites with higher degree of *content awareness*. These evaluation criteria may also be used for *content awareness* evaluation of websites of public libraries. The *content awareness* evaluation criteria also cover some of the websites' usability approach which makes library websites more useful. Detailed accounts of such practices are given in Chapter 4 (cf. Section 4.9). The important points can be summarized as follows:

- Register with search directories
- Popularize through friends, family and employees
- Contact association sites
- Contact publishers and vendors websites
- Submit to announcement sites and newsletters
- Promote something on your site
- Ask other sites for links (city guides)
- Make reciprocal link requests with other libraries
- Use of link building software(s)
- Mention your site in discussion groups
- Respond to blogs
- Article submission
- Use a service or buy links
- Link baiting

There are several methods and there are some healthy as well as un-healthy practices being used for this purpose. Normally, it is observed that libraries are not concerned for getting more *backlinks* or *references* rather they emphasize more on increasing the number of hits which is also a good measure of website popularity and effectiveness. But hits demonstrate temporary access of a client whereas *backlink* citations provide a permanent measure as long as the content is not changed.

Buying links and link baiting are not healthy practices but are extensively used by many websites apart from library. It is very difficult to ascertain whether libraries also adopt such practices. Such practices are not ethical. However, an active librarianship can render services using web as an important channel. This would certainly make the library more visible and further slowly but steadily library will get lot of *backlinks*. There are some additional suggestions, from authors' side, to improve the visibility of websites of library:

(a) Multiple web pages in websites attract more *backlinks*. So library websites should have multiple web pages with variety of information which may attracts more *backlinks*.

(b) Changes in URLs of library websites destroy the existing *backlinks* which reduces WIF. So library websites should not change their URLs frequently.

(c) Valuable informational contents in web pages of library websites attract more *backlinks*. So library websites should provide more user oriented valuable information as web page content.

(d) Smaller lengths of URLs of library website are better indexed by search engines. So, the URLs should be kept smaller in length.

(e) Structured library websites with higher OWPC and CWPC scores indicate higher degree of *content awareness*. So librarians and webmasters should try to make library websites more informative and structured and evaluate time to time with such scales.

(f) Distribution of same information over multiple web pages of library website adversely effects *content awareness* level. So same information should be grouped in one place.

(g) *Backlinks* point to index pages / homepages, digital library pages, journals pages, e-resource pages, e-theses pages etc. So librarians should try to make library websites with details of such information. This attracts more *backlinks* which increases WIF of library websites.

5.7. SOME OBSERVATIONS AND EXPERIENCES

The world is not perfect and hence same is true also for the studies in the area of webometrics. The form of Internet which is seen and searched by search engine is "visible web". According to Deep Web Research 2009 by Marcus P. Zillman, the "Deep Web" encompasses in its vicinity one trillion pages and search engines can only index approximately 20 billion pages. Even the web visibility of the widest part by search engines is only 85% of the total indexed term. The degree of completeness or incompleteness of index differs from search engines to search engines. One search engine may produce one kind of search result which may not tally with the search result of other search engine. Keeping this in mind some scholars has developed their own crawlers but those also cannot be said perfect because of coverage of crawlers and the algorithm used for crawling. However, many of such studies have produced commendable results.

In the study, the above mentioned difficulties were kept in the mind and hence, four search engines are used for the experiments while preparing the text of this book. The results produced by four popular search engines can be said as generic. However, they differ in coverage at many places. The study also supports that Yahoo Site Explorer is better in producing webometric data compared to other three.

The web based tools like Google, Yahoo Site Explorer, MSN, HotBot etc. do produce data of analysis but they continuously keep on changing their algorithm for ranking and indexing the web page. An interesting remark can be observed at one of the blog "Webometric Thoughts" titled "Why I Hate Google: My Ranking has Improved". The responder to the blog says that his website gets three times higher ranking even when he is posting information on his blog less frequently. The reason for this increase he points out is the change made in the algorithm of Google Analytics. This incident points out that it is not reliable always to depend on web based tools for calculation. It is because of the same reason that the present study has used only the data produced by search engines not the analytical tools.

The library websites of highly reputed institutes have will normally have higher WIF. With the time, *backlinks* change due to dynamism of the web which also changes value of WIF. It is also observed that changes in URL structure also destroy existing *backlinks*. Index pages/homepages of library websites attract maximum number of *backlinks* including other pages wherever there is valuable information from users' perspective.

Regarding *content awareness* of library websites, it is to be said that more structured library websites with more informational contents have higher degree of *content awareness* which is also an indicative of better usability of library. The *content awareness* evaluation criteria guide the librarians and webmasters on how to make library websites more useful, more informative, more structured and more attractive.

5.8. FUTURE PROSPECTS IN WEBOMETRICS

The webometric study is an open area of research. However, a study is warranted to look into actual ranking of libraries and their corresponding WIF. In India, there are accreditation for universities and institutes by National Assessment and Accreditation Council (NAAC) but it does not provide any kind of ranking. A study of WIF of already ranked libraries should be done to look into the relationship of WIF and their actual ranking.

Measuring the *content awareness* of libraries is another area which has lot of potential for further research.

REFERENCES

Björneborn, L. & Ingwersen, P. (2001). Perspectives of webometrics. *Scientometrics, 50*(1), 65-82.

Internet Systems Consortium Domain Survey. (2014, January). Retrieved August 12, 2014, from Internet Systems Consortium: http://ftp.isc.org/www/survey/reports/current/

Internet Usage Statistics. (n.d.). Retrieved August 12, 2014, from Internet World Stats: http://www.internetworldstats.com/stats.htm

Larson, R. R. (1996). Bibliometrics of the World Wide Web: an exploratory analysis of the intellectual structure of cyberspace. *In* S. Hardin (Ed.), *Proceedings of the 59th Annual Meeting, ASIS 96, Baltimore, Maryland* (pp. 71-79). Medford, NJ: Learned Information. Available at http://sherlock.berkley.edu/asis96/asis96.html

Search Engine Land. (2013, February). Retrieved August 12, 2014, from Search Engine Land: http://searchengineland.com/google-worlds-most-popular-search-engine-148089

Why I hate Google: my ranking has improved. (December 3, 2009). Retrieved August 17, 2014, from Webometric Thoughts: http://oldwebometrics.blogspot.in/2009/10/why-i-hate-google-my-ranking-has.html

Zillman, M. P. (December 28, 2008). *Deep web research 2009.* Retrieved August 17, 2014, from Law and Technology Resources for Legal Professionals: http://www.llrx.com/features/deepweb2009.htm

BIBLIOGRAPHY

Abdullah, A. R. (2001). A comparative study of academic libraries websites in Malaysia (Master's Dissertation). Faculty of Information Studies, Universiti Teknologi MARA.

Abels, E. G., White, M. D. & Hahn K. (1997). Identifying user-based criteria for web pages. Internet Research: Electronic Networking Applications and Policy, 7, 252–262.

Aguillo, I. F. (1998). STM information on the web and the development of new Internet R & D databases and indicators. Online Information 98: Proceedings (pp. 239-243). Oxford: Learned Information.

Almind, T. C. & Ingwersen, P. (1996). Informetric analysis on the World Wide Web: a methodological approach to "internetometrics". Centre for Informetric Studies, Royal School of Library and Information Science [CIS Report 2].

Almind, T. C. & Ingwersen, P. (1997). Informetric analyses on the World Wide Web: methodological approaches to webometrics. Journal of Documentation, 53(4), 404-426.

Allen, M. (2002). A case study of the usability testing of the University of South Florida's virtual library interface design. Online Information Review, 26(1), 40-53.

Association of Indian Universities. (2006). University Handbook: India (31st ed.). New Delhi: Association of Indian Universities.

Augustine, A. & Greene, C. (2002). Discovering how students search a library website: a usability case study. *College & Research Libraries*, 63(4), 354-365.

Avouris, N., Tselios, N., Fidas, C. & Papachristos, E. (2003). Website evaluation: a usability-based perspective. Lecture Notes in Computer Science, 2563, 217-231.

Backlink Analyzer. (n.d.). [computer software]. Retrieved June 17, 2009, from eKstreme.com. Available at http:// ekstreme.com/backlink-analyzer

Backlink Analyzer. (n.d.). [computer software]. Retrieved August 12, 2014, from SEOTOOLS. Available at http://tools. seobook.com/backlink-analyzer/

Backlink Watch!. (n.d.). [online software tool]. Retrieved August 12, 2014, from BACKLINK WATCH! Available at http://www.backlinkwatch.com/

Badre, A. N. (2000). The effecs of cross cultural interface design orientation on World Wide Web user performance. GVE Research Technical Reports. Retrieved April 24, 2001, from http://www.cc.gatech.edu/gvu/reports/2001/abstracts/01-03.html

Barber, W. & Badre, A. N. (1998). Culturability: the merging of culture and usability. In 4th Conference on Human Factors and the Web. Basking Ridge, NJ.

Bar-Ilan, J. (1997). The “mad cow disease”, Usenet newsgroups and bibliometric laws. Scientometrics, 39(1), 29-55.

Bar-Ilan, J. (1999). Search engine results over time: a case study on search engine stability. Cybermetrics, 2/3(1), Paper 1. Available at http://www.cindoc.csic.es/cybermetrics/articles/v2i1p1.html

Bar-Ilan, J. (2000). Evaluating the stability of the search tools HotBot and Snap: a case study. Online Information Review, 24(6), 439-449.

Bar-Ilan, J. (2002). Methods for measuring search engine performance over time. Journal of the American Society for Information Science and Technology, 53(4), 308-319.

Bar-Ilan, J. (2004). A macroscopic link analysis of academic institutions within a country: the case of Israel. Scientometrics, 59(2), 391-403.

Barjak, F., Li, X. & Thelwall, M. (2007). Which factors explain the web impact of scientists' personal homepages? Journal of the American Society for Information Science and Technology, 58(2), 200-211.

Barnum, C. (2002). Usability testing and research. New York: Longman.

Battleson, B., Booth, A. & Weintrop, S. (2001). Usability testing of an academic library website: a case study. *Journal of Academic Librarianship,* 27(3), 188-198.

Beamer, L. & Varner, I. (2001). *Intercultural communication in the global workplace.* Boston: McGraw-Hill.

Berners-Lee, T. & Cailliau, R. (1990). World Wide Web: proposal for a hypertext project. Available at http://www.w3. org/Proposal.html

Björneborn, L. (2001). Small-world linkage and co-linkage. Proceedings of the 12th ACM Conference on Hypertext and Hypermedia (pp. 133-134). New York: ACM.

Björneborn, L. (2004). Small-world link structures across an academic web space: a library and information science approach (Doctoral Dissertation). Copenhagen, Denmark: Royal School of Library and Information Science.

Björneborn, L. & Ingwersen, P. (2004). Towards a basic framework for webometrics. Journal of the American Society for Information Science and Technology, 55(14), 1216-1227.

Bossy, M. J. (1995). The last of the litter: "netometrics". Solaris, 2. Presses Universitaires de Rennes. Available at http://biblio-fr.info.unicaen.fr/bnum/jelec/Solaris/d02/2bossy.html

Bradford, S. C. (1934). Sources of information on specific subjects. Engineering, 137, 85–86.

Brin, S. & Page, L. (1998). The anatomy of a large-scale hypertextual web search engine. Computer Networks and ISDN Systems, 30, 107-117.

Broder, A., Kumar, R., Maghoul, F., Raghavan, P., Rajagopalan, S., Stata, R., ... Wiener, J. (2000). Graph structure in the web. Computer Networks, 33(1-6), 309-320. Available at http://www.almaden.ibm.com/cs/k53/www9.final

Brookes, B. C. (1988). Comments on the scope of bibliometrics. In L. Egghe & R. Rousseau (Eds.), Informetrics 87/88. Select Proceedings of the first International Conference on Bibliometrics and Theoretical Aspects of Information Retrieval (pp. 29–41). Amsterdam: Elsevier Science.

Brookes, B. C. (1990). Biblio-, sciento-, infor- metrics? what are we talking about? In L. Egghe & R. Rousseau (Eds.), Informetrics 89/90: selection of papers submitted for the Second International Conference on Bibliometrics, Scientometrics and Informetrics (pp. 31-43). Amsterdam: Elsevier Science.

Chakrabarti, S., Dom, B. E., Kumar, S. R.,...Kleinberg, J. (1999). Mining the web's link structure. IEEE Computer, 32(8), 60-67.

Chen, C., Newman, J., Newman, R. & Rada, R. (1998). How did university departments interweave the web: a study of connectivity and underlying factors. Interacting with Computers, 10, 353-373.

Chignell, M. H. & Keevil, B. E. (1996). Developing usable online information for a web authoring tool. In SIGDOC96 Conference. New York: ACM.

Chisenga, J. (1998). A study of university libraries' home pages in Sub-Saharan Africa. *Libri*, 48(1), 49-57.

Chisman, J., Diller, K. & Walbridge, S. (1999). Usability testing: a case study. College & Research Libraries, 60(6), 552-569.

Chu, H., He, S. & Thelwall, M. (2002). Library and information science schools in Canada and USA: a webometric perspective. Journal of Education for Library and Information Science, 43(2), 110-125.

Clausen, H. (1999). User-oriented evaluation of library and information centre websites. New Library World, 100(1146), 5-10.

Clyde, L. A. (1996). The library as information provider: the home page. The Electronic Library, 14(6), 549–558.

Cole, F. J. & Eals, N. B. (1917). The history of comparative anatomy. Part I: a statistical analysis of the literature. Science Progress, 11, 578–596.

Constantine, L. (1999). Usage-centered web design. Retrieved June 5, 2009, from http://web.archive.org/web/ 19991012141354/ http://webreview.com/pub/1999/06/25/feature/constantine.html

Craven, J. (2003). Accessibility and usability of websites. Library & Information Update CILIP Magazine), May, 2003.

Cronin, B., Snyder, H. W., Rosenbaum, H., Martinson, A. & Callahan, E. (1998). Invoked in the web. Journal of the American Society for Information Science, 49(14), 1319-1328.

Csir, F. J. (1996). Evaluation and criteria of the World Wide Web: reference websites (Master's Dissertation). Kent State University.

Cyr, D. & Trevor-Smith, H. (2004). Localization of web design: an empirical comparison of German, Japanese, and United States website characteristics. Journal of the American Society for Information Science and Technology, 55(13), 1199-1208.

Data Doctor Backlink Checker (version 2.0.1.5). (n.d.). Retrieved June 17, 2009, from Pro Data Doctor. Available at http://www.softpedia.com/get/Internet/Other-Internet-Related/Data-Doctor-Back-Link-Checker.shtml

Del Galdo, E. & Neilson, J. (1996). International user interfaces. New York: Wiley.

Dempsey, G. & Sussman, R. (1999). A hands-on guide for multilingual websites. World Trade, 12(9), 68-70.

Dickstein, R. & Mills, V. (2000). Usability testing at the University of Arizona library: how to let users in on the design. Information Technology & Libraries, 19(3), 144-151.

Dinkelman, A. & Stacy-Bates, K. (2007). Accessing e-books through academic library websites. College & Research Libraries, 68(1), 45-58.

Derek J. de Solla Price. (n.d.). Retrieved June 17, 2009, from Wikipedia: http://en.wikipedia.org/wiki/Derek_J._de_ Solla_Price

Dodge, M. (1999). The geography of cyberspace. CASA Working Paper 8. London: Centre for Advanced Spatial Analysis, University College London.

Domain Inbound Links Checker. (n.d.). [computer software]. Retrieved August 12, 2014, from Online Utility.org. Available at http://www.online-utility.org/webmaster/ backlink_domain_analyzer.jsp

Dumas, J. S. & Redish, J. C. (1993). A practical guide to usability testing. [S.l.]: Intellect Books.

Easley, D. & Kleinberg, J. (2010). Link Analysis and Web Search. In Networks, Crowds, and Markets: Reasoning about a Highly Connected World. Chapter 14. Cambridge University Press.

Egghe, L. & Rousseau, R. (1990). Introduction to informetrics: quantitative methods in library, documentation and information science. Amsterdam: Elsevier.

Etzioni, O. (1996). The World Wide Web: quagmire or gold mine? Communications of the ACM, 39(11), 65-68.

Fairthorne, R. A. (1969). Empirical hyperbolic distributions (Bradford-Zipf-Mandelbrot) for bibliometrics description and prediction. Journal of Documentation, 25, 319–343.

Fang, W. (2007). Using google analytics for improving library website content and design: a case study. Library Philosophy and Practice 2007. Retrieved June, 2009, from http://www.webpages.uidaho.edu/~mbolin/fang.htm

Fano, R. M. (1956). Information theory and the retrieval of recorded information. In Shera, J .H., Kent, A.

& Perry, J. W. (Eds.), Documentation in action (pp. 238-244). New York: Rein-hold.

Fernandes, T. (1995). Global user interface design. *Proceedings of the ACM Conference on Human Factors in Computing Systems - CHI '95, Mosaic of Creativity, May* (pp. 363-364). Denver: SIGCHI.

Fichter, D. (2000). Head start: usability testing up front. *Online*, 24(1), 79-81.

Fraser, B., Comden, D. & Bergstahler, S. (1998). Including users with disabilities: designing library websites for accessibility. CHOICE: Current Reviews for Academic Libraries, 35, 35-37.

Frías, E. R. (2010). Application of webometric techniques to the study of accounting and financial variables (Doctoral Dissertation). University of Granada.

Ganski, K. L. (2008). Accessibility of e-resources from theological library websites. Theological Librarianship, 1(1), 38-45.

Garfield, E. (1972). Citation analysis as a tool in journal evaluation. Science, 178(4060), 471-479.

George, C. A. (2005). Usability testing and design of a library website: an iterative approach. OCLC Systems & Services, 21(3), 167-180.

Girardin, L. (1996). Mapping the virtual geography of the World Wide Web. Proceedings of the 5th WWW Conference. Available at http://www.girardin.org/luc//cgv/www5/ index.html

Glänzel, W. (2001). National characteristics in international scientific co-authorship relations. Scientometrics, 51(1), 69-115.

Glossary of Documentation Terms. (1976). London: British Standard Institution, 1976 (BS 5408: 1976).

Google Scholar's Support for Scholarly Publishers. (n.d.). Retrieved June 8, 2009, from Google Scholar: http://scholar.google.co.in/intl/en/scholar/publishers.html

Gross, P. L. K. & Gross, F. M. (1927). College libraries and chemical education. Science, 66, 386-389.

Gullikson, S., Blades, R., Bragdon, M., McKibbon, S., Sparling, M. & Toms, E. G. (1999). The impact of information architecture on academic website usability. The Electronic Library, 17(5), 293-304.

Hall, E. & Hall, M. (1990). Understanding cultural differences. Yarmouth, ME: Intercultural Press.

Harley, D. & Henke, J. (2007). Toward an effective understanding of website users: advantages and pitfalls of linking transaction log analyses and online surveys. D-Lib Magazine, 13(3/4).

Hawkins, D. T. (1977). Unconventional uses of on-line information retrieval systems: on-line bibliometrics studies. Journal of the American Society for Information Science, 28(1), 13–18.

Head, A. J. (1999). Web redemption and the promise of usability. *Online*, 23(6), 20-23.

Henzinger, M. (2000). Link analysis in web information Retrieval. Bulletin of the IEEE Computer Society Technical Committee on Data Engineering, 23(3), 1-7.

Herring, S. C. (2002). Computer-mediated communication on the Internet. In B. Cronin (ed.), Annual Review of Information Science and Technology (pp. 109-168). Medford, NJ: Information Today.

Heydon, A. & Najork, M. (1999). Mercator: a scalable, extensible web crawler. World Wide Web, 2, 219-229.

Hider, P. & Ferguson, S. (2006). An evaluation of the information architectural qualities of Australian library websites. In: ALIA 2006 Biennial Conference. Available at http://conferences.alia.org.au/alia2006/Papers/Philip_Hider.pdf

Hightower, C., Sih, J. & Tilghman, A. (1998). Recommendation for benchmarking website usage among academic libraries. College & Research Libraries, 59(1), 61-79.

History of the World Wide Web. (n.d.). Retrieved from Wikipedia: http://en.wikipedia.org/wiki/History_of_the_World_Wide_Web

Holly, Y. (2005). Content and workflow management for library websites: case studies. Hershey: Information Science Publishing.

Houghton, D. (2000). Building an academic library website: experiences at De Montfort University. Program, 34(3), 269-280.

Huizingh, E. (2000). The content and design of websites: an empirical study. Information and Management, 37(3), 123-134.

Hulme, E. W. (1923). Statistical bibliography in relation to the growth of modern civilization. London: Butler & Grafton.

Ingwersen, P. (1998). The calculation of web impact factors. Journal of Documentation, 54(2), 236-243.

Ingwersen, P. & Christensen, F. H. (1997). Data set isolation for bibliometric online analyses of research publications: fundamental methodological issues. Journal of the American Society for Information Science, 48, 205–217.

Internet Systems Consortium Domain Survey. (2014, July). Retrieved January 21, 2015, from Internet

Systems Consortium: http://ftp.isc.org/www/ survey/reports/ current/

Internet Usage Statistics. (n.d.). Retrieved Janaury 21, 2015, from Internet World Stats: http://www.internetworldstats.com/stats.htm

Jalal, S. K., Biswas, S. C., & Mukhopadhyay, P. (2010). Web impact factor and link analysis of selected Indian Universities. Annals of Library and Information Studies, 57(1), 109-121.

Jeyshankar, R. (2011). Link analysis and Web Impact Factor of Indian nationalised banks. International Journal of Information Dissemination and Technology, 1(3), 171-179.

Jurkowski, O. L. (2005). An analysis of library web sites at colleges and universities serving distance education students. In E. D. Garten, D. E. Williams & J. M. Nyce (Eds.), Advances in Library Administration and Organization, 22 (pp. 23-77). [S.l.]: Emerald Group Publishing.

Keevil, B. E. (1998). Measuring the usability of your website: usability index checklist for websites. Retrieved June, 2009, from http://www3. sympatico.ca/bkeevil/ sigdoc98/checklist/Web Check_Sep13.html

Kent, P. (2006). Search engine optimization for dummies (2nd ed.). Hoboken, NJ: Wiley.

Kessler, M. M. (1983). Bibliographic coupling between scientific papers. American Documentation, 14, 10-15.

Kim, H. J. (2000). Motivations for hyperlinking in scholarly electronic articles: a qualitative study. Journal of the American Society for Information Science, 51(10), 887-899.

King, D. L. (1998). Library home page design: a comparison of page layout for front-ends to ARL library websites. College & Research Libraries, 59, 458-465.

Koehler, W. (1999). Digital libraries and World Wide Web sites and page persistence. *Information Research, 4*(4). Available at: http://informationr.net/ir/4-4/paper60.html

Koehler, W. (2002). Web page change and persistence: a four year longitudinal study. *Journal of the American Society for Information Science and Technology, 53*(2), 162-171.

Kosala, R. & Blockeel, H. (2000). Web mining research: a survey. SIGKDD Explorations, 2(1), 1-15.

Kousha, K. & Horri, A. (2004). The relationship between scholarly publishing and the counts of academic inlinks to Iranian university websites: exploring academic link creation motivations. Journal of Information Management and Scientometrics, 1(2), 13-22.

Krueger, J., Ray, R. L. & Knight, L. (2004). Applying web usability techniques to assess student awareness of library web resources. The Journal of Academic Librarianship, 30(4), 285-293.

Larson, R. R. (1996). Bibliometrics of the World Wide Web: an exploratory analysis of the intellectual structure of cyberspace. In S. Hardin (Ed.), Proceedings of the 59th Annual Meeting, ASIS 96, Baltimore, Maryland (pp. 71-79). Medford, NJ: Learned Information. Available at http://sherlock.berkley.edu/asis96/asis96.html

Lasswell, H. (1948). The structure and function of communication in society. In L. Bryson (Ed.), The communication of ideas (pp. 37-51). New York: Harper & Brothers.

Lawrence, S. & Giles, C. L. (1998). Searching the World Wide Web. Science, 280, 98-100.

Lawrence, S. & Giles, C. L. (1999). Accessibility of information on the web. Nature, 400, 107-110.

Letnikova, G. (2003). Usability testing of academic library websites: a selective bibliography. *Internet Reference Services Quarterly*, 8(4), 53-68.

Leydesdorff, L. & Curran, M. (2000). Mapping university-industry-government relations on the Internet: the construction of indicators for a knowledge-based economy. Cybermetrics, 4(1). Available at http://www.cindoc.csic.es/cybermetrics/articles/v4i1p2.html

Li, X., Thelwall, M., Musgrove, P. & Wilkinson, D. (2003). The relationship between the WIFs or inlinks of computer science departments in UK and their RAE ratings or research productivities in 2001. Scientometrics, 57(2), 239-255.

Link Checker Pro. (n.d.). [computer software]. Retrieved June 17, 2009, from Link Checker Pro. Available at http://www. link-checker-pro.com/

Link Popularity. (n.d.). [online link popularity checker]. Retrieved June 17, 2009, from Add Me.com. Available at http:// www.addme.com/popularity.htm

Link Popularity Check 3.0.3. (n.d.). [computer software]. Retrieved June 17, 2009, From Link Popularity Check. Available at http://www.checkyourlinkpopularity.com/

Ma, Y. (2002). A design analysis model for developing world wide web sites. Journal of the American Society for Information Science and Technology, 53(7), 531-535.

Maharana, R. K., Panda, K. C., & Sahoo, J. (2012). Web impact factor (WIF) and link analysis of Indian Institute of Technologies (IITs): A webometric study. Library Philosophy and Practice (e-journal). 789, 1-11.

Marcus, A. & Gould, E. W. (2000). Cultural dimensions and global web user-interface design. Interactions, 7(4), 33-46.

Marshakova, I. (1973). System of document connection based on references. Nauchne-Tekumicheskala Informatsija (Series 2). 3-8.

McClements, N. & Becker, C. (1996). Writing web page standards. College & Research Libraries News, 57(1), 16-17.

McKiernan, G. (1996). CitedSites(sm): citation indexing of web resources. Available at http://www.public.iastate.edu/~CYBERSTACKS/Cited.htm

McMullen, S. (2001). Usability testing in a library website redesign project. Reference Services Review, 29(1), 7-22.

Mettrop, W. & Nieuwenhuysen, P. (2001). Internet search engines - fluctuations in document accessibility. Journal of Documentation, 57(5), 623-651.

Milunovich, K. (2002). Designing and maintaining Law library websites: some practical considerations. Law Library Journal, 94(3), 487-508. Retrieved June, 2009, from http://www.aallnet.org/products/pub_llj_v94n03/2002-29.pdf

Molyneux, R. E. & Williams, R. V. (1999). Measuring the Internet. Annual Review of Information Science and Technology, 34, 287-339.

Morville, P. (1999). Information, architecture, and usability. Web Architect. Retrieved June, 2009, from http://web.archive. org/web/19991013024942/ http://webreview.com/pub/ 1999/03/12/arch/index.html

Mukherjee, B. (2007). Scholarly communication on the web: an investigation of open access electronic journals in library and information science

(Doctoral Dissertation). Varanasi, India: Department of Library & Information Science, Banaras Hindu University.

Nacke, O. (1979). Informetrie: eine neuer name für eine neue disziplin. Nachrichten für Documentation, 30(6), 219-226.

Nacke, O., Wehmeier, R. & Eisenhardt, O. H. (1980). Informetrie und scientometrie: cui bono? ein dialog, eine liste und ein programm. Nachrichten für Dokumentation, 31, 100–106.

Nalimov, V. V. & Mulchenko, Z. M. (1969). Scientometrics, study of the development of science as an information process. Moscow: Nauka.

Nelson, M. (2005). Academic homepages and Nobel laureates. In P. Ingwersen & B. Larson (Eds.), Proceedings of ISSI 2005 - 10th International Conference of the International Society for Scientometrics and Informetrics (Vol. 1, pp. 193-196). Stockhom: Karolinska University Press.

Neuendorf, K. A. (2002). The content analysis guidebook.. Thousand Oaks, CA: SAGE.

Nielsen, J. (1993). Usability engineering (ed. 13). Boston: Academic Press.

Nielsen, J. (n.d.). How to conduct a heuristic evaluation. Retrieved June, 2009, from http://www.useit.com/papers/heuristic/heuristic_evaluation.html

Nielsen, J. (n.d.). Usability 101: introduction to usability. Retrieved June, 2009, from http://www.useit.com /alertbox/20030825.html

Norlin, E. & Winters, C. M. (2002). Usability testing for library websites: a hands-on guide. Chicago: American Library Association.

Noruzi, A. (2005). Web impact factors for Iranian universities. Webology, 2(1), Article 11. Retrieved from http://www.webology.ir/2005/v2n1/a11.html

Noruzi, A. (2006). The web impact factors: a critical review. The Electronic Library, 24(4), 490-500.

Oppenheim, C., Morris, A., McKnight, C. & Lowley, S. (2000). The evaluation of WWW search engines. Journal of Documentation, 56(2), 190-211.

Otlet, P. (1934). Treatise on documentation. The book on the book. Theory and practice. Brussels: Van Keerberghen.

Owen, J. (2003). Making your website accessible. Library & Information Update, (January 2003). Retrieved June, 2009, from http://www.cilip.org.uk/ publications/ update magazine/archive/ archive2003/january/update0301c.htm

Pirolli, P., Pitkow, J. & Rao, R. (1996). Silk from a sow's ear: extracting usable structures from the web. CHI 96 Electronic Proceedings. Available at http://www.acm.org/sigchi/chi96/proceedings/ papers/Pirolli_2/pp2.html

Potter, W. G. (1981). Introduction to bibliometrics. Library Trends, 30, 5.

Price, Derek de Solla (1970). Citation measures of hard science, soft science, technology and nonscience. In C. E. Nelson & D. K. Pollock (Eds.), Communication among scientists and engineers (pp. 3-22). Lexington: Heath Lexington Books.

Pritchard, A. (1969). Statistical bibliography or bibliometrics? Journal of Documentation, 25, 348–349.

PR Weaver. (n.d.). [computer software]. Retrieved August 12, 2014, from PR Weaver: PR tool for

Search Engine Optimization. Available at http://www.prweaver.com/

Ravden, S. J. & Johnson, G. I. (1989). Evaluating the usability of human computer interfaces: a practical method. Chichester : E. Horwood.

Ravichandra Rao, I. K. (1983). Quantitative methods in library and information science. New Delhi: Wiley Eastern.

Raward, R. (2001). Academic library website design principles: development of a checklist. Australian Academic & Research Libraries, 32(2).

Rich, L. A. & Rabine, J. L. (1999). How libraries are providing access to electronic serials: a survey of academic library websites. Serials Review, 25(2), 35-46.

Robbins, S. S. & Stylianou, A. C. (2003). Global corporate websites: an empirical investigation of content and design. Information and Management, 40(3), 205-212.

Rodríguez i Gairín, J. M. (1997). Impact assessment of information on the Internet: AltaVista, the citation index of the web. Revista Española De Documentación Científica, 20(2), 175-181.

Rosenfeld, L. B. & Morville, P. (1998). Information architecture for the World Wide Web. Sebastopol, CA: O'Reilly.

Rousseau, R. (1997). Sitations: an exploratory study. Cybermetrics, 1(1), Available at http://www. cindoc.csic. es/cybermetrics/articles/v2i1p2.html

Rousseau, R. (1999). Daily time series of common single word searches in AltaVista and NorthernLight. Cybermetrics, 2/3(1), Paper 2. Available at http://www.cindoc.csic. es/ cybermetrics/articles/v1i1p1.html

Rowlands, C. (2000). Usability matters - what is good design? Retrieved June, 2009, from http://web.archive.org/ web/20000815215258/ www.webreview.com/pub/2000/03/10/feature/index3c.html

Rozic-Hristovski, A., Hristovski, D. & Todorovski, L. (2002). Users' information-seeking behavior on a medical library website. Journal of the Medical Library Association, *90*(2), 210-217.

Rozic-Hristovski, A., Todorovski, L. & Hristovski, D. (1999). Developing a medical library website at the University of Ljubljana, Slovenia. Program, 33(4), 313–325.

Rubin, J. (1994). Handbook of usability testing: how to plan, design and conduct effective tests. New York: John Wiley.

Schaffner, J. (2007). Good design for library websites and online public access catalogs [White paper, LIS 488]. Retrieved June, 2009, from http://web.simmons.edu/~schaffne/ whitepaper.pdf

Scientometrics. (n.d.). Retrieved June 17, 2009, from Wikipedia: http://en.wikipedia.org/wiki/ Scientometrics

Search Engine Land. (2013, February). Retrieved August 12, 2014, from Search Engine Land: http://searchengineland. com/google-worlds-most-popular-search-engine-148089

SearchEngineWatch.com. (n.d.). Retrieved June 6, 2006, from Search Engine Watch: http:// searchenginewatch.com/ (currently page not exists)

Search Commands. (n.d.). Retrieved June 5, 2006, from Search Commands: http://www.search commands.com/ (Last accessed on 24.06.09)

Search Thingy Top Ten Search Engines. (n.d.). Retrieved June 5, 2006, from Search Thingy: http://www.searchthingy. com/search.asp

Shukla, A. (2009a). Measuring effectiveness of institutional websites: a case study of central universities of India. Research Digest, 4(3).

Shukla, A. (2009b). Evaluating Indian academic and research library websites based on web impact factor analysis (Doctoral Dissertation). Varanasi, India: Department of Library & Information Science, Banaras Hindu University.

Shukla, A. & Tripathi, A. (2009). Webometric analysis of institutes of national importance in India. IASLIC Bulletin, 54(3), 165-180.

Shukla, A. & Tripathi, A. (2014). Backlinks analyses of institutes of national importance and premier management institutions library websites. Journal of International Academic Research for Multidisciplinary (JIARM), 2(7), 560-575.

Shukla, A. & Vanlalfeli. (2014). Webometric analyses of library websites of Indian Institutes of Technology. Journal of Advancements in Library Sciences, 1(2), 34-48.

Simon, S. J. (2001). The impact of culture and gender on websites: an empirical study. The Data Base for Advances in Information Systems, 32(1), 18-37.

Small, H. (1937). Co-citation in the scientific literature: a new measure of relationship between two documents. Journal of the American Society for Information Science and Technology, 24(4), 265-269.

Smith, A. G. (1999). A tale of two web spaces: comparing sites using web impact factors. Journal of Documentation, 55(5), 577-592.

Smith, A. G. & Thelwall, M. (2002). Web impact factors for Australasian universities. Scientometrics, 54(3), 363-380.

Snyder, H. & Rosenbaum, H. (1999). Can search engines be used for web-link analysis? A critical review. Journal of Documentation, 55(4), 375-384.

Spool, J. (1998). Website usability: the big picture. Retrieved June 5, 2009, from http://web.archive.org/web/19991013021157/http://webreview.com/ pub/web98east/23/spoolx.html

Stover, M. & Zink, S. D. (1996). World Wide Web home page design: patterns and anomalies of higher education library home pages. *Reference Services Review*, 24(3), 7-20.

Sun, H. (2001). Building a culturally-competent corporate website: an explanatory study of cultural markers in multilingual web design. In: Proceedings of *ACM Special Interest Group for Design of Communication* (SIGDOC) 2001, 95-102. Available at http://faculty.gvsu. edu/sunh /resch/acm01.pdf

Tague-Sutcliffe, J. (1992). An introduction to informetrics. Information Processing & Management, 28(1), 1-3.

Tang, R. & Thelwall, M. (2003). Disciplinary differences in US academic departmental website interlinking. Library & Information Science Research, 25(4), 437-458.

Tang, R. & Thelwall, M. (2004). Patterns of national and international web links to U.S. academic departments: an analysis of disciplinary variations. Scientometrics, 60, 475-485.

Thelwall, M. (2000). Web impact factors and search engine coverage. Journal of Documentation, 56(2), 185-189.

Thelwall, M. (2001a). A publicly accessible database of UK university website links and a discussion of the need for human intervention in web crawling. Available at http://www.scit.wlv.ac.uk/~cm1993/papers/a_publicly_accessible_database.pdf

Thelwall, M. (2001f). A web crawler design for data mining. Journal of Information Science, 27(5), 319-325.

Thelwall, M. (2001b). Exploring the link structure of the web with network diagrams. Journal of Information Science, 27(6), 393-402.

Thelwall, M. (2001c). Extracting macroscopic information from web links. Journal of the American Society for Information Science and Technology, 52(13), 1157-1168.

Thelwall, M. (2001d). Results from a web impact factor crawler. Journal of Documentation, 57(2), 177-191.

Thelwall, M. (2001e). The responsiveness of search engine indexes [Electronic version]. Cybermetrics, 5(1), Paper 1. Available at http://www.cindoc.csic.es/cybermetrics/articles/v5i1p1.html

Thelwall, M. (2002a). A comparison of sources of links for academic web impact factor calculations. Journal of Documentation, 58(1), 66-78.

Thelwall, M. (2002e). An initial exploration of the link relationship between UK university websites. Aslib Proceedings, 54(2), 118-126.

Thelwall, M. (2002b). Conceptualizing documentation on the web: an evaluation of different heuristic-based models for counting links between university websites. Journal of the American Society for Information Science and Technology, 53(12), 995-1005.

Thelwall, M. (2002c). Evidence for the existence of geographic trends in university website interlinking. Journal of Documentation, 58(5), 563-574.

Thelwall, M. (2002d). Methodologies for crawler based web surveys. Internet Research: Electronic Networking and Applications, 12(2), 124-138.

Thelwall, M. (2002f). The top 100 linked to pages on UK university websites: high inlink counts are not usually associated with quality scholarly content. Journal of Information Science, 28(6), 483.491.

Thelwall, M. (2003b). Can Google's PageRank be used to find the most important academic web pages? Journal of Documentation, 59(2), 205-217.

Thelwall, M. (2003a). Web use and peer interconnectivity metrics for academic websites. Journal of Information Science, 29(1), 1-10.

Thelwall, M. (2008). Extracting accurate and complete results from search engines: case study windows live. *Journal of the American Society for Information Science and Technology, 59*(1), 38-50.

Thelwall, M. (2011). A comparison of link and URL citation counting. Aslib Proceedings, 63(4), 419 - 425.

Thelwall, M. & Harries, G. (2003). The connection between the research of a university and counts of links to its web pages: an investigation based upon a classification of the relationships of pages to the research of the host university. Journal of the American Society for Information Science and Technology, 54(7), 594-602.

Thelwall, M. & Harries, G. (2004). Do better scholars' web publications have significantly higher online impact? Journal of the American Society for Information Science and Technology, 55(2), 149-159.

Thelwall, M. & Smith, A. (2002). Interlinking between Asia-Pacific university websites. Scientometrics, 55(3), 363-376.

Thelwall, M. & Tang, R. (2003). Disciplinary and linguistic considerations for academic web linking: an exploratory hyperlink mediated study with Mainland China and Taiwan. Scientometrics, 58(1), 153-179.

Thelwall, M., Harries, G. & Wilkinson, D. (2003). Why do websites from different academic subjects interlink? Journal of Information Science, 29(6), 453-471.

Thelwall, M., Vaughan, L. & Björneborn, L. (2005). Webometrics. Annual Review of Information Science and Technology, 39, 81-135.

Thelwall, M., Vaughan, L., Cothey, V., Li, X. & Smith, A. (2003). Which academic subjects have more online impact? a pilot study and a new classification process. Online Information Review, 27(5), 333.343.

Thomas, O. & Willet, P. (2000). Webometric analysis of departments of librarianship and information science. Journal of Information Science, 26(6), 421-428. doi: 10.1177/016555150002600605

Times Higher Education Supplement. (n d.). Retrieved June 2, 2009, from Times Higher Education: http://www.times highereducation.co.uk/

Top Ten Search Engines. (n.d.). Retrieved June 4, 2006, from seoconsultants.com: http://www.seocon sultants.com/ search-engines/

Turnbull, D. (1996). Bibliometrics and the World Wide Web (Technical Report FIS-12-19-1996-1). Faculty of Information Studies, University of Toronto.

University Grants Commission. (n.d.). Retrieved April 27, 2006, from University Grants Commission (UGC): http://www. ugc.ac.in/

VandeCreek, L. M. (2005). Usability analysis of Northern Illinois University Libraries' website: a case study. OCLC Systems and Services, 21(3), 181-192.

Vasantha Raju, N. & Harinarayana, N. S. (2008). An analysis of usability features of library websites. Annals of Library and Information Studies, 55(2), 111-122.

Vaughan, L. & Thelwall, M. (2003). Scholarly use of the web: what are the key inducers of links to journal websites? Journal of the American Society for Information Science and Technology, 54(1), 29-38.

Vaughan, L. & Thelwall, M. (2004). Search engine coverage bias: evidence and possible causes. Information Processing & Management, 40(4), 693-707.

Vaughan, L. & Thelwall, M. (2005). A modeling approach to uncover hyperlink patterns: the case of Canadian universities. Information Processing & Management, 41(2), 347-359.

Walia, P. K. & Kaur, P. (2008). Webometric analysis of library associations' websites of India. IASLIC Bulletin, 53(3), 131-143.

Web search engine. (n.d.). Retrieved June 9, 2009, from Wikipedia: http://en.wikipedia.org/wiki/Search_engines

Web usability. (n.d.). Retrieved June 4, 2009, from Wikipedia: http://en.wikipedia.org/wiki/Web_usability

Westergren, J. (2006). Link building guide. Retrieved June 4, 2009, from http://www.jimwestergren.com/link-building-guide/

What is link building. (n.d.). Retrieved June 7, 2009, from Admin Zone Forum: http://www.theadmin zone.com/forums/ showthread.php?t=25021

White, H. D. & McCain, K. W. (1989). Bibliometrics. Annual Review of Information Science and Technology, 24, 119-186.

Wilkinson, D., Harries, G., Thelwall, M. & Price, L. (2003). Motivations for academic website interlinking: evidence for the web as a novel source of information on informal scholarly communication. Journal of Information Science. 29(1), 59-66.

Wilson, C. S. (1999). Informetrics. In Williams, M. E. (Ed.), Annual Review of Information Science and Technology, 34, 107-247.

Wittig, G. R. (1978). Documentation note: statistical bibliography - a historical footnote. Journal of Documentation, 34, 240–241.

Wordnet search - 3.0. (n.d.). Retrieved June 9, 2009, from WordNet: http://wordnetweb.princeton.edu/perl/webwn

World Wide Web. (n.d.). Retrieved June 8, 2009, from Wikipedia: http://en.wikipedia.org/wiki/World_Wide_Web

Yoon, S. (2002). The antecedents and consequences of trust in online-purchase decisions. Journal of Interactive Marketing, 16(2), 47-63.

Yu, B. & Roh, S. (2002). The effects of menu design on information-seeking performance and user's attitude on the web. Journal of the American Society for Information Science and Technology, 53(11), 923-933.

Appendices

APPENDIX – I : EVALUATION CRITERIA FOR CONTENT AWARENESS OF LIBRARY WEBSITES

108 Points Parameter

Instruction: Provide 0 marks for under construction and HTTP 404 (File not found) message containing web pages in the library website.

1. Does the library have website / web page for itself?

   (1) Yes ( ) [2 Point]

   (2) No ( ) [0 Point]

Definition: Web page is a single hypertext document whereas website is collection of web pages.

2. Does the library website have separate site /sub-site for itself?

   (1) Yes ( ) [2 Point]

   (2) No ( ) [0 Point]

Note: Website is associated with domain name segment preceding the SLD. For ex. 'www.bhu.ac.in' has website 'bhu.ac.in' but 'dlis.bhu.ac.in' has website 'bhu.ac.in' and sub-site 'dlis.bhu.ac.in'. Domain name of Banaras Hindu University, Varanasi is 'www.bhu.ac.in' and sub-domain is 'www.dlis.bhu.ac.in'.

3. Does the library website have?

   (1) Multiple web pages ( ) [2 Point]

   (2) Single web page*

   *If single, then

Does the library web page have the collection of library related content solely?

(1) Yes ( ) [1 Point]

(2) No ( ) [0 Point]

4. Does hyperlink for library website / web page(s) appear in the index page (homepage) of the university / institute website?

(1) Yes ( ) [2 Point]

(2) No*

*If No, then

Does hyperlink for library website / web page(s) appear under Facilities / Infrastructure / About us headings in the index page (homepage) of the university / institute website?

(1) Yes ( ) [1 Point]

(2) No ( ) [0 Point]

If Yes, under which headings ....Facilities / Infrastructure / About us / Other (specify) ....
....

5. Whether the library website / web page(s) provide updating information?

(1) Yes ( ) [1 Point]*

(2) No ( ) [0 Point]

*If Yes, then

Whether the library website / web page(s) revised, modified or updated regularly?

(1) Yes ( ) [1 Point]

(2) No ( ) [0 Point]

If Yes, website / web page modified within .... Week / Month / Other (Specify) ....
....

6. Whether the library website / web page available in another language (except preferred)?

(1) Yes ( ) [2 Point]*

(2) No ( ) [0 Point]

*If Yes, then

If yes, mention the name(s) of languages ....

....

7. Does the library website have separate web page for providing information about introduction or historical details of the library?

(1) Yes ( ) [2 Point]

(2) No*

*If No, then

Does the library website provide information regarding introduction or historical details of the library in any common web page or any other place?

(1) Yes ( ) [1 Point]

(2) No ( ) [0 Point]

8. Does the library website have separate web page for providing information regarding mission statement / aim / objective / purpose of the library?

(1) Yes ( ) [2 Point]

(2) No*

*If No, then

Does the library website provide information regarding mission statement / aim / objective / purpose of the library in any common web page or any other place?

(1) Yes ( ) [1 Point]

(2) No ( ) [0 Point]

9. Does the library website have separate web page for providing library collection information?

(1) Yes ( ) [2 Point]

(2) No*

*If No, then

Does the library website provide information regarding library collection in a common web page or any other place?

(1) Yes ( ) [1 Point]

(2) No ( ) [0 Point]

10. Does the library website have separate web page for providing information regarding electronic resources (e-journals & databases etc.) subscribed by the library?

(1) Yes ( ) [2 Point]

(2) No*

*If No, then

Does the library website provide information regarding electronic resources (e-journals & databases etc.) subscribed by the library in a common web page or any other place?

(1) Yes ( ) [1 Point]

(2) No ( ) [0 Point]

11. Whether electronic resources (e-journals & databases etc.) subscribed by the library can be accessed online?

(1) Yes ( ) [2 Point]

(2) No ( ) [0 Point]

Scope Note: It includes online journals, e-journals, e-databases, free databases & trial databases. Users can access e-journals within campus premises, provide 2 marks if only indicative information is available.

12. Does the library website have separate web page / downloadable files for providing information regarding print / current journals subscribed by the library?

(1) Yes ( ) [2 Point]

(2) No*

*If No, then

Does the library website provide information regarding print / current journals subscribed by the library in a common web page or any other place?

(1) Yes ( ) [1 Point]

(2) No ( ) [0 Point]

Scope Note: It includes print journals, magazines, news papers etc. Downloadable files includes list of print / current journals available in pdf / doc / excel file format, if so provide 2 marks.

13. Does the library website have separate web page / hyperlink for providing information regarding e-books (ebrary) subscribed by the library?

(1) Yes ( ) [2 Point]

(2) No*

*If No, then

Does the library website provide information regarding e-books (ebrary) subscribed by the library in a common web page or any other place?

(1) Yes ( ) [1 Point]

(2) No ( ) [0 Point]

14. Does the library website have separate website / web page for providing information regarding Ph. D. theses / dissertations to the users of the library?

(1) Yes ( ) [2 Point]

(2) No*

*If No, then

Does the library website provide information regarding Ph. D. theses / dissertations to the users of the library in any common web page or any other place?

(1) Yes ( ) [1 Point]

(2) No ( ) [0 Point]

Scope Note: It include information regarding traditional theses, electronic theses, availability of theses abstracts, electronic theses submission, searching and downloading etc.

Note: Don't count the theses collection details under this criteria.

15. Does the library website have separate website / web page for institutional repositories?

(1) Yes	( )	[2 Point]
(2) No	( )	[0 Point]

Note : Don't include 'theses repository' of any institute under this criteria. Mention additional institutional repositories in evaluation criteria no. 40, if found more than one.

16. Does the library website have separate web page / hyperlink for web OPAC / Online Catalogue?

(1) Yes	( )	[2 Point]
(2) No*		

*If No, then

Does the library website provide only information regarding web OPAC / Online Catalogue?

(1) Yes	( )	[1 Point]
(2) No	( )	[0 Point]

17. Does the library website provide access to digital / electronic library?

(1) Yes	( )	[2 Point]
(2) No*		

*If No, then

Does the library website provide only information regarding digital / electronic library in any common web page or any other place?

(1) Yes	( )	[1 Point]
(2) No	( )	[0 Point]

> **Scope Note:** It include all types of digital resources provided by library except e-journals & online journals.

18. Does the library website have / provide separate web page / hyperlink for the subject gateways / subject directories / subject portals?

    (1) Yes ( ) [2 Point]

    (2) No*

    *If No, then

    Does the library website provide information regarding subject gateways / subject directories / subject portals for users in any common web page or any other place?

    (1) Yes ( ) [1 Point]

    (2) No ( ) [0 Point]

> **Scope Note:** It includes technical information gateways, subject portals, subject directories. For ex. BUBL, Infolibrarian, AERADE, ELDIS, ChemDex, History, Intute, InfoLaw etc.

19. Does the library website have separate web page for necessary downloadable materials (various forms, formats, software etc.) of the library (in grouped way)?

    (1) Yes ( ) [2 Point]

    (2) No*

    *If No, then

    Does the library website provide necessary downloadable materials in many web pages of the library website (in scattered way)?

    (1) Yes ( ) [1 Point]

    (2) No#

    #If No, then

Does the library website provide the structure of the necessary downloadable materials in html file format?

(1) Yes ( ) [1/2 Point]

(2) No ( ) [0 Point]

Note : Downloadable materials, generally available in pdf or doc file formats. Sometimes zip file format is also used for downloadable materials. Downloadable forms made in html file format can be copied but requires necessary modifications when pasted in MS Word.

20. Does the library website have separate web page for providing information regarding user membership details?

(1) Yes ( ) [2 Point]

(2) No*

*If No, then

Does the library website provide information regarding user membership details in any common web page or any other place?

(1) Yes ( ) [1 Point]

(2) No ( ) [0 Point]

Scope Note: It includes types of member, no. of documents to be issued, membership procedure, membership fee, overdue charges, membership rules etc.

Note: It doesn't include the record of daily visitors.

21. Does the library website have separate web page for general rules about library usage or any other?

(1) Yes ( ) [2 Point]

(2) No*

*If No, then

Does the library website provide rules about library usage or any other in any common web page or any other place?

(1) Yes ( ) [1 Point]

(2) No ( ) [0 Point]

Scope Note: It includes general rules of library. Membership rules will not be accepted here.

22. Does the library website have separate web page for providing information about institutional / organizational membership details adopted by the library?

(1) Yes ( ) [2 Point]

(2) No*

*If No, then

Does the library website provide information about institutional / organizational membership details adopted by the library in any common web page or any other place?

(1) Yes ( ) [1 Point]

(2) No ( ) [0 Point]

Scope Note: This includes membership of DELNET, INFLIBNET, INDEST, IFLA, OCLC, IASLIC, ILA, UGC-INFONET etc. like associations.

23. Does the library website have separate web page for providing information about institutional / organizational / corporate / industrial / outside / special membership details given by the library?

(1) Yes ( ) [2 Point]

(2) No*

*If No, then

Does the library website provide information about institutional / organizational / corporate / industrial / outside / special membership details given by the library in any common web page or any other place?

(1) Yes ( ) [1 Point]

(2) No ( ) [0 Point]

24. Does the library website have separate web page for providing information regarding new arrivals / recent additions in the library?

(1) Yes ( ) [2 Point]

(2) No*

*If No, then

Does the library website provide information regarding new arrivals / recent additions in the library in any common web page or any other place?

(1) Yes ( ) [1 Point]

(2) No ( ) [0 Point]

25. Does the library website provide information regarding useful links to the library users?

(1) Yes ( ) [2 Point]

(2) No ( ) [0 Point]

Scope Note : It include links to international / national organizations, institutes, associations, libraries, educational websites, online tutorials, news websites, dictionaries, encyclopedias and other reference sources etc.

26. Does the library website have separate web page for providing information regarding recent news / events / happenings of the library?

(1) Yes ( ) [2 Point]

(2) No*

*If No, then

Does the library website provide information regarding recent news / events / happenings of the library in any common web page or any other place?

(1) Yes ( ) [1 Point]

(2) No ( ) [0 Point]

27. Does the library website have separate web page / hyperlink for virtual tour of the library?

(1) Yes ( ) [2 Point]

(2) No ( ) [0 Point]

28. Does the library website have separate web page for working hours & holidays of the library?

(1) Yes ( ) [2 Point]

(2) No*

*If No, then

Does the library website provide information regarding working hours & holidays of the library in any common web page or any other place?

(1) Yes ( ) [1 Point]

(2) No ( ) [0 Point]

Does the library website have separate web page(s) for providing information about staff of the library?

(1) Yes ( ) [2 Point]

(2) No*

*If No, then

29. Does the library website provide information about staff of the library in any common web page or any other place?

(1) Yes ( ) [1 Point]

(2) No ( ) [0 Point]

Does the library website have separate web page / online web form for getting feedback / suggestion by the users of the library?

(1) Yes ( ) [2 Point]

(2) No*

*If No, then

30. Does the library website provide information regarding feedback / suggestion by the users of the library in any other form in any common web page or any other place?

(1) Yes ( ) [1 Point]

(2) No ( ) [0 Point]

Note: Logically, suggestions and feedback are more or less similar things. So, here both are grouped together, though some websites have both at different places. If found anywhere, both then treat as only one.

31. Does the library website have separate web page / online web form for providing information regarding frequently asked questions (FAQs) / ask the librarian / chat with librarian?

(1) Yes ( ) [2 Point]

(2) No*

*If No, then

Does the library website provide information regarding frequently asked questions (FAQs) / ask the librarian / chat with librarian in any other form in anywhere in the website / web page?

(1) Yes ( ) [1 Point]

(2) No ( ) [0 Point]

Note: Logically, frequently asked questions (FAQs), ask the librarian and chat with the librarian is more or less similar things. So, here all are grouped together, though some websites have all at different places. If found anywhere, all then treat as only one.

32. Does the library website have separate web page for sitemap of the library website / web pages?

(1) Yes ( ) [2 Point]

(2) No ( ) [0 Point]

33. Does the library website have separate web page for floor / layout plan of sections / units of the library?

    (1) Yes ( ) [2 Point]

    (2) No*

    *If No, then

    Does the library website provide floor / layout plan of sections / units of the library in a common web page or any other place?

    (1) Yes ( ) [1 Point]

    (2) No ( ) [0 Point]

34. Does the library website have separate web page for providing any contact information or means of communication with the librarian & other section / unit in-charge?

    (1) Yes ( ) [2 Point]

    (2) No*

    *If No, then

    Does the library website provide any contact information or means of communication with the librarian & other section / unit in-charge in a common web page or any other place?

    (1) Yes ( ) [1 Point]

    (2) No ( ) [0 Point]

    If Yes, website / web page provides .... Contact address / E-mail address / Other (specify) ....
    ....

35. Does the library website have separate web page for providing information regarding various sections / units of the library?

    (1) Yes ( ) [2 Point]

    (2) No*

    *If No, then

Does the library website provide information regarding various sections / units of the library in a common web page or any other place?

(1) Yes	( )	[1 Point]
(2) No	( )	[0 Point]

Note: Separate web page for various sections / units of library means a web page which solely has the content of various sections / units of the library whereas common web page may include other library related information also.

Instruction: If the library website has individual web pages for each of the sections / units of the library then provide additional ½ (half) mark for each of the following sections / units mentioned here.

(1)	Circulation Section	( )	[1/2 Point]
(2)	Stack Section	( )	[1/2 Point]
(3)	Acquisition Section	( )	[1/2 Point]
(4)	Technical Processing Section	( )	[1/2 Point]
(5)	Library Administration / Office	( )	[1/2 Point]
(6)	Periodical / Back Volume Section	( )	[1/2 Point]
(7)	Book Bank Section	( )	[1/2 Point]
(8)	Documentation Section	( )	[1/2 Point]
(9)	Micrography / Photography Section	( )	[1/2 Point]
(10)	Computer Section	( )	[1/2 Point]
(11)	Manuscript Section	( )	[1/2 Point]
(12)	Others x n	( )	[1/2 x n Point]

Note: Here n is the number of sections / units

Mention the name(s) of sections / units included in others ....

....

36. Does the library website have separate web page for providing information regarding services to the users of the library?

    (1) Yes ( ) [2 Point]

    (2) No*

    *If No, then

    Does the library website provide information regarding services to the users of the library in a common web page or any other place?

    (1) Yes ( ) [1 Point]

    (2) No ( ) [0 Point]

Instruction: If the library website has individual web pages for each of the services then provide additional ½ (half) mark for each of the following services mentioned here.

(1) Document Delivery Service (Electronic form also) ( ) [1/2 Point]

(2) Inter Library Loan ( ) [1/2 Point]

(3) Issue – Return (Borrowing, Self check in / out) ( ) [1/2 Point]

(4) Reference Service ( ) [1/2 Point]

(5) Photocopy Service ( ) [1/2 Point]

(6) Internet Service ( ) [1/2 Point]

(7) Documentation (CAS, SDI) Service ( ) [1/2 Point]

(8) Book Reservation / Renewal (including online) ( ) [1/2 Point]

(9) Book Bank ( ) [1/2 Point]

(10) Indexing, Abstracting, Database Search ( ) [1/2 Point]

(11) Translation Service ( ) [1/2 Point]

(12) Others x n ( ) [1/2 x n Point]

Note: Here n is the number of services

Mention the name(s) of services included in others

....

....

37. Does the library website have separate website / web page for providing information regarding various departmental / sectional / campus libraries of the parent institute?

(1) Yes ( ) [2 Point]

(2) No*

*If No, then

Does the library website provide information regarding various departmental / sectional / campus libraries of the parent institute in a common web page or any other place?

(1) Yes ( ) [1 Point]

(2) No ( ) [0 Point]

38. Whether library website provides information regarding services for special class patrons (users) in a separate web page?

(1) Yes ( ) [2 Point]

(2) No*

*If No, then

Whether library website provides information regarding services for special class patrons (users) in a common web page or any other place?

(1) Yes ( ) [1 Point]

(2) No ( ) [0 Point]

Instruction: If the library website has individual web pages for the services for various special class patrons (users) of the library then provide additional ½ (half) mark for each of the following services for special class mentioned here.

(1) Services for Children ( ) [1/2 Point]

(2) Services for Challenged (all types)
( ) [1/2 Point]

(3) Services for Prisoners
( ) [1/2 Point]

(4) Services for Alumni Members
( ) [1/2 Point]

(5) Services for Distance Learners
( ) [1/2 Point]

(6) Others x n ( ) [1/2 x n Point]

Note: Here n is the number of services for special class patrons

Mention the name(s) of services for special class patrons included in others ....
....

39. Whether library website provides information regarding special activities conducted by the library for the patrons, specialists, library professionals and others in a separate web page?

(1) Yes ( ) [2 Point]

(2) No*

*If No, then

Whether library website provides information regarding special activities conducted by the library for the patrons, specialists, library professionals and others in a common web page or any other place?

(1) Yes ( ) [1 Point]

(2) No ( ) [0 Point]

Instruction: If the library website has individual web pages for the special activities conducted by the library for the patrons, specialists, library professionals and others then provide additional ½ (half) mark for each of the following special activities mentioned here.

(1) Conferences / Training / Workshops
( ) [1/2 Point]

(2) Educational Courses ( ) [1/2 Point]

(3) Literacy Programmes ( ) [1/2 Point]

(4) User Orientation ( ) [1/2 Point]

(5) Refresher Course ( ) [1/2 Point]

(6) Others x n ( ) [1/2 x n Point]

Note: Here n is the number of special activities

Mention the name(s) of special activities included in others ....

....

40. If the library website / web page provide information regarding following additional items besides above mentioned then provide additional ½ points for each of them.

(1) Library Archive ( ) [1/2 Point]

(2) Image Gallery of Library ( ) [1/2 Point]

(3) Internal Publication Holding ( ) [1/2 Point]

(4) Standards / Patents (IPR) Information ( ) [1/2 Point]

(5) Library Blog ( ) [1/2 Point]

(6) Media Resource Centre ( ) [1/2 Point]

(7) Website Internal Search Engine ( ) [1/2 Point]

(8) Book Fair ( ) [1/2 Point]

(9) Approved Vendors List ( ) [1/2 Point]

(10) Online Tutorials ( ) [1/2 Point]

(11) Virtual (Online) Reference Desk ( ) [1/2 Point]

(12) Recognition / Awards / Appreciations ( ) [1/2 Point]

(13) AV (Multimedia) Collection details ( ) [1/2 Point]

(14) Library Committee ( ) [1/2 Point]

(15) Projects & Consultancy ( ) [1/2 Point]

(16) Chronology of Librarians ( ) [1/2 Point]

(17) User Guidelines ( ) [1/2 Point]

(18) Union Catalogue ( ) [1/2 Point]

(19) Consortia ( ) [1/2 Point]

(20) Others x n ( ) [1/2 x n Point]

Note: Here n is the number of additional items

Mention the name (s) of additional items included in others...

....

41. Are there any broken hyperlinks in library website / web pages?

(1) Yes ( ) [-2 Point]

(2) No ( ) [2 Point]

Note: Broken links include HTTP 404 (File not found), HTTP 403 (Forbidden), the page cannot be found / displayed, non functioning URLs etc. Provide 0 marks for these web links / web pages in the websites.

APPENDIX - II

WEBSITE PERFORMANCE CALCULATION FORMULAE

Overall Website Performance Calculation (OWPC)

$$\frac{\text{Total points obtained} \times 100}{\text{Maximum points}} = \ldots \%$$

Criteria wise Website Performance Calculation (CWPC)

$$\frac{\text{Total points obtained} \times 100}{\text{Maximum points of attempted criteria}} = \ldots.. \%$$

APPENDIX - III

WEBSITE PERFORMANCE GRADE TABLE

(Based On 108 Points Parameter)

Points Range	% Range	Grading	Degree of Awareness
Up to 108	Up to 100	Excellent	Much attention has been paid to the library website for serving the need of patrons. Excellent condition of awareness for maintenance & updation of library website.
Up to 86.4	Up to 80	Very Good	Regular attention has been paid to the library website for serving the need of patrons. Very Good condition of awareness for maintenance & updation of library website.
Up to 64.8	Up to 60	Good	Normal attention has been paid to the library website for serving the need of patrons. Good condition of awareness for maintenance & updation of library website.
Up to 43.2	Up to 40	Average	Less attention has been paid to the library website for serving the need of patrons. Satisfactory condition of awareness for maintenance & updation of library website.
Up to 21.6	Up to 20	Unsatisfactory	Need based attention have been paid to the library website for serving the need of patrons. Unsatisfactory condition of awareness for maintenance & updation of library website.